Dreamers, Schemers and Scalawags

THE FLORIDA CHRONICLES

VOLUME 1

D1166324

Dreamers, Schemers and Scalawags

THE FLORIDA CHRONICLES
VOLUME 1

Stuart B. McIver

Pineapple Press, Inc.
Sarasota, Florida

Dedicated to Laurel

Copyright © 1994 Stuart B. McIver
Copyright © 2011 Joan McIver

All rights reserved. No part of this book may be reproduced in any form or by any means, electronic or mechanical, including photocopying, recording, or by any information storage and retrieval system, without permission in writing from the publisher.

Inquiries should be addressed to:
Pineapple Press, Inc.
P.O. Box 3889
Sarasota, Florida 34230

Cataloging-In-Publication Data

McIver, Stuart B.
Dreamers, schemers, and scalawags / by Stuart B. McIver.—1st ed.
p. cm.—(The Florida Chronicles ; v. 1)
Includes bibliographical references and index.
ISBN 1-56164-034-4 Hb ISBN 1-56164-155-3: Pb
1. Florida—Biography. 2. Florida—history. I. Title. II. Series.
CT229.M38 1994
920.0759—dc20
[B] 201148311
CIP

Hb: 10 9 8 7 6 5 4 3 2 1
Pb: 10 9 8 7 6 5 4 3

Printed and bound in the United States of America

CONTENTS

On the Move

Visionaries

Sportsmen

FOREWORD

Stuart McIver has created a mother lode of generally unknown vignettes about Florida—people, places and things. Most of this book reads more like a "page burner" novel than a work of nonfiction. It grabs your attention right at the beginning and continues to captivate until the end.

Many people think of Florida only in terms of what it is today or has been during the past few decades: pink plastic flamingoes, stuffed baby alligators, theme parks, and sandy beaches. What really went on in Florida in the past century and part of this one is more fascinating than anything modern-day computer enhancement can create. Also, Florida's pioneer con artists could make today's swindlers and snake-oil peddlers seem like saints.

The parade of characters who left footprints in Florida, both large and small, includes such people as Ned Buntline, Andrew Jackson, Miccosukee Sam Jones, Oliver Hardy (of Laurel and Hardy fame), Charles Cory, Wilson Mizner (brother of Addison)—the list goes on and on, too numerous to mention here, but included in this book. No other state can boast such a colorful cast of characters as those who once passed this way.

Of special interest are the chapters on the Seminole Wars, the least known of all American Indian wars, and the memories of those on both sides who suffered through all three of them.

It does not matter if one is a native Florida Cracker or an immigrant from elsewhere; an occasional visitor or someone who has never seen the Sunshine State—this book will be a fascinating read. It is a microcosm of all America, a reflection of times past and gone forever. And what better person to tell this story than Stuart McIver, who is a veritable storehouse of the human side of Florida history.

—Patrick Smith

ACKNOWLEDGMENTS

Many people have contributed to the writing of this book, through providing information, pictures or support. Some worthy souls who should have been on this list may have been overlooked inadvertently. To you, I say "sorry, and thanks, anyway." To the rest, some of whom are now deceased, my thanks go out gratefully. The list includes: Susan B. Anthony, Patti Bartlett, Jo Bigelow, Sam Boldrick, Maggie Bowman, Richard Brooks, Dorothy Bryan, Leslie Cabarga, Ed Carlson, Bob Carr, Representative Bill Clark, Steve Davidson, Nan Denison, Rodney Dillon, Douglas Donn, Jean Dove, Hampton Dunn, Charles and Hamilton Forman, Elizabeth Friedman, Cheryl Frost, Paul George, Sue Gillis, Tom Hambright, Dan Hobby, Dawn Hugh, Gordon Ickes, Betty Mae Jumper, Joe Knetsch, Kevin McCarthy, John Monahan, Joan Morris, Bill Morrison, Jay Morton, Bill Munroe, Mary Munroe, Charles Palmer, Deedee Roberts, Joanne Runkel, Elizabeth Gentry Sayed, Becky Smith, Willard Steele, Patsy West, Matt Wiseley, Nick Wynne and Ronald Young. Special thanks are reserved for my wife Joan and my daughter Laurel who helped me pull all these stories together.

And, finally, I would like to thank the editors of *Florida Sportsman, Boca Raton* and, particularly, *Sunshine* magazine in whose pages shorter versions of these stories first appeared. And, of course, June Cussen and Patricia Hammond, my patient editors at Pineapple Press, who worked with me to bring about this, the first volume in *The Florida Chronicles* series.

STORYTELLERS

Memorable tellers of tales keep showing up on the Florida landscape. The Sunshine State has welcomed the best and the worst, from the sensational dime novels of the preposterous Ned Buntline to the loftier achievements of Zora Neale Hurston and the poet Laura Riding.

CHAPTER 1

Hanging Mr. Buntline

Seminole War sailor lived life even more lurid than his dime novels

Ned Buntline was probably the only American novelist to survive his own hanging.

But then a hanging would seem almost routine in a life as preposterous as Ned's, part of which was lived in South Florida—in the Keys, at Fort Dallas on the Miami River, at Fort Lauderdale and deep in the Everglades.

He was called Midshipman Edward Zane Carroll Judson when he served here from 1839 till 1842 with the U.S. Navy. During the Second Seminole War he was assigned to the Florida Squadron based at Tea Table Key, near today's Islamorada, and later at Indian Key.

In 1844 he assumed the pen name of Ned Buntline, a nautical term appropriate for the flash flood of writings that would pour forth for the next four decades. He developed the "art form" known as the dime novel and wound up writing some 400 of them.

In the Wild West he met a buffalo hunter named William Cody. Ned nicknamed him Buffalo Bill, wrote a play about him and helped make him a celebrity.

In the course of his 63 years he killed at least one man in a duel; married four times, maybe more, since there is some indication that he sometimes had more than one wife at a time; started a riot in New York City and served a year in prison for it; and became a power in the notorious Know-Nothing political party. To throw the whole picture into total confusion, he was active for years as a temperance lecturer, though on occasion drunk on the job. He was also a composer of hymns.

If he were alive today, he would doubtless have singled out his hanging as the low point of a life filled with as many highs and lows as a runaway pendulum.

The first in a series of ups and downs leading to the noose came in

Cincinnati in April, 1845. Financial problems threatened to overwhelm the *Western Literary Journal and Monthly Magazine,* which he and his partner, Lucius Hines, were publishing. Ned skipped town and left Hines with the debts.

But a high followed quickly in Eddyville, Kentucky. Buntline collected a $600 bounty for single-handedly capturing two murderers. He didn't use his bounty to rescue his partner. Instead he moved on to Nashville, Tennessee, and used the money to found another magazine, *Ned Buntline's Own.*

In 1846 he paid a little too much attention to an impressionable teenager, pretty Mary Porterfield. Robert Porterfield, her husband, was not amused. In the resulting gunfight, Ned killed Porterfield.

When Buntline was brought up for arraignment, Porterfield's brother shot at him in court. In the confusion Ned jumped through a window.

Unfortunately, he was soon recaptured, not by the law but by an angry mob. That night they hanged him to an awning post. As his life was ebbing away, friends appeared and cut him down. After his ordeal, the grand jury refused to indict him.

* * *

Edward Judson's colorful life began either on March 20, 1823, or August 26, 1822, at either Stamford, N.Y., or Philadelphia. Fiction mingled with fact throughout his life. As a small boy, he ran away to sea and served as an apprentice in the Navy. In 1838 he earned a Midshipman's commission for heroism in a drowning incident in New York's East River.

That same year the Florida War, as the Second Seminole War was called, began to threaten marine interests along the southeast Florida coast. Midshipman Judson was dispatched to Tea Table Key with a naval unit, newly assembled by Lieut. John T. McLaughlin. Officially, it was named the Florida Squadron. Its personnel called it the Mosquito Fleet.

Ned served as executive officer aboard the schooner *Otsego.* He saw service on both the east and west coasts and ventured back deep into a mysterious and little known part of Florida, the Everglades, with the greatest of all the Indian fighters, Lieut. Col. William S. Harney.

"I love a Florida winter," he would later write in the *Western Literary Journal.* "I do not mean one of your northern winter evenings, only rendered clear through the intense frigidity of the stiffened atmosphere . . . but I allude to one where the bright-faced moon and dancing stars look down on forests clothed in the rich beauty of perennial greenness, on an earth covered with flowers—spangled with luscious, air-perfuming fruit. On such a night, when the sky was smiling at itself in the brook-mirror below it, we hauled up our

Ned Buntline's drama, "Scouts of the Prairie," starred Buffalo Bill. Left to right: Ned Buntline, William F. "Buffalo Bill" Cody and Jack "Texas Jack" Omohundro. (Library of Congress)

boats at Fort Dallas, in the mouth of the river Miami, en route for the Everglades."

In the *Journal* he published five flamboyant accounts of the Florida War: "A Cruise in Lake Okeechobee," "A Chase in the Everglades," "The Capture and Trial," "Indian Key, its Rise, Progress and Destruction," and an untitled article about a march to Seminole hunting grounds. He wrote about such powerful Indian leaders as the medicine man Sam Jones.

After his troubles in Cincinnati and Nashville, Buntline moved his *Ned Buntline's Own* to New York City. He wasted little time in getting into trouble again. His magazine, a rowdy, sensationalized, super-patriotic publication, contended that Kate Hastings operated a disorderly house in New York.

On Duane Street a well-dressed Kate suddenly appeared, shouting, "You dirty, mean, sneaking, paltry son of a bitch, how dare you publish me in your paper?" She then pulled out a horsewhip and gave him a hiding on the streets of New York. Not even 30, Ned had already suffered through a hanging and now a public horsewhipping.

Ned hated foreigners, particularly Brits. When the famous English actor William Charles Macready came to New York, Ned's magazine compared him unfavorably with the American tragedian Edwin Forrest. Unfortunately, both were appearing in *Macbeth* at the same time.

When Shakespeare's witches fussed over their bubbling cauldron, boos and hisses were followed by eggs, oranges and rotten apples. "So foul and fair a day I have not seen," intoned Macready, and he proved to be right.

Fanned up by Buntline's inflammatory writings, a mob of ten thousand attacked the Astor Place Theater. Thirty-four people were killed, another 141 injured. For his vigorous leadership role in the riot, Ned was sentenced to a year in prison on Blackwell's Island.

In the early 1850s several secret societies together formed the American Party in virulent opposition to foreigners in general and Catholics in particular. For a political party it displayed one strange quirk, a holdover from its secretic origin. When someone not a party member asked them about their political policies, they answered, "I don't know." Ned, a member, dubbed the organization the Know Nothing Party.

Active with the super-patriotic, flag-waving, anti-Catholic party, Ned managed to start another riot on election day in St. Louis in 1854. Again deaths occurred, and again Ned was indicted. He escaped by jumping bail. Two decades later he came back to St. Louis with a traveling road show. He was promptly arrested.

At about this time Ned began to turn out dime novels, a sensationalized form of fiction which featured swashbuckling heroes, one-dimensional villains and highly moral themes. He published some in his own magazine, then for the leading publisher of dime novels, Beadle & Adams. The novels, published every other week, cost a dime or, if short, just a nickel. Readers could subscribe to a series of the stories for $2.50 a year.

Among Ned's classics over the next four decades were: *Ned Buntline's Life Yarn; Stella Delorme, or the Comanche's Dream; The Virgin of the Sun; The Red Revenger; The Idiot Spy; Buffalo Bill* and *The White Wizard, or The Great Prophet of the Seminoles*.

His *White Wizard,* all 52 chapters of it, is a tale of the Second Seminole War. It ranges from the Ten Thousand Islands into the Big Cypress Swamp

Beadle's Dime New York Library

Copyrighted in [illegible], by Beadle & Adams.

Vol. II. Published Every Two Weeks. Beadle & Adams, Publishers, [illegible] William Street, New York. Ten Cents a Copy. $2.50 a Year. No. 16

The White Wizard;

or,

The Great Prophet of the Seminoles.

By Ned Buntline.

CHAPTER I.

Along the whole southern and western coast of Florida, from the ancient Fort of St. Marks to Key West, there were no settlements, and only a few Spanish fishing stations at Tampa Bay, Manitee, Boca Grande, and Sanabel, at the date when we draw the curtain of the drama which we offer to the reader, nearly forty years ago.

[illegible]

Ned Buntline's *The White Wizard* took place in the Florida Everglades. (Sun-Sentinel) and the Everglades, from St. Augustine to Havana to New York City. Its cast of characters include a future president, Colonel Zachary Taylor, and such major Indian leaders as Chekika, Coacoochee and Osceola. Its lead character, however, bears the name of the fierce medicine man Arpiaka, better known as Sam Jones. This character bears no resemblance to Sam, who hated the white man as much as Buntline hated foreigners. He is instead a white man adopted by the tribe.

During the Civil War Ned enlisted in the Union Army. He rose to the rank of sergeant before being dishonorably discharged for drunkenness in 1864. Thereafter he called himself "Colonel."

After the war he was touring the West as a temperance lecturer when he met a spectacular buffalo hunter named William F. Cody at Fort McPherson, Nebraska. Ned gave him the name Buffalo Bill, and in 1872 wrote a play about him, *The Scouts of the Prairie.*

For its opening in Chicago the play sported a memorable cast. The Sioux and Pawnee roles were filled by Chicago actors found walking the streets. Cody, of course, played Buffalo Bill; John B. Omohundro, a Virginian, appeared as Texas Jack; an Italian dancer, Guiseppina Morlacchi, whose legs had been insured for $100,000 when she first introduced the cancan to America, played the Indian maiden, Dove Eye, and the versatile Ned Buntline appeared as Cale Durg.

Ned did not award himself the greatest of roles. In Act l he pauses in the action to give his temperance lecture, after which he is captured by the Indians and given a hard time at the "Torture Post." He is then killed off in the second act—not soon enough according to reviews. The *Chicago Inter-Ocean* regretted that he hadn't been killed before the temperance lecture.

Buntline lived out his last days back at Stamford. He continued to give temperance lectures, write hymns and turn out dime novels. After his death from a heart attack in 1886, literary critics Stanley J. Kunitz and Howard Haycraft gave their assessment of his career:

"He was the real father of the dime novel. Cheap, boisterous, an incorrigible liar and a generally bad egg, he nevertheless prided himself on his piety, and lectured indefatigably in favor of temperance. His writing was all trash and he himself a rascal of the first order, but he has his place in the history of American eccentrics and the development of American fiction."

Even his obituaries were fictional. Near the end he wrote several different versions and sent them to different papers. One fiction he tried to perpetuate in all of them was his Union Army rank as a colonel. At the time of his death he was applying for a Civil War pension—as a private.

CHAPTER 2

A Genius of the South

Zora Neale Hurston was Florida's first major black female novelist

She was broke and alone when she died in 1960 in a Fort Pierce welfare home. Her body was taken to the Garden of the Heavenly Rest, where it lay in an overgrown and unmarked grave for 13 years.

Then author Alice Walker learned about the sad fate of the fellow black novelist whom she had come to revere.

Walker won the 1983 Pulitzer Prize for her novel *The Color Purple,* which was turned into a hit movie starring Whoopi Goldberg and Oprah Winfrey. But in 1973 she had not yet become famous, so she was able to go to Fort Pierce and pose as the niece of Zora Neale Hurston. This way, Walker figured, she could convince people that she had a good reason to search for the grave of "Aunt Zora."

A young woman named Rosalee, who worked at the funeral home that had handled Zora's burial, guided Walker to the Garden of the Heavenly Rest, a cemetery strangling in waist-deep weeds. Walker waded in, steeling herself against sandspurs, ants, bugs and snakes.

"Zora!" Walker yelled. "Are you out here?"

Startled, Rosalee grumbled, "If she is, I sure hope she don't answer you. If she do, I'm gone."

When they finally found the grave, the novelist said to her guide, "Thank you, Rosalee. Zora thanks you too."

"Just as long as she don't try to tell me in person," Rosalee said.

Later, at the Merritt Monument Company, Walker saw the headstone she wanted: a top-of-the-line black stone called Ebony Mist. Unfortunately, Walker was still a struggling writer and couldn't afford the fancy gravestone, so she settled for a plain gray vertical marker on which her tribute was engraved:

ZORA NEALE HURSTON
A GENIUS OF THE SOUTH
1901–1960
NOVELIST, FOLKLORIST
ANTHROPOLOGIST

* * *

Today it's easy to find Zora's grave. At the Garden of the Heavenly Rest, cleaned up somewhat since 1973, the lone vertical tombstone stands out conspicuously, which is only fitting, because Zora Neale Hurston was no ordinary mortal.

From the small, all-black town of Eatonville in central Florida, Zora ventured into the big world of New York City. There she became a leader in the cultural movement called the Harlem Renaissance of the 1920s. While a student at Columbia University, she studied with Franz Boas, America's greatest anthropologist.

Zora wrote plays, short stories, magazine articles, scholarly papers and seven books. Four of her books were novels, one was an autobiography, and two were fascinating accounts of black folklore in the American South and the Caribbean.

She was a complex, often contradictory woman, equally at home with New York's poets, playwrights and jazz musicians, rural Florida's turpentine workers and migrant laborers, and witch doctors in New Orleans and the West Indies.

Zora was a warm, people-loving woman, but both her marriages were short-lived failures. She strutted through life with a boisterous sense of humor, yet contemplated suicide at a low period of her life.

Her political views kept her in constant hot water with other blacks. A black who had achieved success on a grand scale, she had little sympathy for those who complained about the "system." She had been raised in a self-governing, all-black town, and as the daughter of a Baptist preacher, found a segregated society a comfortable world. She took delight in the rich culture of black people and in no way wished it to be integrated with the whites' way of doing things. Zora spoke out against the 1954 Supreme Court desegration decision that energized the civil rights movement.

In 1950 she worked for conservative George Smathers, who unseated liberal senator Claude Pepper in what is still considered the dirtiest political compaign ever waged in Florida.

A year later Zora wrote a story for *The Saturday Evening Post* praising the country's leading conservative Republican, Sen. Robert Taft, who lost his

Zora Neale Hurston (Florida State Archives)

party's nomination to Gen. Dwight D. Eisenhower. No wonder she was at odds with the National Association for the Advancement of Colored People.

"I was born in a Negro town," wrote Zora. "I do not mean by that the black backside of an average town. Eatonville, Florida, is and was, at the time of my birth, a pure Negro town—charter, mayor, council, town marshal and all. . . . It was the first attempt at self-government on the part of Negroes in America."

At the age of 17, Zora left Eatonville to attend Morgan Academy in Baltimore and Howard University in Washington, D.C. In 1926, she won a scholarship to Barnard College, the women's division of Columbia University in New York.

Her short stories quickly gained her a powerful foothold in the Harlem Renaissance. In her typically outrageous fashion she called fellow black writers the niggerati.

She worked for a time as secretary to Fannie Hurst, a famed white novelist much concerned with racial prejudice. Hurst once integrated a restaurant in Vermont by passing Zora off as an African princess. Said Zora, "Who would think that a good meal could be so bitter?"

In 1927 Zora returned to rural Florida to collect folklore under the sponsorship of Columbia's Department of Anthropology. Back in Eatonville she collected stories, then headed for the lumber and turpentine camps of Polk County. To gain acceptance in these communities, she passed herself off as a

Jacksonville bootlegger's woman on the run. She ended this phase of her research only after she nearly got into a knife fight with another woman.

From there, she moved to New Orleans to research the world of voodoo. There she gained the confidence of Samuel Thompson, a descendant of the legendary Creole conjurer Marie Leveau.

To initiate Zora into voodoo, Thompson required her to lie naked for 69 hours face down on a couch, without food or water and with her navel touching a snake skin.

It was a dangerous test, this trip into the occult, and Zora wrote very little about the experience, remarking only that "for 69 hours I lay there. I had five psychic experiences and awoke at last with no feeling of hunger, only one of exultation."

Zora continued her research on folklore in Miami and the Bahamas, but still found time to work on a play she was writing in collaboration with another famous black author, Langston Hughes. She was in the Bahamas when the killer hurricane of 1928 struck south Florida. Years later it would be used as a pivotal event in her greatest novel, *Their Eyes Were Watching God.*

Her first book on folklore, *Mules and Men,* was published in 1935 by the J.B. Lippincott publishing company, which had also published her first novel, *Jonah's Gourd Vine,* the previous year.

Her 1936 book *Tell My Horse* explored the folklore of the Caribbean, including a memorable chapter on zombies — soulless bodies supposedly called back from the dead. At a hospital in Haiti, she claimed to have photographed a zombie that had a "blank face with dead eyes." Yet she was never able to penetrate the mysterious world of zombies.

However, Haiti seemed to inspire Zora.

When she returned to New York, she plunged into a story that had been taking shape for months. For seven weeks Zora poured out the words that had been "dammed up inside her," then sent the manuscript to Lippincott.

Their Eyes Were Watching God is a story of the love of an older woman of means for a younger, free-spirited laborer. It is set in Eatonville and ranges to the shores of Lake Okeechobee, where the deadly hurricane of 1928 brings tragic results. It is a superb book, filled with memorable characters, and remains to this day one of the finest books ever written by a native Floridian about Florida.

After Lippincott published another novel and her autobiography, Zora changed publishers. The switch grew out of her friendship with Florida novelist Marjorie Kinnan Rawlings, whose publisher was Scribner's.

Zora's *Seraph on the Suwanee* was released by Scribner's in 1948, and the timing could not have been worse. An incredible cloud shrouded the first wave of generally favorable reviews.

Their Eyes Were Watching God was Zora Neale Hurston's most famous novel. (Sun-Sentinel)

On Sept. 13, 1948, New York police knocked at Zora's door. She was arrested and charged with committing sodomy with a 10-year-old boy. Scribner's bailed Zora out of jail and helped her find a lawyer. Her passport finally provided her with an airtight alibi. She had been in Honduras, collecting folklore, when the incident with the boy was supposed to have occurred.

Zora's lawyer went to Manhattan District Attorney Frank Hogan and laid out the facts. Hogan looked into the case and learned that the child was disturbed, and that the boy's mother bore a deep resentment against Zora for once advising her to get psychiatric help for her son. Six months later the charges were dismissed.

But the traumatic experience devastated Zora. She had hoped there would be no publicity, since the case involved a child. But someone in the district attorney's office had leaked information to the *Baltimore Afro-American,* a major black newspaper.

An inaccurate, sensationalized story about the charges ran one week after the publication of *Seraph on the Suwanee*. At first Zora contemplated suicide. Instead, she disappeared, only to resurface a few months later in Miami

Beach. Zora, now 49, had been hired as a maid at a mansion on Rivo Alto Island, off Miami's Venetian Causeway. She was paid $30 a week, plus room and board. Her employer found out who she was when she saw Zora's byline over a *Saturday Evening Post* story.

Being a proud woman, Zora refused to admit that she took the job because she needed the money. Instead, she claimed she took it as a break from writing.

"You can only use your mind so long," she said. "Then you have to use your hands. . . . A writer has to stop writing every now and then and just live a little."

In the last decade of her life, Zora was unable to complete a publishable manuscript. Moving from Belle Glade to Eau Gallie to Merritt Island, she struggled to eke out a living, mostly by teaching and selling magazine and newspaper articles.

In 1959 she moved to Fort Pierce, where she worked as a substitute teacher, wrote freelance articles for the *Chronicle,* a local black weekly, and struggled to finish a novel on King Herod. Her health continued to decline as she fought a lingering tropical disease, a stomach ulcer, a weight problem, gall bladder attacks and finally a stroke.

In October, 1959, Zora entered the St. Lucie County Welfare Home, where she died of "hypertensive heart disease" on the night of January 28, 1960.

Family, friends and publishers donated money for her funeral.

"They said she couldn't become a writer recognized by the world," C.E. Bolen, publisher of the *Chronicle,* said in his eulogy. "But she did it. The Miami paper said she died poor. But she died rich. She did something."

In 1979 a mural was unveiled in the state capitol in Tallahassee depicting famous Floridians. Among them was Zora Neale Hurston. Unfortunately, the mural's Zora was an impostor. Renee Faure, the artist who painted the mural, said she had no photo of Zora so she substituted the face of another woman. A true likeness of Zora finally was painted on the mural in 1985.

Since then, the author has received a good deal of respect. Two plays have been written about her, many of her best books are back in print, a biography has been written, books of criticism have been published and now the Zora Neale Hurston Festival of the Arts is held each January in Eatonville.

And why not? As C.E. Bolen put it, "She did something."

CHAPTER 3

Poet in a Citrus Grove

Laura Riding left author Robert Graves to live in Indian River country

Down a sandy, unpaved private road some two dozen people, some from as far away as England, Ireland and Switzerland, came to the modest Cracker house to pay homage to the poet. Laura Riding had died on Labor Day, 1991, after living a half century in obscurity, hidden away in a citrus grove in the little Indian River community of Wabasso.

The assembled group included two from London, the poet's bibliographer and the poetry critic of the esteemed British newspaper *The Guardian,* and her biographer, who lives in Jacksonville. They shared their memories of an eminent literary figure—poet, critic, novelist, editor, publisher—with Wabasso neighbors who had seen her as a housewife and a grove owner who also wrote.

At 90 she had already outlived the famous contemporaries—some friends, some enemies and some friends turned enemies—who had helped her blaze a Bohemian pathway through her early years.

If the ghosts from that unconventional phase could have appeared at the memorial service, what a cast of characters Wabasso would have seen.

Robert Graves, poet, critic, biographer and novelist, with whom she lived as mistress for 12 years.

Lawrence of Arabia, who found her as "glamorous as a movie star" with "all the qualifications for an imperial role in real life," according to a Graves biographer.

The legendary Gertrude Stein, a close friend whose short book, *An Acquaintance with Description,* she and Graves had published.

Many famous writers who moved in and out of her life: Allen Tate, John Crowe Ransom, Siegfred Sassoon, T. S. Eliot, Virginia Woolf and W. H. Auden.

T. S. Matthews, editor of *Time* magazine, a friend who would become an enemy. At least, he introduced her to the only man she really loved, her second husband, Schuyler Jackson, beside whom she now lies in sandy Indian River soil at Winter Beach Cemetery.

The ghosts would not have recognized the Wabasso Laura, just as her latter-day admirers and neighbors would not have believed the tales from her days with Graves. It is as though one Laura lived in Europe, then returned to America as a totally separate woman.

Her biographer, Elizabeth Friedman, of Jacksonville, sees it differently. "She was a serious woman," she says. "She didn't change over the years."

The unifying force was a life-long search for truth, first through poetry and finally through an exhaustive inquiry into the precise meaning of words.

Laura Riding was an enigmatic woman. A half century of her life was lived in Florida, yet she never wrote a word about a land she loved.

A *femme fatale* with a magnetic appeal, she appears almost homely in photographs and paintings.

Still young, and at the height of her powers, she suddenly stopped writing poetry. Wrote Matthews: "Laura is one of those literary curiosities, a poet who renounced poetry—not because it was too much for her but because she was too much for it—a writer whose reputation grew, whose myth took deeper root, during the . . . years in which she lived a recluse and wrote, in effect, nothing; word of whom spread . . . after she stopped writing."

Her standing in the eyes of other poets, critics and academics, particularly in England, is so high that critic Robert Nye, writing in the British *P.N. Review* declared that the only English poet "fit to be mentioned in the same breath" with her is Shakespeare. Yet she has remained obscure and little read. Friedman, quoted in the *Vero Beach Press-Journal,* said of her: "Her work is accessible if one is very conscious of word use and one is precise in word definitions. . . . In her mind, there are no synonyms. Every word has a precise meaning."

And worst of all, a woman of invincible will and immense ego, she found herself defined for most of her adult life through her relationship with a man whom she dominated, the celebrity author Robert Graves. His biographers, says her biographer, give a distorted, often untrue and decidedly unflattering portrait of Riding. These accounts are indeed sensationalized, hard to believe in light of the person her neighbors saw in Wabasso.

* * *

The poet was born Laura Reichenthal January 16, 1901, in New York City. Her parents were Jewish but, as she said, "not religiously so." She enrolled in Cornell University with the aid of three scholarships, an early recognition of her remarkable intellectual gifts.

In her second year at Cornell she married Louis Gottschalk, a teaching assistant in history. By 1923 she was busy writing both fiction and poetry, using the pseudonym Laura Riding. A number of her early poems were published by the Fugitives, a school of southern writers that included such important poets as Tate, Ransom and Robert Penn Warren.

Along the way, Laura, enmeshed in an unhappy marriage, began a brief affair with Tate. It resulted, rumor said, in a botched abortion which left her with internal problems. Although she loved children, she was fated never to give birth to any.

Ransom suggested that Laura, by now divorced from Gottschalk, send some of her poems to Robert Graves. Perhaps he could help get them published in England. A friendly response from Graves induced her to set out for the British Isles. Unexpectedly Graves found himself with a "lady secretary" as he sailed to Egypt for a teaching job, along with his wife, four children and their nurse.

"Friendship at first sight" was the way Graves later described the meeting between himself, his wife Nancy and the visitor from America in the first week of January, 1926. Friendship was not long in blossoming into what the French call *ménage à trois*. Laura called it "the three life."

Robert and his artist wife, Nancy, were both somewhat vulnerable, he from a mother-dominated childhood coupled with World War I shell shock, she from a nervous temperament aggravated by an unruly thyroid. Laura, strong-willed and confident, gave Robert disciplined intellectual and artistic guidance. To Nancy she brought cheerful companionship and a steady hand at managing the day-to-day needs of living.

Graves wrote to his old friend Sassoon: "It is extremely unlikely that Nancy, Laura and I will ever disband . . . " Some members of Robert's family were less happy with Laura's grip on him, charging that she had "vampirized him from the first." Others were pleased with her kindness to him.

Graves, unhappy in Cairo, broke his teaching contract and returned with his entourage to England. They moved first to the little Oxfordshire cottage that Robert rented from his mother.

Nancy then made an unconventional proposal. She suggested that Robert and Laura go to London and immerse themselves in serious writing. A little later she suggested that all three of them visit Austria for a while. Strange as the "three-life" might seem to others, it was for them a comfortable arrangement, at least for a while.

Riding and Graves, both workaholics, were pouring out books, poems and articles, some individually, some in collaboration. Such books as Graves' *The English Ballad,* Laura's *Contemporaries and Snobs* and *Anarchism is Not Enough* and their joint *Anthologies Against Poetry* and *A Survey of Modernist*

Poetry made a substantial contribution to scholarly literature but brought little income to their household.

Appearing suddenly, like a kindly rain in a desert, T. E. Lawrence, "Lawrence of Arabia," brought them temporary relief from money worries. His publisher wanted a popular biography of the hero. Lawrence, aware of Graves' financial woes, insisted on Robert as his biographer. The 1927 book, *Lawrence and the Arabs,* eased the money worries for a time.

In Paris Riding and Graves visited the famous *avant-garde* author Gertrude Stein. A lesbian, Stein observed that Laura was generally most attractive to slightly masculine women or slightly feminine men. She found Laura someone who "gets into your tenderness as well as your interest."

Meanwhile, in the midst of their busy writing schedule, Laura and Robert started the Seizin Press, a small publishing company dedicated to producing hand-printed books of high quality. "Seizin" is an archaic word for possession; what they possessed was their own printing press.

In the winter of 1929 Geoffrey Phibbs, a rebellious young Irish poet, joined the Riding-Graves group, thus converting the "three-life" into the "four-life." The results were disastrous.

Phibbs' wife Norah, an illustrator, was not accepted at first. Geoffrey was somewhat smitten by Robert's wife, Nancy, while Laura was attracted to Phibbs. When Laura, a juggler who already had too many balls in the air, saw that Geoffrey was unhappy with his wife left out, she tried to bring Norah into a "five-life."

Tension was building in a game without a scorecard or, worse yet, without rules. Laura, consumed with jealousy, was pretending to be more than human, a goddess who, she felt, embodied "Finality." In Paris, Laura, realizing that Geoffrey was going to stay with Norah, exploded into a tantrum in a restaurant. Norah wrote later that "God" had thrown herself on the floor, gone into hysterics, kicked her legs in the air and screamed. The manager assigned two waiters the task of removing Laura from the premises.

Three weeks later Laura cracked up. The night of April 26 she, Robert, Nancy and Geoffrey embarked on an argument which lasted past midnight, then after a brief rest resumed on the fourth floor of their London flat. Geoffrey declared he was "not going to continue to live with or near Laura."

It was too much for her. She tried first to kill herself by drinking the disinfectant Lysol. When it had no effect, she crawled out onto a window ledge, smiled and said, "Goodbye, chaps."

Then with a shout she hurled herself toward almost certain death on the concrete pavement below.

Robert began running downstairs, hoping he could save her somehow.

Laura Riding (Sun-Sentinel)

Then, perhaps realizing the odds were too long, he flung open a window on the third floor and followed her to the concrete below.

Nancy kept her head. She called Robert's sister, Rosaleen, a doctor, then phoned for an ambulance. She and Geoffrey hurried downstairs, fearful of what they would find.

What they found was Robert, in remarkably good shape, and Laura, in great agony, apparently near death. Geoffrey, unable to stand the suffering, left. Nancy stayed at the scene. Rosaleen arrived promptly and gave Laura a shot of morphine to ease her pain.

Rosaleen had Riding taken to Charing Cross Hospital, where she had received her medical training. The report was dismal: four broken vertebrae, a pelvis broken in three places and a severely bent spinal column. If she lived, it was unlikely that she would ever walk again.

Since attempted suicide was a crime in Great Britain, the police moved in quickly to question the witnesses. Phibbs spun a weird tale of the four-life, describing Laura as "a sort of vampire" whom he had come to regard as "mad."

Police for a time suspected Graves of attempted murder. Could he have pushed her, then in a tidal wave of remorse thrown himself out the window? In time they concluded that she had simply jumped. Now the wait began. When, if ever, would Laura recover enough to stand trial?

Within a week Rosaleen was able to write to her brother John: "She's going to live—and I think to walk—but their problems are all unsolved—and are like the most incredible Russian novel."

Within the turmoil that swirled around him, Graves decided it was time to put his past life behind him by writing a frank autobiography of his early years, particularly his terrible war experiences. He would call it *Good-bye to All That* and it would bring him critical acclaim, fame and money—and alienation from his family.

But first he faced another problem—Laura's trial. Courtroom testimony would expose the juicy story of the "four-life." Laura would probably be deported and scandal would tarnish the Graves family name.

Graves had an influential friend in government, Eddie Marsh, who worked as secretary for Winston Churchill at the Exchequer. Graves had been introduced to Churchill by Lawrence of Arabia, who had visited Laura regularly at Charing Cross Hospital. The charges were dropped.

For Robert it seemed the time to say good-bye to all that, even to his children and his aging parents. He and Laura decided to leave England. In France Gertrude Stein recommended the Spanish island Majorca: "paradise, if you can stand it!"

On the Mediterranean isle they found a place to live cheaply. In the little village of Deya, Robert and Laura rented a primitive stone cottage named Casa Salerosa, nestled beside a terrace of olive trees.

Other writers and artists were not long in showing up. First there was the Scottish poet Norman Cameron, who built a small bungalow near them. Soon they were joined by Elfriede, a lusty German girl. Elfriede later said she had been "procured by Laura for Norman." Unfortunately, while waiting for Norman, she had fallen in love with Robert. The result was an unwanted pregnancy. Laura insisted on an abortion.

Afterward Riding evicted Elfriede. When the beautiful German girl returned unexpectedly, Laura went after her with a whip. Robert mercifully intervened, declaring he had seen enough violence in the war. By this time

Cameron, feeling sorry for the beleaguered Elfriede, finally got around to falling in love with her.

Others began to arrive, among them Tom Matthews, who would play a major role in their lives. Matthews, accompanied by his wife Julie and their two children, had taken a leave of absence from his job with *Time* Magazine to work on a novel.

Forty-five years later Matthews wrote vivid descriptions of Robert and Laura. Robert, he wrote, was "gangly-tall, muscular but shambling; with his broken nose and wildly staring eyes, swarthy coloring and frizzy black hair as unruly as the sun's corona, he looked like a bandit from an earlier century."

Of Laura, he wrote that she was "as primly neat as Robert was gawky. She never had a hair out of place, and her clothes, which were old-fashioned, never seemed odd. When she was in full regalia her dignity matched and enhanced costume. . . . "

When Matthews found himself bogged down, Riding offered to help. Her help, he later said, was "the clutch of an octopus brain." Her suggestions, changes and rewrites drastically altered his book.

"I put up what resistance I could," he wrote, "but my mind was no match for Laura's, and I think I lost every argument. Once a whole paragraph of mine came through her scrutiny with no word changed; I felt as if I had won the Nobel Prize." This is an interesting admission coming from a man who would later become *Time*'s editor-in-chief. He would also become the third husband of author and journalist Martha Gellhorn after she divorced Ernest Hemingway.

While Tom and Laura struggled with a novel that would become *The Moon's No Fool,* Graves began work on his greatest success, the historical novel *I, Claudius*. In his story of the Roman Empire one of the most memorable characters is the scheming, manipulative Livia. She stopped at nothing, even murder, to gain her ends. Some have speculated that her character was based on Laura.

I, Claudius, published in 1934, was followed a year later by *Claudius the God*. Both were critical and commercial successes. Riding first bad-mouthed the genre, then decided she would show Robert the way to write a "proper" historical novel. Her *A Trojan Ending,* published in the United States by Random House, earned a few favorable reviews but unfortunately very few readers.

In 1936 the Spanish Civil War forced them to leave Majorca. They returned to London, where Graves was now a celebrity.

Alexander Korda made plans to produce a movie about Claudius, starring Charles Laughton in the title role. The project was scrapped when Merle Oberon, cast as the film's Messalina, was injured in an automobile accident.

Four decades would pass before Claudius would emerge on film as the most successful television series ever produced by the British Broadcasting Company.

The following summer Laura completed work on her manuscript for *Collected Poems,* the book which many regard as her masterwork. Schuyler Jackson, reviewing it for *Time* in 1938, wrote: "This book, for an English-speaking person marooned in the middle of the 20th century, would be the book of books for him to have along."

Calling her "probably the most difficult and at the same time the most lucid of present-day poets," Jackson declared that Riding and the German writer Rainer Maria Rilke were the only two true poets of the era.

Jackson was a close friend of Matthews from their days together at Princeton University. Tom had long hoped to bring Schuyler and Laura together. Now the possibility loomed especially attractive to her.

Things were changing for Riding and for Graves. Robert was becoming interested in Beryl Hodge, the wife of his friend Alan, and Laura was intrigued with the idea of returning to her native land—and meeting Jackson.

In the spring of 1939 Riding and Graves sailed for America. At the dock in New York she met Jackson, described in a Matthews book as "arrestingly handsome. His head was round, with a broad, high brow; cheekbones marked, mouth and jaw firm, lips thin. . . . His shoulders were broad and his body well muscled."

With Schuyler, his wife Kit, and Tom and Julie Matthews, Riding and Graves drove then to Princeton, New Jersey, where they divided their time between the Matthews' home and Schuyler's nearby farm.

Soon Laura had recruited Jackson to work with her on a dictionary, a long-time Riding-Graves project. Her powerful personality was already reaching out to him and at the same time was slowly wearing Kit down. One night at dinner Kit leaned forward, laid her head on the table and began crying.

"Schuyler and Laura were falling in love . . . in front of our fascinated, wincing but unseeing eyes," wrote Matthews. It was more than the fragile Kit could take. She went mad.

For Graves the American visit was also proving disastrous. He saw Laura slipping away. Then one day she disappeared into Schuyler's bedroom and did not emerge for two days.

Robert returned to England without Laura. It was over and he knew it.

After Kit divorced Schuyler, he and Laura were married in the spring of 1941 at Elkton, a small Maryland town famous for quickie weddings. Schuyler, like Graves, left behind four children.

Three years earlier Jackson had visited the east coast of Florida. Near Vero Beach a little citrus town named Wabasso, population about 300, had caught his eye.

They bought a grapefruit grove and a Cracker house, nestled among the trees and sheltered from the sight of the Florida East Coast Railway by a stand of Australian pines. What a contrast to London, Paris, Majorca! Their neighbors were citrus growers, pickers and shippers. Ironically, the biggest packing house in Wabasso was owned by one Robert Graves, prominent grower and later chairman of the Indian River County Commission.

Their house was a small box-shaped dwelling with a steeply pitched tin roof. Schuyler had an office to himself; Laura wrote in the large room running the width of the house. A shelf above her work table held the 10 volumes of the Oxford English Dictionary.

Her return to America brought a sharp break with her past, not just with Graves but with the work that had been her life's passion. She renounced poetry as an inadequate vehicle for telling the truth, and in collaboration with Schuyler began work on a book on language, entitled *Rational Meaning: A New Foundation for the Definition of Words*.

Far removed from distractions, other than the FEC's lonesome whistle, Laura and Schuyler labored hard on their project. Laura cooked the meals and kept the house. She had become a housewife.

"Schuyler kept the place up," said Mrs. Nelly Bass, one of their neighbors. "He was an ordinary, old-fashioned active person."

Mrs. Bass remembers Laura fondly. Laura often visited with the Bass family and was particularly kind to their children. She remembered their birthdays and brought them gifts.

"I never went to her house," said Mrs. Bass. "'If you come to my house,' she told me, 'you have to make an appointment.' I told her I never make any appointments with anybody but my doctor."

Neither of the Jacksons could manage money. Schuyler's father set up a trust for him, providing just enough for them to live on. At Schuyler's death the trust was designed to shift to his four children.

Schuyler's death came on July 4, 1968. Nelly Bass recalls the day: "Schuyler pulled off his work shoes and left them there by the front door. Then he went in and died. She wouldn't let anybody move those shoes. They just sat there by the door."

After the death of Schuyler, Laura, said Mrs. Bass, stayed up all night, fearful of break-ins.

"My rooster bothered her," said Mrs. Bass.

By now an old woman with long white hair, she walked with the help of a cane, perhaps the legacy of her London leap. The people of Wabasso saw nothing of the "vampirish" Laura that emerged from the books about Graves. She baked cookies for the children in the schools nearby. She was generally well liked and respected by her neighbors. They knew she was a writer and they respected that.

She continued laboring on *Rational Meaning*. The precise meaning of words—this was what commanded the attention of this remarkable intellect.

"The last time I saw it, the manuscript was a foot high," said Maggie Bowman, Indian River County commissioner and an old friend of Laura's.

An environmentalist, Laura got to know the commissioner through the Pelican Island Audubon Society, which Bowman headed. Riding had heard water pumps going night and day, supplying water for a golf course on ritzy John's Island. She concluded that saltwater intrusion threatened Wabasso's shallow wells.

"It was an intelligent, well-reasoned analysis of the problem," said Bowman. "We took it to the St. Johns River Water Management District and the matter was corrected."

After the death of her husband, Laura knew financial hardship. A few royalty payments helped, as did a Guggenheim Fellowship in 1973 which paid her $2500 a year. Fortunately, her wants were few. She did not consume alcohol. A chain-smoker when young, she had given that up. She had no electrical bills to pay—the house had no electricity and no heat.

In 1988 she suffered a massive heart attack. Pat O'Brien, who worked in health care, arranged for nurses for her through Medicare and in the last years of her life became a close and trusted friend.

One cold, winter's night while he was working as a volunteer drug counselor he received a call on his car phone at 1 a.m. The nurse at the Jackson home told him she was freezing. There was no heat except a kerosene stove, and neither of them knew how to light it.

In the car was a 16-year-old street-smart drug dealer who luckily knew kerosene stoves. By a lucky coincidence he was also the son of a nurse that Laura particularly liked. He fixed the stove, then stayed for another two hours talking to her until the early morning hours.

"She would probably be at her best talking to an Einstein, but she could also talk at Odie's level," said O'Brien. "When she died he was in jail for a shooting. I went by and told him and he cried."

Near the end she suffered intense pain, partly from her heart condition and partly from severe sciatica. She often ignored her medication, O'Brien said, because she wanted a clear mind when she was working or when she was reading something particularly difficult.

On January 16, 1991, Laura Jackson celebrated her 90th birthday. The next month she was awarded the prestigious Bollingen Prize for Poetry. The honor came late. By now her health was deteriorating rapidly. On Labor Day at Humana Hospital in Sebastian her heart finally gave out.

One of the finest tributes came from Pat O'Brien: "God blessed me to let me know a woman as special as Mrs. Jackson. She was one neat lady."

SILVER SCREEN

From the days of the silent films to the glitzy color of today Florida has drawn moviemakers. Jacksonville once battled it out with Hollywood for the role of America's film capital. The state's passing parade of film celebrities has included directors D.W. Griffith and John Huston, the "ton of jollity" known as Oliver Hardy and such cartoon characters as Betty Boop, Popeye the Sailorman, and Superman.

CHAPTER 4

When Silents Were Golden

Before talkies, moviemakers feasted on Florida's tropical scenery

In 1925 a Miami developer named Charles Apfel said he was told by several scientists that a devastating Arctic current would soon menace Hollywood and the rest of Southern California. That being the case, he reasoned, why not take advantage of Florida's land boom and move the nation's film capital to the balmy subtropics?

A man of action, Apfel quickly purchased the Gomez Grant, a Spanish land grant of more than 12,000 acres just south of Stuart that dated back to the early 1800s, when Spain still ruled Florida.

On this land, Apfel planned to develop a town of 20,000 residents and call it the City of Olympia. Nearby he would build studios, sets and palatial mansions for the Hollywood moguls and stars who had fled California's new ice age. This section would be called Picture City.

Over the next few months Apfel laid out curving streets and sidewalks and built concrete street lamps. But that's as far as it went. The developer had a great idea, but his timing was off. By 1926 the Florida boom had gone bust, and along with it, a fledgling movie industry. And, of course, California's ice age never did arrive.

What remains of Apfel's Olympian dreams?

Drive along Dixie Highway in Hobe Sound and you will see a few old sidewalks, weathered paving, tired-looking lampposts and streets with names such as Juno Circle, Venus Street, Mercury Street and Vulcan Avenue. That's all that remains of what he hoped would become the "Los Angeles of Florida."

Even before Charles Apfel came along with his ill-timed vision, the movies had discovered Florida. In 1908, three years before California attracted its first big studio, Jacksonville was working hard to become filmdom's winter capital.

A fat Georgia boy named Oliver Hardy got his start there. Before getting himself into "another fine mess" with Stan Laurel, he made over a hundred comedies for Pop Lubin's studio and the Vim Comedy Company.

As early as 1910, Lubin discovered that palm trees made a romantic backdrop for the movies. His film *A Honeymoon Through Snow to Sunshine* closed with tropical sequences shot in Miami and Palm Beach.

Other moviemakers quickly learned that Florida's tropical ambience could double as backdrops for tales of the South Seas; that swamps made creepy locales for terrified heroines; that beaches could be used as deserts, and that the cameras could roll almost every day in the Florida sunshine.

Between 1915 and 1926 more than 120 movies were shot along the Gold Coast, most of them heavily into the exotic.

A good example was *A Woman There Was,* a 1919 Fox movie starring Hollywood's greatest vamp, Theda Bara. Miami Beach served as the stand-in for a South Seas island where Theda, playing a native chief's daughter, falls in love with a missionary. In the dramatic climax, she gets stabbed by her fellow natives but still manages to help the missionary escape from the island.

About the same time, the Fox company was also turning Miami into India. An elaborate Hindu temple was built on Seybold Creek, north of Miami, for a movie titled *Jungle Trail.* One scene called for temple priests to sacrifice a luscious princess by pitching her into a lagoon infested with sacred crocodiles. Naturally, the crocs were portrayed by low-wage Florida alligators.

While the princess was willing to be a good sport, the movie's hero, William Farnum, was less than enthusiastic about a scene where he was supposed to leap into the water, pummel a few gators and rescue the princess from certain death.

Fortunately, the director found a stand-in who didn't mind the gators—Henry Coppinger, the man credited with concocting the "sport" of alligator wrestling. Coppinger later passed along this rather peculiar trade to the Seminoles. For years, the Indians would rely on alligator wrestling to attract tourists to their villages. It was just as well, because the demise of the Florida film industry was a bitter blow to the Seminoles, many of whom had made a good living portraying the bloodthirsty natives of South Pacific islands and far-off jungles.

One of those Indians was Tony Tommie, the first Broward County Seminole to be educated in the white man's schools. Tommie was also a talent scout and casting director. Many Seminoles had also found work in Palm Beach, where a 20-episode serial titled *Gloria's Romance* was filmed in 1916.

In the serial, a madcap young heiress on her way to Palm Beach crashes her car into the ocean. She then has to make her way on foot through alligator-infested swamps to Palm Beach (geography was obviously not the strong

Legendary vamp Theda Bara, to the right of the cross, played a native chief's daughter in a South Seas movie, "A Woman There Was," shot on Miami Beach. (Historical Association of Southern Florida)

point of the scriptwriters). Of course, she would first be captured by the Indians in an episode titled *Caught by the Seminoles,* which followed an episode called *Lost in the Everglades.*

Gloria's Romance was made not by any of the better known production companies of the day, such as Fox, Pathe or Famous Players Lasky, but by one of the nation's biggest newspapers, *The Chicago Tribune*. The sole purpose of the movie was to boost the newspaper's circulation.

Max Annenberg, the *Tribune*'s circulation manager, discussed the project with stage impresario Flo Ziegfield. The great Ziegfield, of Ziegfield Follies fame, liked the idea and wondered if there might be a starring role in it for his wife, Billie Burke. Anxious to stay on the good side of Ziegfield, Annenberg said that Billie could play the leading role of the young heiress.

"Wait," said Ziegfield, "is there any chance for glamour?’

Yes, Annenberg told him, there would be plenty of glamour, including a society ball, a courtroom scene, and a sickbed scene in which Billie, for some inexplicable reason, would wear many priceless jewels.

"Money?" asked Ziegfield.

"Plenty," said Annenberg, "$75,000."

"Double it or no deal."

"But that would be more than any other actress has ever been paid," Annenberg protested.

"Well, Billie is the best actress who ever lived," insisted her husband.

Two weeks later the two men settled for the unheard-of figure of $130,000, along with a few perks: at least ten costume changes for Billie, a present of a powder-blue Rolls-Royce with Billie's initials in gold on each door, jewels from Cartier and a lavish Palm Beach home she could retain for a while for her personal use after shooting ended.

Filming started in the fall of 1915 and was completed by the following spring. Along the way the producers exposed nearly a million feet of film, almost six times as much as more efficient serial makers.

On May 18, 1916, the serial was unveiled to the public with the kind of fanfare that only Ziegfield could generate. It was the only serial ever to have its premiere on Broadway.

Unfortunately, *Gloria's Romance* was an expensive flop. But Billie Burke continued to appear in movies and, 23 years later, earned everlasting fame as the Good Witch Glenda in *The Wizard of Oz.*

Gloria's Romance also paid dividends for Ziegfield. The movie introduced him and his flamboyant designer, Joseph Urban, to the Palm Beach scene. Urban designed Mar-a-Lago, now owned by real estate tycoon Donald Trump, for Marjorie Merriweather Post, the cereal heiress.

Three years after the completion of *Gloria's Romance,* a film crew arrived in Fort Lauderdale to shoot *The Great Gamble,* a 15-episode serial produced by the Western Photo Play Company for Pathe.

Tony Tommie rounded up his Seminole buddies to play the usual menacing savages. Their most bloodthirsty act was to capture Anne Luther and Charles Hutchison, the film's stars, and prepare to burn them at the stake. In typical serial fashion, Luther and Hutchison were rescued before the Indians could torch them.

Hutchison, known as the "Thrill-A-Minute Stunt King," also had to leap from a Florida East Coast Railway train into New River. And Luther had a harrowing scene on a temporary bridge over Cypress Creek near Pompano. The structure collapsed on cue as her car crossed the stream. She escaped from the waters only to be captured by the Seminoles.

Also in 1919, Famous Players-Lasky, which would later become Paramount Pictures, brought in the famed dancer Irene Castle and a company of 20 to film scenes in Fort Lauderdale, Palm Beach and Miami for *The Firing Line,* based on a popular novel by Robert Chambers.

"Lovely Irene Castle," the publicity release gushed, "will dance into your heart in this big, brilliant, colorful drama of life at gay Palm Beach. . . . Charming gowns, stirring adventure, laughter and love and tears amid the flowers and fountains of Florida."

Once again the film gave employment to the Seminoles and brought to the screen a well-known Fort Lauderdale con man named Bert Lasher. Bert played the role of guide to a hunter in scenes shot in an isolated area that would later become Wilton Manors. He even managed to wangle parts in a hunting sequence for two of his hunting dogs, Joe and Prince.

In the fall of 1919 Fort Lauderdale finally managed to reel in the biggest catch of them all—D.W. Griffith, America's greatest silent film director. More than any other individual, Griffith had moved the cinema toward an art form with such classics as *Birth of a Nation, Intolerance* and *Broken Blossoms.*

But the film he made in Fort Lauderdale, *The Idol Dancer,* was just another potboiler that used Florida palms and beaches to create one more South Seas

D.W. Griffith, America's greatest director of the silent era, sits beside his cameraman during filming of "The Idol Dancer" on the shores of the New River. (Fort Lauderdale Historical Society)

island. No one objected, of course. Griffith was bringing excitement to Fort Lauderdale, along with jobs for Indians, blacks and a number of young women around town. Furthermore, the home folks would have the opportunity to mingle with Richard Barthelmess, a major star of his day, and Clarine Seymour, a promising starlet.

When Griffith hit town, he brought with him a crew of more than 50 actors, cameramen and technicians. They moved into the Hotel Broward in downtown Fort Lauderdale, even though construction of the hotel was not yet completed. The first signature on the new hotel's register was David Wark Griffith.

A replica of a South Seas village was built on the grounds of the Las Olas Inn, which boasted a superb stand of coconut palms. The movie crew was amused by the small-town modesty of Fort Lauderdale schoolgirls who played bit parts. When makeup men applied brown paint to their faces and arms to transform them into dusky South Seas maidens, the girls had no objections. But when it came to leg makeup, they were shocked and insisted on doing the job themselves.

Griffith stayed on after *The Idol Dancer* to shoot *The Love Flower,* starring many of the same performers. Most of the second film was shot in Miami, which in the early 1920s was rapidly becoming South Florida's hot spot for filming.

In 1923 another top director came to Miami. Rex Ingram, who had directed Rudolph Valentino in *The Four Horsemen of the Apocalypse,* arrived to make *Where the Pavement Ends,* starring Ramon Navarro. A derelict sailing vessel was hauled up on Miami Beach and converted into a trading station and cafe where much of the film's action took place.

As it turned out, 1923 was the high point in south Florida's silent filmmaking. Twenty-one movies were produced on the Gold Coast that year. Production remained strong through 1926, but then the boom ended. By 1929, the year of the stock market crash, not a single movie was being made in south Florida.

Farther north, Jacksonville's bid for movie stardom had died almost a decade earlier, a victim of reform-minded politicians and religious leaders who thought the industry too sinful and high-handed to be tolerated in their town.

Moviemaking dried up in South Florida for different reasons. The real estate collapse of 1926 was a major factor, of course, but so was the arrival of the talkies. Hollywood became preoccupied with learning how to put sound on film, and for years most filming was done on accoustically designed "sound stages" in Hollywood, eliminating the demand for exotic locales such as Florida.

Director Rex Ingram and his star, Edith Terry, take a break in filming "Where the Pavement Ends" on Miami Beach. (Historical Association of Southern Florida)

Development also played the role of spoiler as far as moviemaking in Fort Lauderdale was concerned. "I hardly know Fort Lauderdale," Richard Barthelmess told a reporter when he returned to south Florida a few years after making *The Idol Dancer.* "All the natural beauty is giving way to progress. I'm afraid we won't be able to film here much longer."

CHAPTER 5

Another Fine Mess

Oliver Hardy of Laurel and Hardy launched movie career in Jacksonville

Before Laurel and Hardy of Hollywood came Plump and Runt of Jacksonville. Big comic, little comic, Mutt and Jeff, a winning formula for a movie comedy team.

In Hollywood, the pairing of courtly, portly Oliver Hardy, the quintessential fat man, with skinny, pasty-pale, sharp-chinned Stan Laurel created many a "fine mess." It also generated uncontrolled laughter on a global scale. It still does.

To the Boys, as the movie pros called them, the combination brought wealth, adoration, acclaim. Even an Oscar.

The two good-hearted bumblers usually embarked on doomed, dim-witted ventures, then found themselves swept away by a tidal wave of hilarious setbacks. Stan invariably broke into comic tears, lifted his derby and scratched his head in justified bewilderment.

In the face of disaster Ollie always strove mightily to maintain his dignity, never easy when his shirt and tie were being mutilated before his unbelieving eyes or a grand piano was landing on top of him in a lily pond.

As the relentless turn of events dawned slowly, always slowly, on Ollie, his expressive face invariably registered a patient disbelief which soon dissolved into impotent indignation. Who can gaze without laughing at Ollie as he twiddles his tie, fusses with his derby or builds a slow burn at the latest dirty trick life has visited upon him? Another fine mess. Another hilarious comedy.

* * *

For Oliver Norvell Hardy, a popular Jacksonville cabaret singer who billed himself at Cutie Pearce's roadhouuse as "The Ton of Jollity," the classic big/little pairing emerged for the first time in 1916, not in California's swinging Tinseltown but in a conservative Deep South city.

When Hardy arrived, there were more motion picture production crews operating in northeast Florida than in Los Angeles. Jacksonville, Florida's biggest city with a population of close to 60,000, was battling New York and California to become the movie film capital, or as the *Florida Times-Union* put it, "the Klondike of the growing motion picture industry." By 1916 some 30 film companies operated beneath the Jacksonville sun, employing a thousand actors and hordes of extras.

To this world, just 200 miles south of his home town of Milledgeville, Georgia, 21-year-old Oliver Hardy came in 1913. He worked as a cabaret singer and as an actor with the Lubin Film Company. Then, in 1916, the right vehicle came along—a series of one-reel comedies planned by the Vim Comedy Company. The series was entitled Plump and Runt.

Hardy, at six feet two and well over 200 pounds, was hardly in the running for the role of Runt. That honor went to a small, acrobatic circus clown named Billy Ruge, sharp-chinned like Stan Laurel.

To the role of Plump, Hardy, just 24 years old, brought far more than singing skills, which were, after all, of no value in those silent-film days. He had already acted in 60 one-reelers, most of them with Lubin.

Vim, based in the New York area, leased the Florida Yacht Club clubhouse and began turning out comedies from "the best outdoor studio this side of Los Angeles," according to *Moving Picture World.* The biggest problems came from thunderstorms.

On the shores of the St. Johns River in the city's fashionable Riverside district, Vim first teamed Plump with Runt in January, 1916, more than a decade before the pairing of Laurel and Hardy. Plump and Runt were a couple of slapstick hobos. Their first comedy was *A Special Delivery,* to be followed by some 34 more one-reelers.

In these films Ollie picked up the little acrobat and tossed him around, said biographer John McCabe, "like a medicine ball." Despite his rotundity, Hardy was both strong and athletic. He had played football and baseball and later in Hollywood was for a time the best golfer in the movie colony.

McCabe, an authority on the Boys, called the Plump and Runt comedies "diverting one-reelers, all of them marked by a charming, even elegant, crudity."

Among the titles in the Plump and Runt series were such films as *Nerve and Gasoline, Bungles Lands a Job, Human Hounds* and *Love and Duty.* In 1917 Vim, which produced 156 one-reel comedies in Jacksonville, paired Hardy with the popular comedienne Kate Price for 14 more films.

Author Richard Alan Nelson, the leading authority on early Florida moviemaking, wrote: "In this grind-'em-out training ground, long before his teaming with Stan Laurel, Hardy developed the talent and mannerisms that would later influence his screen persona as the lovable 'Ollie.'"

Jordan R. Young, who studied the Plump and Runt films, felt that he detected "possibly the first-sown seeds of the Laurel and Hardy concept. Besides many of the comedies sounding like typical L & H situations, the character relationships and plot developments coincide frequently, sometimes to an incredible degree."

In Jacksonville Hardy acquired his lifelong nickname, "Babe." Near the Lubin studio a little Italian named Enzo ran a barber shop which served the movie crowd. After shaving Ollie, always a pink-cheeked cherub, Enzo would rub his face with talcum powder, saying "Nice-a babe-e-e. Nice-a babe-e-e." The Lubin actors picked up on it, shortening it to "Babe."

In the Duval County seat Hardy also wooed the first of his three wives, Madelyn Saloshin. She was a talented pianist with the pit orchestra at the Orpheum Theatre, where he appeared as a singer. Though she was roughly a decade older than he, they married in 1913. He was just 21. His mother, who lived in Milledgeville, was furious at the elopement.

Oliver Hardy was responsible for the breakup of Vim. Attorney Louis Burstein ran Vim's Jacksonville operation. His partner Mark Dintenfass sent money down from New York to pay the actors in cash every Saturday. The problem was that Burstein was skimming money from their pay envelopes.

By accident Hardy discovered the salary list. He saw immediately that New York was sending down more money for him than he was getting. He exploded: "Hey, you dirty bastards—you're only paying me so much, but you're charging the guy in New York to pay a lot more."

The scandal wrecked the company. Hardy stayed in Jacksonville a while, acting in comedies produced by the King Bee Film Company, headed by none other than Burstein. He also sang at the Hotel Burbidge, where his wife Madelyn conducted a ragtime band.

By 1917 Jacksonville's movie industry was busily shooting itself in the foot. Moviemakers were setting off false fire alarms to get action shots of fire trucks. Some 1,380 extras hired for a mob scene went out of control, became a mob and wrecked downtown property. Religious groups were alarmed when bank robberies were filmed on Sunday. That year the mayor, J.E.T. Bowden, one of the industry's staunchest supporters, was defeated for reelection by 834 votes.

Soon the movie industry was making its decision in favor of California. In the late fall of 1917 Babe Hardy himself headed west, leaving behind his native South. But not really. Years later he would reveal that he developed the character Ollie in the Laurel and Hardy comedies as "a Southern gentleman." Traces of his Southern accent stayed with him to the end, particularly in words like "certainly" and "anniversary."

* * *

For Laurel and Hardy the road to the movies took different paths. Stan, born in northern England, raised in Scotland, came from a show business family. In British music halls, he understudied the great Charlie Chaplin. It was inevitable that his comic genius would lead him to Hollywood.

Ollie first reached the silver screen by a geographically more direct route—across the state line from Georgia to Florida. Norvell Hardy was born on January 18, 1892, near Augusta in the little north Georgia town of Harlem. When Norvell was only 11 months old, his father, Oliver Norvell Hardy, a Civil War hero, died. Later Norvell, proud of the father he never really knew, took his name and became Oliver Norvell Hardy.

When Ollie was nine, the family moved to Milledgeville, where his mother, Miss Emily, ran a hotel. The boy, who was already displaying considerable singing talent, was fascinated by the "theatricals," as the show business guests who stayed at the hotel were called.

Before he was 10, young Norvell, a talented boy soprano, had run away with Coburn's Minstrels, a troupe headed by Charles Coburn, a third cousin of a famed actor who would later become a close friend of Hardy's. A wise man, Coburn wrote Emily Hardy and suggested that the boy be allowed to travel with them until he got the show business fever out of his blood, which, predictably, proved to be a matter of just a few weeks.

Norvell, though lovable, was a headstrong youth, difficult to manage for a widow struggling to support five children. She provided him with singing lessons and even gave the young teenager train fare to go to Atlanta to hear the world's greatest tenor, Enrico Caruso. For him it was one of the most moving experiences of his life.

Miss Emmie could be tough when she had to be. Norvell, aged 14, decided to prove his manhood with a fancy maple leaf tattoo inscribed on his inner right forearm. His mother, not one bit amused, stormed over to the tattoo parlor and horsewhipped the tattooist.

Norvell never lasted long at any of the schools he attended—the Atlanta Conservatory of Music, Georgia Military College or Young Harris College in the Georgia mountains. In later life he came to regret his lack of education and became an omnivorous reader of news magazines to try to make himself an informed citizen.

On occasion he sang popular songs at the Milledgeville Opera House before finding his niche in 1910 as a boy of 18. When the Electric Theatre became the town's first movie house, he landed a job as projectionist. In addition he took tickets, swept out the theater, acted as backup manager and sang to illustrated slides. At the Electric Theatre he saw films for three years—and he learned from them. In particular, he studied the art of the "take," an actor's reaction to screen events. His slow-burn "take" became one of his trademarks.

"I knew," he said many years later. "I knew. I thought to myself that I could be as good—or maybe as bad—as some of those boys."

In 1913, when Hardy was 21, a friend returned from a vacation in Florida. He told tales of a growing film colony at Jacksonville, just 200 miles to the south.

Norvell quit his job and headed south to the bustling Florida city on the banks of the St. Johns. He promptly found work as a vaudeville and cabaret singer at the Orpheum Theatre, which paid him $40 a week, and at Cutie Pearce's roadhouse.

Since Hardy worked mostly at night, he was free during the day to watch the moviemakers, particularly the Lubin Film Company at the Florida Yacht Club clubhouse.

He liked the comedy players so much he volunteered to work as company water boy just to be near the action. One day a director, needing a fat boy for his next comedy, asked Norvell if he was available for a film to be entitled *Outwitting Dad.*

Thus was launched in April of 1914 a major motion picture career. Lubin hired Ollie for $5 a day for three days a week.

Four years later Hardy first met Arthur Stanley Jefferson, whose movie name was Stan Laurel. Stan starred in *The Lucky Dog,* while Ollie appears in it briefly as a heavy.

The two went their separate ways, honing their acting skills, occasionally appearing in comedies together but never as a starring team. Ollie, billed as Babe Hardy, even appeared as a Kansas farmhand in the first *The Wizard of Oz,* a 1925 seven-reel film.

That same year he appeared, too, in *The Paperhanger's Helper,* a two-reeler which he recalled later with fondness: "I think of that picture once in a while as being the start of the Laurel and Hardy idea as far as I was concerned."

A decade after Hardy arrived in Hollywood, the master of comedy films, Hal Roach, paired him again with Laurel in *Putting Pants on Philip,* regarded by many as the first true Laurel and Hardy movie. Ollie played the role of Piedmont Mumblethunder, confronted with the problem of getting his visiting cousin from Scotland to trade his kilt for trousers. In later comedies the Boys were always called Stan and Ollie.

Oliver Hardy, second from right, with friends at Jacksonville, circa 1916. (Florida State Archives)

Pants was followed in late December of 1927 with the L and H comedy that finally told the fans and the studio that a major comedy team had arrived. *The Battle of the Century* was a pie fight to end all pie fights, literally. To make this two-reeler the studio purchased a day's total output of pies from the Los Angeles Pie Company—four thousand pies to be thrown, pushed or fallen into. The fans loved it—seven laughs a minute for 20 minutes for its preview showings.

From that date until the death of Babe in 1957, the two comics stayed together as performers and as friends. When the movie industry phased from silent to sound films in the late 1920s, they made the switch without missing a gag.

The Laurel and Hardy films, both short subjects and features, totalled 89, among them *Saps at Sea, A Chump at Oxford, Swiss Miss, Babes in Toyland* and *Sons of the Desert.* Thirty-two of their films were silent.

In 1932 the Boys starred in a three-reel classic. For 30 minutes their fans saw them stumble through a long, hard day, struggling to deliver a piano to a house on the top of a hill, accessible only by interminable stairs. The blunders, and the gags, are unending. *The Music Box* won them an Oscar for the year's best short subject.

Stan was the creative member of the team, the giver of plots, ideas and gags. Ollie always saw himself purely as a comic actor and left the shaping of the comedies to his partner. Thus there was no friction between them about their roles nor about the content of their films. Both disliked smut and mean-spirited humor.

In their early days they spent little time together away from the studio. Laurel was a workaholic. He toiled for long hours, then hung around with other moviemakers, talking shop on into the night.

On the other hand, Hardy preferred to associate with people outside the industry, bank presidents and business executives. He could hardly wait to get to the golf course. Babe was the perpetual club champion at the Lakeside Golf Club as well as the best dancer at the club.

One of his favorite golf partners was Bing Crosby. Bing, the master crooner, admired Hardy's singing. While golfing, the two of them sang duets. The two were also horse racing fans, participating as founding investors of Del Mar Race Track. Babe, also, once owned a racing stable.

Friends recall Ollie as a man of elaborate courtesy, a kindly, good-natured man with a great zest for living. He was not, however, without his demons. Till late in life he was tormented by his size. He never learned to like being called "Fatty." But then not until his health began to deteriorate did he learn to control his appetite.

Both Stan and Ollie had their marital woes. Both were married three times and for each of them only their third marriage was a good one.

By the end of World War II the movie world had changed. There was no longer a niche where even the wondrous talents of the Boys seemed to fit. Their last film together was *Atoll K,* a confused European-made movie released in 1951. It bombed, but their popularity soared again. Television found them.

Late in their lives, in the mid-1950s, they turned to stage appearances in Great Britain and then on the Continent. Touring together with their wives for weeks on end they found they had become the closest of friends. In an industry where egos doomed many long-term alliances they remained friends to the end.

Oliver, whose weight sometimes reached 350 pounds, suffered a severe heart attack on September 15, 1956. Eleven months later he died, following of a series of strokes. He was 65. Stan died eight years later at 70.

With so many of their films available in video stores, Laurel and Hardy are far from forgotten. A book of poems by Michael Heffernan (University of Georgia Press) even bears the name *The Cry of Oliver Hardy* and observes:

"How he would dance with dread and tweedle his derby

"And send his clear soprano up from all his tonnage. . . ."

The Boys are remembered in festivals in their home towns. Stan is honored

Badge for Sons of the Desert international convention at Clearwater Beach in 1990. (Ronald Young)

each year in Ulverston, Lancashire, England, and Ollie in Harlem, Georgia, where the annual Oliver Hardy Festival is held each fall.

Laurel and Hardy are remembered, too, through the Sons of the Desert, an international fan club named after one of their funniest films. More than 200 tents, as the clubs are called, meet in 14 countries and once a year get together for an international convention.

Stan came up with a perfect motto for the club, a phrase that captures the glory of the Boys:

"Two minds without a single thought."

CHAPTER 6

Cartoon Madness

Betty Boop, Popeye and Superman once sported around Miami studio

"It is because of Max's (and Dave's) myopia that you will take your family to Orlando instead of to Miami to visit 'Fleischerland.'"

Thus wrote author Leslie Cabarga in his *The Fleischer Story,* a book about Max and Dave and other quarreling siblings, who did indeed for one brief, shining hour bring to Miami their version of "Fleischerland."

Theirs was, of course, a far cry from today's Disneyworld. Instead of a Magic Kingdom and an Epcot, they brought in an animation studio and with it people with such exotic job descriptions as inbetweeners and opaquers.

Battling hard to keep up with the incomparable cartoon creations of Walt Disney—and battling among themselves—the brothers Fleischer moved their studio from New York to Miami in 1938.

For three and a half years Fleischer animators spun out cartoons from their studio at the corner of Miami's N.W. 17th Street and 29th Avenue. Spurred into motion by the pens of talented artists, the delectable little Betty Boop charmed fans of all ages while Popeye popularized spinach. "Faster than a speeding bullet," the studio's Superman rocketed his way into America's hearts.

Then, suddenly, in December of 1941 the war with Disney ended just as America's war with Japan and Germany was beginning.

* * *

Movie cartooning was in its infancy when *Gertie the Dinosaur,* drawn by Winsor McCay, burst upon a delighted public in 1914. It was so popular that a wave of artists, many of them newspaper and comic strip cartoonists, entered the pioneering field—among them Max and Dave Fleischer, two talented brothers whose parents had moved from Austria to New York in 1887.

In a field so new there were no textbooks, schools or training aids, animators had to be innovators, ideally a mixture of artist and inventor. How to make a drawing move—this was the problem they faced.

Movie animation not only called for cartooning skills, but also demanded new techniques for photographing artwork. It wasn't as simple as having a camera expose nearly 1500 separate frames of film a minute as actors played their roles in front of its lens.

Cartoons had to expose their 1500 frames one frame at a time. Each picture had to advance the movement just a little bit. When projected the characters would move naturally across the screen. Or so the animators hoped.

It was a slow process, too slow to be profitable. McCay took two years and 10,000 drawings to complete *Gertie,* a one-reeler that ran less than ten minutes.

Max Fleischer, who led the brothers into the mad, mad world of animation, had the skills for this strange, new universe. He was a talented artist. At the *Brooklyn Daily Eagle* he had drawn the comic strip "Little Elmo." And he was an inventive man. He developed new inking techniques and invented equipment that gave him some two dozen patents, among them the Rotoscope, a device to trace figures from live-action film onto paper, frame by frame.

With the Rotoscope the process of drawing was speeded up, and movements of cartoon figures became less jerky. Still, in 1916 it took Max, Dave and Joe Fleischer a full year of hard work to make a one-minute experimental film, *Out of the Inkwell,* featuring a clown. Less than a minute long, it required 2400 drawings.

In the years ahead the Fleishers made training films for the U.S. Army in World War I, produced a one-hour film on Einstein's Theory of Relativity, combined live actors and cartoon figures on film six decades before *Who Framed Roger Rabbit?,* made the first cartoon with sound in 1926 and turned out their popular bouncing-ball sing-along short subjects.

Still financial problems plagued their Inkwell Studios. In 1929 Dave, a gag and idea man, and Max joined Paramount Pictures in setting up a new corporation, Fleischer Studios, Inc. Paramount owned 51 percent of the company's stock. Younger brothers Joe and Lou also worked at the studio but not as partners.

By this time a powerful force was asserting itself in the cartoon world. With the introduction of an appealing character named Mickey Mouse in a 1929 short called *Steamboat Willie,* Disney began his domination of the field.

Meanwhile, Fleischer Studios gave the world Miss Betty Boop in 1932 and a year later brought Popeye the Sailor onto the screen. Betty, with her squeaky voice, was a curvaceous cutie, characterized by Leslie Cabarga as a Jewish American Princess. Dressed in a skimpy black dress, accented by a garter on her left leg, she danced through her long cartoon life, always on the edge of inflaming the Hays Office, Hollywood's office of censorship. Once a bare breast popped out of her low-cut dress and flashed across the screen for 1/24th of a second.

The character Betty Boop had been created by a superb artist named Grim Natwick, so skilled at drawing the female form that Disney would later lure him to Hollywood where he would draw Snow White. For his next, and greatest, star, Max turned to the funny papers.

Long a fan of E. C. Segar's comic strip, "Popeye," Fleischer negotiated with King Features Syndicate to bring the crusty sailor to the screen. Popeye, backed up by Olive Oyl, J. Wellington Wimpy and Bluto, was for a time even more popular with filmgoers than Mickey Mouse.

Despite the success of Popeye, the studio was constantly playing "catch-up" in its battle with Mickey Mouse and Donald Duck. In 1937 Disney released the first feature-length cartoon, 80 wonderful minutes of *Snow White and the Seven Dwarfs*. Film animation would never be the same.

By now, Max's professional jealousy of Disney was almost out of control. His California rival always seemed to keep one step ahead, from technical aspects to story lines. In his book about Hollywood, *Just Tell Me When To Cry,* Max's son, movie director Richard Fleischer, wrote: "At my parents' house 'Disney' was a dirty word. If you said it at dinner, you were sent away from the table. My father, let alone being a full-fledged, authentic genius, was the nicest, sweetest, kindest, funniest, most tolerant man who ever lived. But mention 'Disney' in his presence and his whole personality changed. An internal, seething anger would seize him."

Paramount told Fleischer it wanted a full-length cartoon feature to compete with Disney. The immediate problem for the brothers was space. Their New York studio at 1600 Broadway was not large enough for a project of that size. They would have to relocate.

At the same time labor problems arose. Employees, trying to form the Animated Motion Picture Workers Union, picketed the studio. Max, described by animator Shamus Culhane as a "benevolent" boss, was stunned. "His reaction," wrote Culhane, "was one of outraged fatherhood."

Max concluded that he should relocate to an anti-union state. Florida, which fit that profile, could offer another advantage. Two years earlier the state had established special tax breaks for new motion picture studios.

Besides, Max and his wife Essie already owned a home on the Miami waterfront and, some said, four city blocks on which the new studio would be built.

In February, 1938, the announcement was made that Fleischer would build

Drawings of Betty Boop (Leslie Cabarga)

a $300,000 animation studio in Miami. Paramount bankrolled the construction with a 10-year loan to Max and Dave.

Max told the press that he felt his workers would be happier and healthier in a warmer climate.

"They need loose clothing so their imaginations can work," he said.

Groundbreaking began in March and in September the new, fully air-conditioned studio was completed. The halls of the studio were dimly lit so animators could rest their eyes while walking along the corridors.

Not everything went smoothly. The latest sound recording equipment was installed, then had to be taken apart after a live grasshopper infiltrated the installation, creating mysterious sound effects.

Fleischer's impact on Miami was immediate. All construction contracts were awarded to local firms. The need for a larger staff led to an arrangement with the Miami Art School to add classes in animation techniques. About 400 workers were trained by the school and then hired.

Two hundred artists had come down from New York and an additional hundred were hired from Hollywood, adding up to a staff of 700 with a weekly payroll of $18,000, a big boost to the Miami economy in the depression year of 1938.

Not all Fleischer ways proved acceptable to Miami. The famous black orchestra leader, Cab Calloway, had starred in the Fleischers' 1932 cartoon, *Minnie the Moocher,* both as a singer and as a live actor who dissolved into a ghost walrus. After Cab visited Lou, the musical Fleischer, at his home, Lou found a note slipped under his door. It read:

"Don't have any more niggers in your house." It was signed: "The Ku Klux Klan."

The story the studio had picked to follow Disney into the world of features was *Gulliver's Travels*. Jonathan Swift's classic satire was a particular favorite of Max's. Max, who wanted to make a film with social significance, wrote in his autobiography:

"I believe a picture should have universal appeal. A child will enjoy every second of it without the slightest realization that behind it was political satire. On the other hand, the adult can enjoy the humor and read through it and there find its political satire, nevertheless entirely free of propaganda."

In an interview he also said: "Gulliver's Travels contains no horror stuff—no evil spirits to scare the youngsters." This was an obvious dig at Disney, who had taken criticism when the wicked queen scared kids so much they wet their pants, an act that dismayed theater owners all over the country who had to clean up the seats.

Gulliver's 74 minutes on the screen took 700 artists 18 months to complete. According to Cabarga, they brushed 12 tons of paint on 500,000 cels—transparent celluloid—and backgrounds to create 115,700 separate scenes. Sixteen tons of drawing paper were used and the movie's elaborate script was 27 miles and 385 yards long.

Talented people worked on the film—animators Grim Natwick and Shamus Culhane, Jessica Dragonette and Lanny Ross as the singing voices of the love interests and Ralph Rainger and Leo Robin, who wrote the music and lyrics. Max is listed as producer and Dave as director, although the two no longer worked well together, frequently refusing to speak to each other.

When the film premiered at the Sheridan Theatre on Miami Beach on December 18, 1939, it was well received. In New York the following week it played to record crowds.

Reviews, though generally favorable, usually pointed out that *Gulliver* fell short of *Snow White*. Disney himself is reported to have said: "We can do better than that with our second-string animators."

By now Disney had simply moved the cartoon up to a new level of artistry—not just in the look of his artwork but also in story telling and character development. The Fleischers were at their best at popping gags on the screen. Furthermore, the look of their cartoons was darker, grittier, gutsier, a reflection, many critics have observed, of the New York scene. Disney projected a brighter, more colorful view of America's small towns and open countryside.

Meanwhile, Max Fleischer had to keep a staff of 700 busy. In February,

Princess Glory and Prince David in scene from "Gulliver's Travels." (Leslie Cabarga)

1940, *Way Back When a Triangle Had its Points,* the first of a dozen Stone Age Cartoons, was released. "Everything you saw on Hanna-Barbera's *Flintstones* series we had done in the Stone Age series first," recalled animator Joe Oriolo. Joe Barbera had worked for Fleischer some 20 years before the popular Flintstones surfaced.

At about the same time Paramount gave Max an assignment he didn't want. Intrigued by the success of a comic book called *Superman,* Paramount bought the rights to produce it as an animated cartoon. To try to talk the parent company out of this mad scheme, Max quoted a high production cost to make each cartoon, between $90,000 and $100,000, about four times as much as a typical cartoon.

Go ahead, Paramount said, and Fleischer embarked on a difficult venture. Instead of imaginary people and animals, they would have to work with relatively realistic characters in a story line without gags. It hadn't been done before.

In Hollywood Paramount's Barney Balaban called a young script writer still in his 20s into his office.

"You're going to write *Superman,*" he said to Jay Morton.

Morton, born in Hollywood, had written westerns for Hoot Gibson and Ramon Navarro. As a child, he had also acted in the first series of Our Gang comedies. He played Stinky. Another member of the Gang was a young Swedish-American named Joe Yule. His name was changed to Mickey Rooney.

Morton's new assignment would take him far from the movie capital. He was handed a Pan-American ticket to Miami and a stack of comic books to read on the three-day flight. In those days planes did not fly at night.

"I'd never written for animation," he said to Max and Dave. "Just eight minutes to tell a story."

Said Max: "Let us send you through the studio." Morton found Max "a wonderful person to work with."

The grand tour introduced Morton to a new world. He visited the animation department where the most talented of the artists drew the first and the last scenes in a given move across the screen. He saw the inbetweening department where inbetweeners drew the pictures needed to move characters from the start of the move to its end. He watched the opaquers who painted the backs of the acetate cels with opaque paints so the backgrounds wouldn't show through. He visited the inking department to observe how inkers traced pencil sketches in ink on cels. He watched background artists create the scenes in front of which the characters performed their gags.

Morton spent four or five months "learning the ropes" and learning about Superman. He met with the comic book's creators, Jerry Siegel and Joe Schuster.

As he worked on his scripts—a script took him about two months to write—he struggled for just the right words to describe Superman.

"Mightier than a roaring hurricane."

"Capable of zooming to heights far beyond man's vision."

"Traveler of the skyways, high above the earth."

And then, finally, he found the phrasing he was looking for:

"Faster than a speeding bullet; more powerful than a locomotive; able to leap tall buildings with a single bound . . . this amazing stranger from the planet Krypton—the man of steel, SUPERMAN."

The sound of the planet Krypton exploding was achieved by simply wrenching an apple apart and amplifying the sound.

In September of 1941 the first of the Superman cartoons was released, followed by another in November. They were well-received but it was now too late for Fleischer Studios.

Dave and Lou had flown to Los Angeles to supervise the scoring and editing of the feature, *Mr. Bug Goes to Town*. Lou returned first and was called into Max's office.

Max showed him a telegram he was sending to Paramount. It stated that he would no longer work with Dave. Lou tried to talk him out of sending it. Finally, Max agreed but it was too late. The telegram had already been sent.

Paramount's reaction came quickly. The Fleischers still owed $100,000 on the $300,000 loan which was due in 1948. Paramount demanded immediate repayment of the loan.

Unable to meet the demands, the Fleischers were forced to give up their studio. Paramount renamed it Famous Studios and in 1943 moved the operation to New York.

In researching *The Fleischer Story* Leslie Cabarga found a number of reasons for the breakup of the studio. When some of the people involved threatened a lawsuit, his publisher, Nostalgia Press, refused to publish the book unless the controversial material was withdrawn. In its place he printed an offer to send interested parties the missing section for $1.50 each. Roughly 300 people accepted the offer.

Then in 1987, 11 years later, DaCapo Press brought out an expanded and updated version of the story. By this time the parties who threatened the lawsuit were dead and Cabarga's observations were included in the latest book.

The root of the problem, he concludes, was clearly the inability of Max and Dave to get along. Paramount was unhappy at the long periods when neither would speak to the other. Joe was angry at Max for blocking his efforts to become a partner.

Paramount and Max were disturbed that Dave was carrying on an extramarital affair with his secretary, whom he later married. Dave, on the other hand, claimed he had learned that Max and Paramount were siphoning off profits to another corporation.

"Dave told a story about a man from Paramount taking him and Max to a ratty shack in the Florida Keys with three girls," wrote Cabarga. "Dave says he slept on the porch that night to avoid the risk of being personally compromised in any way."

Max's son Richard believed Paramount wanted the Fleischers out so it could control any future sales to a new medium, television, looming on the horizon.

The brothers continued to live active lives. Max sold his waterfront Miami mansion—offering price, $40,000—then went to work for Jam Handy Films in Detroit. He wrote a book about Noah and the Ark, then went to work for an animation studio in New York. He died in 1972 at 89. His rivalry with Walt Disney had been so intense that it was still on his mind in the final moments of his life.

Hardening of the arteries to the brain had all but robbed Max of the power to speak, but when his daughter Ruth visited him in the hospital, she showed him an issue of *Life* magazine with Walt Disney's face on the cover. When Max tried to speak, Ruth leaned closer and caught his faint comment: "Son of a bitch."

Dave worked for Columbia Pictures, then Universal Pictures. Lou went to work grinding lenses, then later moved to California where he gave music lessons. Joe stayed on with Famous Studios, finally retiring to Hollywood, Florida, where he died in 1979. Charles stayed in Miami after the studio closed and at 74 was killed in a fall from a ladder.

Of all the Fleischer staff the one who made out best was Jay Morton. He returned to Hollywood but kept in touch with Miami. In the 1950s he published a chain of weekly newspapers, then served on the Dade County Metro Commission. He continues to write the story line for feature Superman films.

The achievement of his, however, that affects the lives of the most Americans was an invention he made and patented after cutting his foot at the beach on a discarded tab from a can. He invented the pop-top, the kind that stays with the can.

CHAPTER 7

Key Largo's Unholy Rollers

Moviemakers parlayed religious bet into winning dice—and cult favorite

The classic John Huston film *Key Largo* brought fame to an obscure island in the Florida Keys long before the island's underwater state park became a mecca for scuba divers and tourists. Much of its Florida renown, however, was based on a misconception that persists today: that the movie actually was filmed on Key Largo. One book on the Keys reports that "Most of the movie was filmed inside of the Hotel (Caribbean Club)."

In fact, Humphrey Bogart, Lauren Bacall, Edward G. Robinson, Claire Trevor and the rest did almost all of their work on the movie in—where else?—Hollywood, California. The stars played their parts on a sound stage set constructed to look like the Caribbean Club. Only a few exteriors were shot in the Keys.

But *Key Largo* did have a strong Key Largo connection. It involved director Huston and screenwriter Richard Brooks, who traveled to the island to begin work on the movie. Brooks, who would later write and direct such memorable pictures as *Elmer Gantry, Sweet Bird of Youth* and *Cat on a Hot Tin Roof,* recalled that strange visit in the late summer of 1947: "A man named Tom Hanley met us in Key West and drove us up to Key Largo. John Huston didn't even believe there was such a place. We were the only ones at Mr. Hanley's hotel. Mr. Hanley brought in a lady to make the beds and cook for us."

The hotel was actually the Caribbean Club, which nestled among coconut palms along Florida Bay. It had been a private fishing club built in 1938 by Carl Fisher, developer of Miami Beach. In 1945 Hanley bought it, added a six-room wing and began operating it as a hotel and illegal gambling casino.

Huston did not like the Maxwell Anderson play *Key Largo,* for which Warner Brothers had bought the screen rights. He liked the title but he wanted a new story line. This meant that Brooks worked hard on the script while Big

John sat on the hotel's Florida Bay pier and fished. It was a tame existence for a legendary hell-raiser like Huston.

Hanley corrected that. By this time he had ascertained that life on Key Largo was much too serene for a high-stakes gambler like Huston. One day, while the director was on the dock, a truck arrived and unloaded a craps table and a roulette wheel, months before the winter season when Hanley usually welcomed in the high-rollers.

"Now our lives are laid out more sensibly," Huston said to Brooks. "I'll still fish during the day, you can write, and in the evenings we'll put on neckties and go to the tables, just the two of us."

Casino owner Hanley was pleased that Huston was living up to his reputation as a heavy bettor. In a short time Huston lost more than $25,000, and Brooks roughly $6,000. "About all I was getting for the script," the writer recalled.

Despite their losses at the hands of a croupier named Ziggy, the moviemakers held no grudges. In his script Brooks wrote in a character named Ziggy. The real life Ziggy later went into the restaurant business in Islamorada.

Soon a few other movie people just happened to start showing up: Huston's wife, Evelyn Keyes, with her pet monkey, Dodie; producer Sam Spiegel; and director Anatole Litvak. Something else arrived: the leading edge of a West Indian hurricane.

As the winds howled, John Huston's sonorous voice mused: "Does anyone here know what Immaculate Conception means?"

"It's got something to do with Christ," said Spiegel.

"I'll go along with Sam," said Litvak.

Then, Huston asked, "Mr. Hanley, are you a Catholic?"

"Yes, sir. I'm a practicing Catholic."

"Do you know what Immaculate Conception means?"

"It means Jesus was born without sin."

"Mr. Hanley, I'm out about $28,000, Mr. Brooks about $7,000. That's $35,000. Want to bet $35,000 you're wrong? Double or nothing?"

Hanley, a prudent Irishman, insisted he was right, but he wanted a smaller bet—much smaller.

Brooks and Hanley went outside in the howling wind to call a Miami monsignor over a crankup phone. When the call went through, Hanley handed the phone to Brooks.

"Father, we're having a religious dispute," said Brooks.

"Are you gambling?"

"Well, it's only a small bet. We want you to tell us what the Immaculate Conception means."

"Mary was born without sin."

After he repeated it for Hanley, they went back in and Huston handed Hanley a piece of paper on which he had written: "Mary was born without sin."

Hanley paid off the bet—$100.

"This is religious money," said Brooks.

"We'll find out how religious it is," said Huston, heading for the craps table.

He didn't have much time. They needed to get to the Miami airport, and already water covered the road to the mainland. They agreed on 20 minutes of play.

In those 20 minutes Huston won back most of what he had lost and Brooks cut his losses to about $4,500. Futhermore, they made it to the airport and then proceeded to make a film which has earned for itself the status of a cult favorite.

Brooks's conclusion: "It must have been good religious money."

LOCATION, LOCATION, LOCATION

The three most important factors in real estate, salesmen and developers have a habit of saying, are "location, location, location." To the Florida buyer it is particularly important that the location be above water. This has not always been the case. The state has been the home of scams, conmen, booms and busts and at least one flood which put nearly everybody's land under water.

CHAPTER 8

Boom, Boom, Boom

Real estate binge burned out suckers and sellers alike

M. Allen Hortt was a pro. He had been in the real-estate business a dozen years. Why should he care if his paperwork backed up on him as long as frenzied buyers kept throwing beautiful green money at him as fast as he could say, "You got a deal"? So how did he describe himself at the height of the Florida Land Boom, the biggest, wildest real estate binge America ever saw?

"Almost a nervous wreck."

But then, that was the way of the boom, unhinging people by luring them on with dreams of instant wealth, untold power and madcap pleasures, orchestrated to the rhythms of the Jazz Age and lubricated by Prohibition's forbidden bathtub gin. The boom's exotic witchery swept the Sunshine State in the Roaring '20s like a tropical fever without a cure. It would simply have to burn itself out, and by 1926 it had done just that. In the process it burned out countless real-estate salesmen, brokers, suckers, speculators, binder boys, thieves, con artists, politicians and even an occasional policeman.

Take the case of Patrolman Johnson, a Georgian who came to work as a cop in a sinful Miami that had grown from 30,000 stable citizens in 1920 to 200,000 maniacs by 1925. Crime in the city proved too much for Johnson. In the heat of the summer of '25 he cracked and tried to gun down that most lawless of all perpetrators—a jaywalker.

Born of the boom were new cities like Hollywood-by-the-Sea and Coral Gables that survived and lived to boom another time; new towns which survived but lost their identities, like Kelsey City, which became Lake Park, and Fulford-by-the-Sea, now North Miami Beach; and countless others that went no further than a saleman's flier or a rough plat, like Okeechobee Highlands and Okeechobee Shores, and Poinciana, a project so deep in the Ten Thousand Islands that buyers had a hard time finding out if their lots were under water. The boom reached out from the Gold Coast to Pensacola in the

Panhandle; to Tampa, St. Petersburg, Sarasota and Naples on the Gulf Coast; and to inland towns like Lakė City, Sebring and Babson Park.

M. A. Hortt, a cowboy from the Old West, witnessed, and somehow survived, the boom from a real-estate office in Fort Lauderdale. Shortly before the upturn, the astute Hortt had purchased 10 acres on the New River for $5,000. As the boom began to gather momentum, he priced the tract at $15,000 and a few days later raised it to $25,000, then raised it a week later to $35,000.

Five men from Long Branch, New Jersey, offered him $30,000. He refused. By the time they got back to him with another offer he had raised it again, to $40,000. The men decided to take a walk along the river to consider the latest figure.

"If a customer comes along while you're making up your minds, and I sell it for $50,000, don't get sore at me," Hortt told them. By the time they got back, Hortt had indeed sold the tract for $50,000 to a man who drove up in a car and wrote out a binder check for $10,000 on the spot.

Hortt sold a tract near Deerfield Beach for $50 an acre. Two days later he resold it for the buyer for $200 an acre. Within a week the price had jumped to $600, and in less than six months the property sold again for $5,000 an acre.

Yes, the money was great in those days. But how to keep up with the paperwork? Clearing a title abstract took about 90 days, and lots were selling and reselling two or three times a week.

But who really cared? Everybody was making money, having fun, and there was just no time to worry.

On September 3, 1925, for example, the Shoreland Company placed its 400-acre Arch Creek section of Miami Shores on the market. The sand pumped into the area had not even settled, but the buyers were ready to go. The doors of Shoreland's Miami office on Flagler Street opened at 8:30 the morning of the sale. They closed at 11 a.m.

The reason? They had run out of property to sell. At the main office and the field offices rioting customers threw nearly $34 million in cash and checks at the sales force.

Shoreland had to close its offices for five days to catch up with its bookkeeping. It was then the company found that the offering had been oversubscribed by more than $11 million.

Miami was so jammed with people that cots were rented through the "hot bed" system, two or more people sharing each bed on 12-hour shifts. The Miami office of the prestigious Mizner Development Corporation, which was busy developing ritzy Boca Raton, operated out of the kitchen of a downtown restaurant.

Newspapers and magazines ran mouth-watering stories about instant fortunes. A South Carolina stenographer paid $350 for a lot and sold it a few weeks later for $65,000. A derelict upgraded two bottles of bootleg gin into $60,000. Anybody could play, anybody could win.

T. H. Weigall, an unemployed British journalist, saw a sign in a New York window, declaring "One Good Investment Beats a Lifetime of Toil. YOU can do what George Cusack, Jr., did!" What George, Jr., did was make $500,000 in Florida real estate, or so the sign said.

Weigall climbed aboard a south-bound train and stepped off into Miami's August heat. He found himself in a mob scene of crowds, auto horns, drills and hammers. "It was real-estate madness," he wrote. "Hatless, coatless men rushed about the blazing streets, their arms full of papers, with perspiration pouring from their foreheads. Every shop seemed to be combined with a real-estate office; at every doorway crowds of young men were shouting and speech-making . . . proclaiming to heaven the unsurpassed chances . . . they were offering to make a fortune."

Weigall got a job writing press releases for the Coral Gables Corporation. His sales pitches ran in the local newspapers, often unchanged, since over-worked editors had little time to read copy. By 1925 *The Miami Herald* had become the nation's largest paper in advertising lineage, with the *Miami Daily News* in fourth place. On July 26, 1925, the *Miami Daily News* published the largest single issue ever printed at that time in the United States: 504 pages in 22 sections.

One of the most successful cities to emerge from the boom was Coral Gables. The head man at the Coral Gables Corporation was George Merrick. At one time he had wanted to be a poet, but that dream ended when his preacher father died. George dropped out of Columbia University and returned to run the family plantation, the largest producer of fruit and vegetables in south Florida. As the boom spread, that land became Coral Gables and Merrick's "City Beautiful" became the poem he longed to write.

At the boom's peak in 1925, as many as 25,000 people were engaged in selling real estate in Miami, a city that numbered only 200,000, many of them housewives and children. The most notorious of the property peddlers were known as "binder boys," a grubby lot from the great cities of the Northeast, easily identified by their white knickers, which were usually in need of washing. Like a horde of locusts, the binder boys swarmed into south Florida in 1925, eager for a quick buck. Their weapon of choice was the binder, which is simply an option on a piece of property, sometimes secured for as little as one percent of the asking price. The binder boy would then sell the option, which might be resold a dozen times before the first real payment on the property was due.

As long as prices kept rising, the binder boys made money. In the process they wrecked any chance local government had of keeping orderly records of who owned what. A decade later county clerks were still trying to figure it out.

Some believe the boom began as early as 1920, others as late as 1924. All agree that the peak was reached in 1925. That year 971 subdivisions were platted in Miami, 174,530 deeds were filed by the Dade County clerk, and 481 hotels and apartment houses were built.

Even so, construction could not keep up with the crush of people. The cost of living boomed out of sight. Miami companies had to build housing for their employees if they wanted a work force. Maintaining a police department proved almost impossible—the cops kept quitting to sell real estate. The Ku Klux Klan offered to handle the police function. The city said no.

Why did such a rampage happen? Many reasons: prosperity, pent-up demand following World War I, dreams of instant wealth, Florida's kindly tax structure, heavy advertising, the what-the-hell mood of the Roaring '20s. But perhaps the biggest factor of all was a four-wheeled contraption that started rolling all over America after the war. Many people drove their first automobile to see for themselves what this bumptious, boisterous Sunshine State was all about. They came from the cities of the North—New York, Chicago, Philadelphia—and from hick towns in the South and Midwest. On Florida's new roads they got the chance to check out their flivvers at death-defying speeds. At 45 miles per hour, Florida offered the nation's highest speed limit.

The boom came early to Broward County. A three-column headline in the *Fort Lauderdale Sentinel* of July 30, 1920, read:

BUILDING BOOM STARTED
AND WILL CONTINUE

That year, Rio Vista on the south side of the New River was platted, while on the north side Idlewyld was founded by Hortt and his partners Bob Dye and Tom Stillwell, publisher of the *Fort Lauderdale Daily News* and the *Sentinel*. Idlewyld was the first Fort Lauderdale community to be built on "made" land, from river bottom fill dropped in amongst the mangroves.

These, however, were modest ventures compared to the huge project that burst on the Broward scene in July, 1921. Joseph Wesley Young, who had already made and lost a real-estate fortune in California, was intrigued by the vast stretch of open oceanfront land that lay south of Dania.

Young looked at the marshy wetlands and saw a great city. When he reached Lake Mabel, now Port Everglades, he envisioned a world seaport. Returning to his hometown of Indianapolis he developed the grand design for his new city: "There will be a wide boulevard extending from the ocean westward to the . . . Everglades," he wrote. "This will be a city for everyone—from

Land sale at Hollywood-by-the-Sea. (Fort Lauderdale Historical Society)

the opulent at the top of the industrial and social ladders to the most humble of working people."

His staff wanted to name the city after Young. He overruled them and named it Hollywood-by-the-Sea. At the height of the boom, it would for a brief time become Broward's largest city, bigger even than the older county seat, Fort Lauderdale.

In California, Young had pioneered marketing techniques that are still in wide use today. Instead of simply selling lots and houses, he developed complete communities, with homes, shopping areas, public buildings, streets and parks. He built hotels, such as the Hollywood Beach Hotel and the Great Southern Hotel. He organized the Hollywood Publishing Company to pour out an endless stream of sales publications. To clear the land for his world seaport, he even brought in a troop of French-Canadian lumberjacks, the forerunners of the annual French-Canadian trek to Hollywood that continues today.

Like Young, Frank Croissant, who had won a 1916 contest as "America's greatest salesman," wasn't about to let the boom pass him by. Arriving in Fort Lauderdale in 1924, he purchased 1,193 acres south of the New River for $1.25 million. Croissant, who had developed Calumet City, Illinois, for Henry Ford, brought 96 of his best salespeople to Fort Lauderdale to kick off Croissant Park on December 27, 1925. By New Year's Day, 1926, they had sold more than $3 million worth of lots.

A small man with a booming voice, Croissant looked ahead with the optimism of a horseplayer, which he was. He owned a racing stable, a stud farm and 110 thoroughbreds. After Croissant Park sold out, he proceeded to

Croissant Park in Fort Lauderdale used a beauty contest to sell lots in 1924. (Fort Lauderdale Historical Society)

develop Croissantania, north of Fort Lauderdale. He described it as "my masterpiece."

Another Broward developer was a West Virginian named Charlie Rodes, who made enough money selling real estate to visit Venice, Italy. There he observed the Venetian technique for using fill to create long, thin peninsulas in which every lot was on the water. He brought "finger-islanding" to Fort Lauderdale and called his development off Las Olas Boulevard "Venice," which in turn gave the city its nickname, "The Venice of America."

Architect Addison Mizner had made a fortune designing elegant homes for Palm Beach swells. He might have kept that fortune if he hadn't caught boom fever. In April 1925, he announced plans for a 16,000-acre development at Boca Raton, then a modest farming town in southern Palm Beach County. A huge hotel would be built on the beach and a smaller but still luxurious hotel called the Cloister Inn, which later became the Boca Raton Hotel and Club, would rise on the shores of Lake Boca Raton.

Mizner's Palm Beach connections gave him celebrity backup, among them Irving Berlin, Elizabeth Arden, actress Marie Dressler and General Coleman du Pont, whose name dripped money. When Mizner and his brother, Wilson, offered Boca Raton lots for sale in Miami and West Palm Beach, an opening-day record of $2,100,000 in sales was set, and Mizner Development Corporation stock soared from $100 a share to $1,000.

"Get the big snobs and the little snobs will follow." That was the unofficial slogan coined by Harry Reichenbach, a flamboyant Hollywood press agent who handled publicity for Addison and his scamp brother, Wilson. Brother Wilson was even more contemptuous. "A platinum sucker trap," he called it as the money poured in.

But even a platinum sucker trap has to end sometime. Today it's difficult to tell just when the music died.

The troubles began in the summer of 1925. In Miami a squad of 20 agents from the Internal Revenue Service began checking the profits of speculators. Since profits were mostly paper, any demand for income-tax payments in cash caused severe nervousness. Some of the biggest of the wheeler-dealers began scaling back their madcap ventures. Bad sign. Booms feed on good news, not bad.

In August the Florida East Coast Railway, overwhelmed by the crush of passengers and cargo, declared an embargo to give its crews a chance to perform routine maintenance. Railroad cars started backing up. By winter more than 7,000 southbound freight cars sat helplessly outside Jacksonville. Desperately needed building materials couldn't get through. Construction slowed.

Miami turned to the seas to bring in supplies. On January 10, 1926, a 241-foot barkentine, *Prins Valdemar,* was wrecked in Government Cut. For nearly a month, the big sailboat blocked the entrance to the Port of Miami. Offshore, a hundred ships, carrying 45 million board feet of lumber, waited, while builders gnashed their teeth.

The nation's press, which had helped feed the boom with stories of instant profits, now fueled its collapse. One of the most crushing items ran in *The New York Times* in late 1925. Coleman du Pont was a practical joker, given to handshake buzzers and squirting flowers. Wilson Mizner rated him a fool, a serious miscalculation. The time came when du Pont had had enough of the high-handed methods of Wilson and Reichenbach. When he announced his resignation from the Mizner company, du Pont did it with flair—a letter to the *Times,* published on November 28:

"I've never been connected with a failure in my life," he wrote, "and this thing is sure to fall with these people in charge."

The impact was enormous. The big-money supporters of the Mizner company fled the scene. Sales had totaled over $25 million in the first six months. Suddenly, they stopped.

All over Boomland the story was the same. Buyers forfeited on their payments and the original owners took back the properties only to find themselves unable to pay the taxes. Land auctions followed, with people taking whatever they could get. Lots in Miami were selling for a tenth of their top prices.

That summer a small calamity struck Hollywood, an omen of things to come. In February Joe Young had opened Tent City, a motel under canvas just to the south of Hollywood Beach Hotel. In July the first hurricane to hit south Florida in 16 years struck. Tent City was blown away.

In June, 1926, Allen Hortt married Lenora Goozee, a schoolteacher he had met on a trip to Alaska. They left for Europe for a two-month honeymoon. On their return Hortt found that the building and loan company where he had deposited $50,000 had suspended withdrawals. He rushed back to Fort Lauderdale to straighten the matter out. He arrived on September 17.

The killer hurricane of 1926 arrived on the 18th.

The storm was bad enough, with a death toll of more than 600, but the headlines in northern papers were even worse:

"SOUTH FLORIDA WIPED OUT . . . .
1,000 DEAD IN FLORIDA STORM,
3,000 HURT . . . ."

The little that was left of the boom died in the storm, a punctuation mark that placed a period at the end of a period. Mizner's company tottered into bankruptcy, and the poet Merrick had to trade his dream of Coral Gables for a fishing camp in the Upper Keys. Joe Young lost Hollywood along with his dream of a world seaport, but somehow Port Everglades came into being in 1928 without his support.

Prudent as the binge neared its end, M. A. Hortt got his affairs in order and somehow weathered the bust. Born in the little Utah town of Orderville, he must have been asking himself at the end of the boom if the south Florida he had moved to might better have been named Disorderville.

CHAPTER 9

The Jester of the Boom

Wilson Mizner brought laughs to real estate binge

Florida was invented for Addison Mizner's younger brother. For a seasoned con man like Wilson, the Gold Coast in the Roaring 20s had it all—a wild real estate boom, a flock of get-rich-quick schemers, and a mob of panting suckers eager to be taken.

How ironic that the talented, flawed scion of the illustrious Mizner family of northern California should come here not to loot the land, but for reasons out of character. Or in his case, lack of character.

Wilson Mizner grew up in a world of privilege. "To my embarrassment, I was born in bed with a lady," Wilson later remarked of his 1876 birth. The lady was a society matriarch who called her youngest son "Mama's angel Birdie" and proceeded to spoil him rotten.

When his father was named Envoy Extraordinary and Minister Plenipotentiary to Central America, the Mizner family was introduced to the joys of diplomatic immunity, perhaps the root of Wilson's belief that he could get away with anything. In Gold Rush days in Nome, Alaska, he put on a black mask, armed himself with a revolver and entered a candy store, shouting, "Your chocolates or your life!" His friend, the police chief, knew that only Wilson could have done it, but no charges were brought. Later Wilson was named deputy sheriff. Friends and associates included such noted pistoleers as Wyatt Earp and Bat Masterson.

In a sense, the versatile Wilson was a true Renaissance man, a master of many skills, most of them sleazy. A saloon singer for awhile, he later ran a badger game, oversaw illegal gambling joints around the country, and engaged in cardsharking on luxury ocean liners. Wilson once ran a banana plantation in Guatemala after trying his hand at managing prizefighters. He started with a trained bear and then moved up in class to one of boxing's greatest middleweight champions, Stanley Ketchel.

Wilson had a way with words. He wrote Broadway stage plays and

Hollywood screen plays. In the movie capital he was one of the owners of a famous Hollywood restaurant which he named the Brown Derby, after the headgear of two of his idols, Governor Alfred E. Smith of New York and Bat Masterson.

Most memorable of all, he was the unchallenged master of the wisecrack, the quotable one-liner. *Bartlett's Quotations* wouldn't have been the same without him.

"The first hundred years are the hardest."

"If you copy from one author, it's plagiarism. If you copy from two, it's research."

"Treat a whore like a lady and a lady like a whore."

"Faith is a wonderful thing, but doubt gets you an education."

"A good listener is not only popular everywhere, but after a while he gets to know something."

"Be nice to people on the way up because you'll meet them again on the way down."

In New York Wilson wrote plays and ran a theatrical hotel called the Rand. He posted two house rules: "Carry Out Your Own Dead" and "No Opium Smoking in the Elevator." He joked about his own opium smoking, convinced he could take it or leave it. He in fact invented the term "user."

Then one night he was beaten up and left for dead in a mid-Manhattan alley, no mean feat since he was six feet four and weighed 220 pounds. He never told anyone what happened. At first he couldn't. His jaw was broken. During his hospital stay he was given morphine, a much stronger drug, to ease the pain. Soon he was hooked.

When Addison heard of his brother's swift descent into addiction, he brought Wilson to Palm Beach. By now Addison had become the ritzy resort's premier architect. Specialists worked hard to cure Wilson, but he kept backsliding with his favorite combination, a highball laced with laudanum. Finally, Wilson decided the specialists weren't going to get the job done. He dismissed them, quit "cold turkey," suffered through withdrawal and cured himself. He never went back to drugs.

When the Mizner corporation acquired a large tract of land in the little town of Boca Raton—Addison dropped the "e" from "Ratone"—Wilson surprised everyone, including himself, by going to work. What caused this miraculous transformation? Apparently, it was Wilson's realization that here in Boca Raton he finally had the opportunity to make money, real money.

As secretary-treasurer of the Mizner Development Corporation, Mizner came perilously close to going straight. But just in time, the larceny in his madcap soul reasserted itself. In the process, his excesses wrecked his

Wilson Mizner, at left, with his architect brother Addison and movie star Marie Dressler. (Historical Society of Palm Beach County)

brother's master plan. Some would even say his miscues unraveled the wildest real estate boom in history and plunged the state of Florida into a deep depression, well ahead of the rest of the country.

To publicize the fabulous new resort of Boca Raton, Wilson brought in an old buddy of his from Klondike Gold Rush days, publicist Harry Reichenbach. Reichenbach's sales philosophy was, "Get the big snobs, and the little snobs will follow." Reichenbach's principal tool was the skillful use of celebrity names. Titles from Europe, society figures such as Vanderbilt and du Pont, and show business stars like Irving Berlin and Marie Dressler all combined to dispense a magnetic aura. Little snobs supposedly would follow.

Work moved ahead on Addison's grand hotel and on the great thoroughfare they had named Camino Real. Money poured into the company at $2 million a week. The boom's exhilarating hysteria finally brought forth the old Wilson Mizner.

The lure of buried pirate treasure was employed to sell property in Boca Raton. The Mizner publicity mill sent forth the claim that the bloodthirsty Blackbeard had once used Boca as his base, leaving behind a vast fortune in treasure. One night Wilson and Reichenbach ventured out to Boca Raton Inlet and buried replicas of artifacts and phony doubloons fabricated by Mizner Industries. Reichenbach made sure photographers were on hand at the moment the treasure was "discovered."

Wilson's fine hand showed up next in Boynton Beach. The brothers had bought a 900-acre strip of land near Boynton Beach. Dubbed the Mizner Mile, it was earmarked for the construction of a $10,000,000 Ritz-Carlton hotel.

But there was a problem with the Mizner Mile. A highway ran between the property and the ocean. Most of the area's residents were Finnish farmers who regarded the beach as their own playground.

Wilson's solution was direct—and high-handed. Build a new road on the western edge of the Mizner Mile and tear up the old highway. Result: 900 acres of Mizner land on the ocean.

The Finnish farmers did not approve. With clubs, pitchforks and shovels, they tried to storm a wooden barricade Wilson had built across the old highway.

In the glow of road flares and automobile headlights, Wilson could be seen shaking his fist at the farmers and cursing them with great eloquence in Finnish, a language this multitalented man had learned in the Klondike. An inappropriate and ostentatious twist was Wilson's garb. Always dapper, he was wearing a top hat, white tie and tails, not normally the dress of choice when ripping up roadway.

Wilson and the Boynton Beach mayor were arrested for destruction of

Statue at entrance to Boca Raton Hotel and Club. (Florida State Archives)

public property. The brothers had to drop their plans to develop the Mizner Mile.

At the Mizner Development Corporation Wilson sat on the board of directors with such business powers as General T. Coleman du Pont, a tall, raw-boned man who arrayed himself in white knickers and white silk knee-length socks. The General, a title that harked back to his National Guard service, was a strange combination of business tycoon and practical joker. In addition to a powerful position in the family munitions business, he owned the Equitable Life Assurance Society as well as a string of hotels that included the Waldorf-Astoria in New York. His practical jokes made endless use of such pedestrian mechanical devices as exploding cigars, dribbling highball glasses and water pistols.

Wilson concluded that the General lacked class.

Classy or not, General du Pont was the biggest investor in the Boca Raton venture. What he didn't realize was how much Reichenbach and Wilson were exploiting the du Pont name to hype the development.

The General became uncomfortable with some of the more grandiose claims. He didn't really believe that no other resort in the world measured up to Boca, which was still in its startup phase. The statement that "yachts discharge directly at the lake entrance to this hotel" bothered him, too, since the hotel at that time was still on the drawing board and the pier only a rickety wooden platform. What disturbed the General most was the fear that the use of his name in company promotions might obligate him to stand behind these claims if financial disaster struck.

General du Pont demanded that Wilson and Reichenbach be thrown out of the company. To buttress his argument, he flaunted a photostat of a newspaper clipping which reported Wilson's 1919 conviction for operating a Long Island gambling house.

Wilson battled back with skills honed in a lifetime of shady dealings. At the county jail he persuaded a female prisoner to write du Pont a letter, claiming the General was responsible for her pregnancy. The move only strengthened du Pont's resolve.

The General proceeded to release under his own name a statement condemning the promotional practices of Wilson and Reichenbach. The statement ran throughout Florida but also in the nation's financial capital, New York. Boom psychology can't stand bad press. The Boca Raton nosedive set in immediately.

The brothers opened the Cloister Inn in February, 1926. The timing couldn't have been worse. The boom was over. Now the Mizners were attracting more lawsuits than customers.

They had hoped the little snobs would follow the big snobs. Now, said Wilson, it was a case of little suckers hunting down big suckers with baseball bats.

"I never open my door but a writ blows in," Wilson wrote a friend.

By early 1927 Wilson had had all of Florida courtrooms he could take. He climbed into his huge Packard, which he called "the stonecrusher," and motored out of Florida for the last time.

Wilson returned to his home state, settling this time in Hollywood. He described it as "a trip through a sewer in a glassbottomed boat." His kind of town.

In those days the movies were just moving into the era of the talkies. Jack Warner's *The Jazz Singer* was the smash hit. Wilson's brilliant witticisms plus his inside knowledge of the argot of the underworld made him invaluable as a writer.

In partnership with a former husband of Gloria Swanson and Jack Warner, Wilson opened the Brown Derby. The food was mediocre but the gathering of stars was glittering. Wilson sat in Booth 50 and delighted the faithful with a continuing stream of one-liners. The wit was still sharp, but he was slowing down now. "It's getting so people no longer count the silverware when I come to dinner," he complained.

But years of preposterous words and deeds had created a legend. Anita Loos, who had written *Gentlemen Prefer Blondes,* called him "America's most fascinating outlaw." When she wrote the script for the movie *San Francisco,* she based its leading character on Wilson. The role was played by Clark Gable. Later in her autobiography, Miss Loos revealed that Wilson had been her one great love.

His only marriage was to a wealthy widow and it ended predictably in an early divorce. The institution was simply not designed for Wilson.

In his 57th year he found himself paying his dues for a long life of high living. "A bum ticker" was the way he summed up his trouble. But his irreverent attitude toward death stayed with him to the end.

When he learned that his valiant middleweight, Ketchel, was dying of gunshot wounds, he said, "Tell 'em to count ten over him and he'll get up."

Told that Addison was dying, he telegraphed: "Stop dying. Am trying to write a comedy."

He did not, however, take the death of his brother lightly. The bond between them was close and the loss of Addison was a shattering blow to Wilson. Within two months he had followed his brother to the grave, characteristically cracking jokes to the end:

"I want a priest, a rabbi, and a Protestant minister. I want to hedge my bets."

When a clergyman offered consolation in Wilson's final minutes he replied, "Much obliged, Padre, much obliged. But why bother? I'll be seeing your boss in a few minutes. I don't expect too much. You can't be a rascal for 40 years and then cop a plea the last minute. God keeps better books than that."

CHAPTER 10

Here's Johnny

Carson helped sell bean patch as new city of Coral Springs

Henry (Bud) Lyons looked upon western Broward County's vast, empty land as "little more than a bean patch." His heirs viewed it as productive ranchland.

But when James Hunt surveyed the same wild, open country, he dreamed of a city rising from the Everglades, a city he would one day name Coral Springs.

Just after World War I, Lyons, a native Georgian, began buying land west of his home in Pompano. Much of the land was under water, a matted jungle of cypress, myrtle, wild willow and sawgrass infested with malarial mosquitoes, wildcats, wild hogs, rattlesnakes, cottonmouth moccasins and alligators.

Bit by bit, Lyons accumulated property through routine purchases, and by trading a mule or an old Model-T Ford for a piece of land. After the Florida land boom collapsed in 1926, he bought property on the delinquent tax rolls.

By the early 1940s, Lyons owned more than 20,000 acres in western Broward, stretching far into the Everglades. A 1939 article in *Country Home Magazine* dubbed him "the titan of the bean patch."

To drain the land, Lyons built canals, ditches, locks and levees and installed pumps along 60 miles of waterways. As dry land emerged, he brought in workers from the Bahamas to burn off vegetation and prepare the soil for planting. Soon he was shipping out two crops of winter vegetables a year.

In 1939, he began to experiment with Brahma cattle, a breed hardy enough to withstand south Florida's heat and insects. When Bud died in 1952, Lyons' heirs converted the farmland into ranchland for 5,000 head of cattle.

The conversion was not made easily. Rustlers and hunters cut down fences, shot the locks off gates and killed deer, wildcats, wild hogs and cattle. Finally, the Lyons family was forced to organize armed posses. Men with shotguns and rifles patrolled the ranch in pickups, roaming the 60 miles of dirt roads Lyons had built. Almost overnight, the "bean patch" had been turned into Wild West Broward.

In 1947, a series of hurricanes and floods led to the creation of the Central and Southern Florida Flood Control District. Tax dollars were used to build a mammoth network of drainage canals, levees and pumping stations. As the swamps began drying up, developers smelled huge profits. All over West Broward the new, dry land was earmarked to become developer cities and retirement communities.

And suddenly, from Fort Lauderdale, a second "titan of the bean patch" made his entrance. James S. Hunt was a sophisticated city boy who had learned salesmanship in the automobile business in Detroit.

After World War II, he moved to Fort Lauderdale to test his sales skills in real estate. Eventually, he formed a partnership with Joseph Taravella, who had served under him in the Navy, and Stephen Calder, a Broward real-estate man since the boom days of the '20s. They called their venture Coral Ridge Properties, named after the coral ridge that ran through northeast Fort Lauderdale. From Sunrise Boulevard in Fort Lauderdale to Pompano Beach, Coral Ridge Properties developed an area of some 8,000 houses and 7,000 oceanfront apartments, including luxury, highrise condominiums along the Galt Ocean Mile.

By the early '60s, Hunt was beginning to run short of land. But he dreamed of building a city from scratch, far from the noise, pollution and urban congestion of Fort Lauderdale. Of course, that was out of the question in the eastern part of the county. He was forced to look west for his slice of virgin real estate.

Meantime, Henry Lyons' widow, Lena, had become a classic example of "land rich, cash poor." While her farm and ranching income had declined, property taxes continued to come due. Lena had more land than she needed, but she was in desperate need of ready cash.

Who could pay her what she wanted? Who had reason to buy land from her? Certainly not other farmers or ranchers. But developers—there was another matter.

In the summer of 1961, talks began at Coral Ridge Properties' small office in Fort Lauderdale. Four decades earlier, Lyons had rejected an offer of $1,000 an acre for his land. Now, Hunt was offering Lyons' widow $259 an acre for 3,860 acres.

"You've got a week to decide or I knock a quarter of a million off the price," Hunt told Lena. Within days, Lena accepted the offer—with one stipulation. "I want to do something for my kinfolks at Christmas," she said. "We've got to close by then."

Hunt accepted, knowing it was a near-impossible task. Title searches led through a maze of old tax bills and deeds dating back to a bizarre 1911 frontier-land lottery. But lawyers from both camps pitched in, and on

1965 Coral Springs land rush drew prospective buyers. (Coral Ridge Properties)

December 14, 1961, James Hunt handed Lena Lyons an impressive Christmas present—a check for $1 million.

In return, he received title to the land that one day would become Coral Springs. Hunt's initial idea was to create a retirement city, as other developers were doing in the western part of the county. One suggestion was a retirement village for National Maritime Workers union members. But the idea fizzled.

So Hunt created a working title—Quartermore—for his still unplanned development. If a broker bought three acres, another acre—a "quarter more"—was thrown in with the deal. Pompano Springs was considered for the development's permanent name and rejected. However, from that suggestion was spawned the name that stuck: Coral Springs.

Once the development's name was selected, Coral Ridge Properties moved to incorporate the new town. Requirements included a city charter and a minimum of five people living on the land.

Hunt adapted the Fort Lauderdale city charter to his needs by writing in the name of his new city. To create instant population, the company towed three wooden shacks to what today is Riverside Drive. Five people—four of them Hunt's employees—were then recruited to move in. On July 10, 1963, Coral Springs was chartered by special act of the Florida Legislature.

James Hunt was determined to bring the look of Old Virginia to his new city: white columns, red brick, verandas, maybe even a magnolia or two. Hunt also wanted a covered bridge to carry traffic north and south over a canal in

The Hills subdivision, but mostly to serve as a landmark. A wooden structure perched atop a steel span bridge in Florida. But somehow it fell short of true landmark status.

Hunt then came up with another idea. He had once seen a chewing tobacco sign on a covered bridge. It had just the touch he wanted, old-fashioned and Southern. He called the chairman of the American Snuff Company in Atlanta and asked him to put a tobacco sign on the bridge.

The chairman himself came down to supervise the production of the sign, which advertised two of his company's products: Peach Sweet Snuff ("Sweet as a Peach") and Bull of the Woods Chewing Tobacco.

In early 1965, after pouring $9 million into the development, Coral Ridge Properties held a huge land sale. At this stage, the company's property had 5 1/2 miles of paved roads, waterways, model homes and, of course, a covered bridge.

Now came the moment of truth, the big sales pitch on March 21, 1965. It was billed as the state's "Largest Land-Rush Discount Land Sale and Barbecue." Some 350 people, 30,000 manhours and $100,000 went into its preparation.

Drum majorettes, cheerleaders and Scottish bagpipers created a carnival-like atmosphere. To make certain the promotion packed in potential buyers, two celebrites were recruited—Guy Lombardo, who brought along his entire orchestra, and a new TV personality, Johnny Carson, who was just emerging as the host of NBC's *Tonight Show.*

A crowd of 10,000 showed up. They ate six tons of barbecue and hot dogs, drank 2,500 gallons of soft drinks and were treated to a tour of the model homes. Visitors were engulfed in a torrent of salesmanship. Soon the guests were hearing about a bustling, thriving city of 60,000 people, living in a community of parks, wide, safe streets and spacious lots. The forecast turned out to be modest; in its first 25 years the city passed 75,000 in population.

The selling price for homesites in The Meadows began at $2,695, in The Hills at $9,000, in the Country Club area at $7,500 and in the Village Green at $5,500. Home prices for the models in The Meadows ranged from $15,000 to $20,000 and in The Hills they started at $20,000.

One buyer was Johnny Carson, who purchased 54.6 acres along Royal Palm Boulevard. In 1970, he sold it for five times what he paid.

But Coral Ridge Properties' biggest sale came just one year after the Great Land Rush. In July, 1966, Westinghouse Electric Corporation bought the development company—for $36 million.

A young Johnny Carson and bandleader Guy Lombardo help sell land in Coral Springs at 1965 land rush. (Coral Ridge Properties)

CHAPTER 11

The South Florida Sea

Flood of 1947 covered five million acres with water

South Florida was beginning to look like the Mojave Desert. In the Everglades, muck caught fire and blazed out of control, darkening the skies along the coast. Saltwater moved inland through drainage canals and the underlying rock, threatening the precious drinking water of South Floridians.

Throughout much of 1944 and 1945, citrus growers and cattlemen looked at the skies and wondered: Will it ever rain again?

But by September, 1947, they were asking: Will the rain ever stop?

That year, some 100 inches of rain fell on south Florida, more than tripling the region's total rainfall for 1945 and ending one of the worst droughts in Florida history. In a few weeks the rain had drenched farmland and filled lakes and canals. Then, in the space of just 25 days, two hurricanes and a tropical disturbance dumped enough water on an already saturated area to inspire the return of Noah and his Ark.

When the sun finally broke through again in November, it shone down on an inland sea—five million acres of water stretching from Lake Okeechobee across the Everglades and the Big Cypress Swamp to Broward and Dade counties.

Ninety percent of eastern Florida, from Orlando to Flamingo, was under water. In Davie, with its vast acreage in citrus groves and cattle lands, the water was waist deep; in Fort Lauderdale, waves were washing across Las Olas Boulevard. Weary horses and cattle stood forlornly on levees in western Broward and Palm Beach counties, sharing what little high ground remained with deer, wildcats, raccoons and rattlesnakes.

People whose property was threatened by water backed up by dams and locks attempted to dynamite them but were faced down by people packing guns to guard the dams that were holding back the waters from their homes and farms. In a primitive struggle for survival, neighbor confronted neighbor.

The Great Flood of 1947 started on March 1 when a squall line dumped a welcome six inches of water on the parched agricultural lands of the upper Everglades. Rain was plentiful in April and May, and then in June became so heavy that chairman Dewey Hilsabeck called an emergency meeting of the Everglades Drainage District (EDD). EDD had jurisdiction over a vast network of drainage canals, dams, levees, locks, water-control structures and hurricane gates.

By opening the hurricane gates at Lake Okeechobee, for example, EDD could drain excess water from the upper Glades into the lake, purposely kept low for just such an emergency. But when the torrential rains came in 1947, EDD was starved for funds to run its flood control program. Chief engineer Lamar Johnson was a worried man when he learned that a hurricane had formed on September 9 in the Atlantic. Slowly the hurricane worked its way across the Caribbean, battering Puerto Rico and the Bahamas, and then took direct aim at Florida.

Suddenly the huge storm swerved north, and south Florida breathed a sigh of relief. Out of the blue, however, the hurricane turned, came back, and on September 17 smashed into the mainland. Its winds were clocked at 155 miles per hour at the Hillsboro Lighthouse.

Almost immediately, all hell broke loose. In Fort Lauderdale, the New River overflowed its banks, and whitecaps broke over downtown, flooding luxury homes on the finger isles. Saltwater destroyed Dania's tomato crop, and rainwater drowned the orange groves of Davie and the beanfields of Pompano Beach. Migrant workers near Lake Okeechobee were evacuated to higher ground. In West Palm Beach the National Guard was called out, and President Harry Truman declared a state of emergency.

Especially ominous was the head of water pouring into Lake Okeechobee from the Kissimmee River Valley. Because the lake was already full, the water had just one place to go—south to Fort Lauderdale and Miami through swollen canals.

Fears were high at Belle Glade, on Okeechobee's south shore, already under water. A hurricane tidal wave had drowned nearly 2,000 people in the area in 1928, a tragedy still horrifyingly vivid to many living on the lakeside.

Farm dikes near the lake were crumbling. The levee at one farm collapsed completely, flooding 3,000 acres of beans and celery. To help drain water on the lake's south shore, boards were removed from the South Bay locks. The released water then roared south down the North New River Canal, which would shortly deliver it to Davie.

That night a small group of men crept in and restored the boards. The Palm Beach County sheriff called them "vigilantes," assuming they came from Davie. The district removed the boards, but again the vigilantes replaced them.

Fort Lauderdale's main north-south street, Andrews Avenue, was under water during 1947 flood. (Fort Lauderdale Historical Society)

"Somebody out there might get shot," the sheriff warned.

In Davie, things were already in bad shape. A local cattleman had asked the courts for an injunction to block the closing of a dike west of town because, though the closed dike would help citrus groves to the east, it would continue to flood his land. This was the heart of the problem. Relief for the cattlemen meant disaster for the grove owners, and vice versa.

No quick solution was in sight—and then, unbelievably, things got worse.

A small tropical disturbance hit south Florida on September 28, dropping seven inches of rain in a 24-hour period. Abnormally high tides backed up the water into rivers and canals.

"Fifty miles of water from the Everglades is moving this way," Sheriff Walter Clark warned a terrified Broward County as he deputized armed guards to protect county dikes.

Water began pouring into Pompano Beach, flooding the section of town near Hammondville Road. By October 2, people were being evacuated from their flooded homes in Davie to the Naval Air Station at the Fort Lauderdale airport. People still living in Davie listened in dismay to reports of a head of water, now 60 miles long, pushing its way south from the upper Glades.

Only one thing worked in their favor: A temporary dam near the State Road 84 bridge had been thrown up by the Army Corps of Engineers. This would ease the problem—or so everyone thought.

But as the water began to drop in Davie, it began to rise in Hacienda Flores,

Golfers had little chance to play as flood waters turned the Fort Lauderdale Country Club course into a giant water hazard. (Fort Lauderdale Historical Society)

a housing development to the east. Hacienda developers asked the Corps of Engineers for permission to dynamite the new dam, and when the Corps refused, developer P. C. Collier called for a meeting of residents.

"If nothing has been done by meeting time," said Collier ominously, "we'll remove the dam by whatever means are necessary."

"No one is going to blow up the dam," retorted Sheriff Clark, trying to maintain calm. "If the dam should be removed, it will be done in an orderly manner and under the proper supervision."

Conflict and confusion were developing everywhere. Policy changes moved as swiftly as the flood currents. One day after approving the highway department's request to open the locks, the Broward Drainage District asked the state to close them again.

Just as quickly, the district reversed itself on the State Road 84 dam. Board members met at the dam in the rain and were greeted by 200 people carrying shovels and shouting, "Blow it up!" The board promptly voted to open the dam.

Later, P. C. Collier reported that the waters in his groves had dropped 11 inches in 12 hours. In Davie, however, water rose eight inches in the same period. Citrus man Harry Earle estimated that 700,000 trees had been lost in the flood.

People began consoling themselves with the thought that the situation could not possible get worse. They were wrong.

On October 10, a headline in the *Fort Lauderdale Daily News* read: "Storm Develops Off Coast. New Tropical Storm 500 Miles From Miami."

On the morning of October 11, more thunderstorms greeted south Florida, but to Broward residents already numbed by the incessant rain, it just seemed like more of the same.

That night many people went to movie theaters in downtown Fort Lauderdale to forget their troubles. Then, sometime around dusk, the storm suddenly blossomed into a small but intense hurricane with winds of 100 mph. As moviegoers left the theaters they found themselves wading through rising water that was flooding the lobbies. Mannequins could be seen floating inside department stores.

As much as 15 inches fell on Fort Lauderdale that night. In some parts of Broward flood waters stood eight feet deep. In downtown Miami, the water was more than four feet deep along Flagler Street.

By Monday, Davie was virtually uninhabited. State Road 84 and West Dixie Highway were under water. Game warden J. R. Giddens, who had struggled vainly to keep hunters from shooting the deer that had taken refuge on the levees west of Davie, said the water was six feet deep in his home in West Dixie. Water was inches from the eaves of new houses in Hacienda Flores.

"Broward County from the air today is one vast lake which stretches from a point a few miles west of the ocean for the full 45 miles westward to Collier County, where the lake continues," read one newspaper story. "The flood stretches from Hialeah on the south northward to the Conners Highway (near Lake Okeechobee) and beyond in Palm Beach County."

Tempers were rising even faster than the water. When the Fort Lauderdale City Commission ordered the use of dynamite to open the "old" Fort Lauderdale inlet, the *Fort Lauderdale Daily News* lashed out at "the stupidity of (our) city leaders," who, it said, had procrastinated for 48 hours before deciding to ignore protests by the wealthy property owners on Harbor Beach. Downtown was blockaded 24 hours too late, charged the paper, which encouraged voters to "call on new leaders" in an upcoming election.

One day after the inlet was blasted open, however, incoming tides refilled it with sand. This didn't prevent Fort Lauderdale voters from turning out in record numbers to bounce the mayor and three commissioners from office.

Even less popular was EDD chief engineer Lamar Johnson. A Broward Sheriff's deputy found a man armed with a rifle hiding behind some sandbags

Business as usual at a Hialeah bar in spite of flooding. (Historical Association of Southern Florida)

at a canal. The man was waiting to shoot Johnson, who was due to arrive shortly.

Finally, in November, the rains ended and the waters began to recede. But the controversy over the opening and closing of dikes and dams persisted. A Broward grand jury was hastily formed to investigate the matter.

Hamilton Forman, a powerful Broward dairyman who had suffered considerable losses due to the flooding, charged in a carefully documented statement that 50 to 75 percent of the damage in Davie and virtually all the damage in Fort Lauderdale had been caused by EDD policies.

On March 24, 1948, EDD chairman Dewey Hilsabeck and chief engineer Lamar Johnson were hauled before the grand jury. Johnson, describing himself as the "favorite whipping boy of Broward County," later wrote:

"The room was small, the atmosphere frosty, and the faces unfriendly, except for the one Negro juryman. I was not invited to be seated. I stood behind the least antagonistic member of the jury, the Negro, to testify. Their questions were terse; my answers, I am afraid, convinced very few. . . . I was not sure as I left whether I should go back to work or get my affairs in order in preparation for a jail sentence."

The EDD's defense was based primarily on the contention that it was trying to clear all flood waters as quickly as possible. The rainfall was so great that the moves proposed by various Broward interests would not really have helped, Johnson said. In addition, the EDD was trying to avoid bloodshed and the destruction of district structures.

Within a week the grand jury returned its verdict. It recommended no action against Hilsabeck or Johnson and called for repair of the flood-damaged works.

Out of the turmoil of the 1947 floods came a new agency which is known today as the South Florida Water Management District. The district includes all or part of 16 counties, with a population of five million and an area totaling 18,000 square miles and 1,400 miles of canals and levees.

Looking back at the days of the Great South Florida Flood, Lamar Johnson wrote in 1974: "The substantial levees of the conservation areas separate the Everglades waters from the strictly local flood waters. As a result, they have built subdivision-type developments almost to these levees, confident of their flood protection.

"It is my opinion, however, that anytime that area gets a foot or more of rainfall overnight, the shades of 1947's flood will be with them again."

Sooner or later, south Florida will find out if he is right.

MOVERS AND SHAKERS

From the days when Florida became a United States territory until the days when the Depression bankrupted Key West, the land has faced a bizarre and varied array of challenges. These ranged from the need to create a territorial constitution to the problem of a governor who committed suicide to the presence of a hell-raising third-party presidential candidate on Florida's sandy soil. Solving the state's problems has called for the skills of people who could make things move even while they were shaking in their boots.

CHAPTER 12

Old Hickory's Term

Jackson was the only Florida Governor to make it to the White House

You had to figure a man who could buy land for 10 cents an acre on the Tennessee frontier and later sell it for $3 an acre would somehow find his way down to Florida.

Andrew Jackson did more than just find his way down here. And he turned out to be considerably more than just a land salesman.

Major General Jackson waged war in a Florida owned by Spain during the War of 1812 and the First Seminole War in 1817–18. He attacked and captured the Spaniards' West Florida capital, Pensacola, twice, even though the United States was not at war with the Spanish, a nicety that disturbed him not a bit.

He disturbed Spain, though, so much so, in fact, that the Spanish, terrified of the American they called "the Napoleon of the Woods," were agreeable to turning the long, skinny peninsula, *La Florida,* over to the upstart New World nation in 1821. The cost to the United States: just $5 million.

Jackson's third entry into the capital was a triumphant one. This time he strutted in as the first United States governor of the newly acquired Territory of Florida.

To this day Jackson remains the only Florida governor to make it to the White House, thus giving the state a rare honor. Only eight other American states have seen their governors attain the Presidency.

"Old Hickory"—a nickname his toughness earned him—was a war hero of epic scale. He had whipped the British at New Orleans and the Creek and Seminole Indians in Alabama and West Florida.

Jackson became one of America's greatest presidents. In polls of 20th-century historians he is consistently ranked among the half dozen best of all the country's leaders. One of his major achievements was making the government more responsive to all citizens, not just to the wealthy and privileged. He is generally regarded as the founder of the modern Democratic Party. In recent years, however, he has been widely criticized for his harsh treatment of the frontier Indians, in particular the Cherokee and the Seminoles.

Old Hickory was a hell-raiser, heavy into gambling on cockfights and horse racing. Always a hothead, he once shot a man to death in one of his many duels. Another time he tried to horsewhip Colonel Thomas Hart Benton, who would become a power in the U.S. Senate. Instead, a shootout resulted. Jackson entered the White House in 1829 with surplus lead still in his body.

General Jackson was a dangerous man to cross. Colonel Don Jose Callava, the last Spanish governor of West Florida, was fated to learn to his great humiliation just how tough Jackson could be.

On March 3, 1821, the U.S. Senate confirmed President James Monroe's appointment of Jackson to serve as Florida's territorial governor. Salary: $5,000 plus expenses.

Jackson entered Spanish West Florida on June 17, encamping about 15 miles west of Pensacola. He sent his beloved wife, Rachel, ahead to the city where she could be housed more comfortably.

He preferred to stay outside until he could set up a meeting which paid proper respect to the new governor. His overtures were greeted with a variety of stalling gambits by Callava, who was just as determined that Spanish face would prevail at the meeting. "I would sink the place and him with it," wrote Jackson, angered at Callava's insistence that the American call on him rather than the other way around. Far faster than he dreamed, the handsome, dignified Castillian was drifting dangerously close to Old Hickory's notoriously low boiling point.

A month after his arrival in Florida, Jackson finally entered the city at 6:30 on the morning of July 17, 1821. A tall, gaunt, almost emaciated man on horseback, Jackson still bore across his face the scar from a British officer's slashing sword, inflicted on him as a 13-year-old soldier in the Revolutionary War. Tired and sickly, he was anxious to get his days of public service behind him so he could retire at 54 to his Tennessee plantation. He had no love for the flat, swampy land around him, so unlike the rolling hills of Nashville.

He ate breakfast with Rachel to the music of U.S. military bands which followed him into Pensacola. Then Jackson and his staff passed between lines of American and Spanish troops in Plaza Ferdinand and entered Government House. There the agreement was signed by Old Hickory and Colonel Callava. A week earlier East Florida had been transferred to U.S. control in a ceremony in St. Augustine.

A gun salute fired by the U.S. Fourth Regiment artillery was answered by guns aboard the *U.S. Hornet,* anchored in Pensacola Bay. Jackson listened then as the Fourth Infantry band played "The Star Spangled Banner." It had been written in Baltimore during the War of 1812, the war that had made him a national hero.

Governor Jackson gazed upon his capital and saw a dilapidated city of some 713 residents, a little more than a third of them black. Even Government House was unfit for occupancy. He described it as "in a ruinous state . . . unsafe." The soldiers' barracks were uninhabitable. Heavy traffic and drenching rains produced streets of mud, aswarm with undesirable types: soldiers of fortune, gamblers, swindlers and land speculators.

Jackson's pious Presbyterian wife found it a city of evil. Rachel wrote a friend: "The Sabbath profanely kept; a great deal of noise and swearing in the streets; shops kept open; trade going on, I think, more than on any other day."

The governor shut down all theaters and gambling halls on Sunday. Violators could be fined $200. A delighted Rachel exclaimed: ". . . fiddling and dancing not heard any more on the Lord's day, cursing not to be heard."

Jackson was concerned primarily with setting up an orderly, American-style government. He established a board of health, set up registration for inhabitants who wanted to become American citizens and created courts, guaranteeing, among other rights, trial by jury. He also divided Florida into two counties, Escambia to the west of the Suwannee River, and St. Johns to the east. South Florida was still an unsettled wilderness.

Jackson "Americanized" the town through cultural activities. The day he arrived in town an American theater, the Commonwealth, was opened. In August he brought in a printing press and established a circulating library with some 50 newpapers in its reading room.

In mid-August, Henry M. Brackenridge, mayor of Pensacola, brought to Jackson's attention the plight of Mercedes Vidal. Nothing could inflame the wrath of this frontier knight more than a damsel in distress. A free quadroon—a person with one-quarter Negro blood—Mercedes was the illegitimate daughter of a Spaniard who had died in 1806, leaving behind large landholdings to several of his half-caste children.

Executor of the will was Forbes and Company, a large Scottish trading company represented by John Innerarity. The tall "Hispanicized" Scot had become a close associate of Callava, who remained in the city during the transition period.

For 15 years Innerarity had withheld Mercedes' inheritance. Eventually, she obtained enough documents to raise serious questions about the company's handling of the will.

After the Americans arrived, Vidal engaged as her attorneys the mayor and Richard Keith Call, a longtime associate of Jackson. She told them she had learned that the remaining documents were being held by Domingo Sousa, one of Callava's clerks, prior to shipment to Havana.

Governor Andrew Jackson (Florida State Archives)

Brackenridge shrewdly concluded it would be best to bypass the federal judge appointed by President Monroe. Judge Eligius Fromentin, a Jesuit priest, had been expelled from France during the French Revolution. He came to Maryland where he married a woman of wealth. Described as "wily, conspiritorial, suave and urbane," he was close to both Innerarity and Callava.

Terrified by the ferocious governor, Sousa told him the papers were at Callava's house. Jackson immediately sent a guard to demand the papers. Dining at his home with none other than Judge Fromentin and Innerarity, Callava airily told the guard a royal commissioner was not subject to such demands.

First lady Rachel Jackson (Florida State Archives)

Over the next few days Jackson persisted and Callava kept stalling. The governor told one of his colonels:

"Sir, you will furnish an officer, sergeant, corporal and 20 men and direct the officer to call on me by half past eight o'clock for orders. They will have their arms and 12 rounds of ammunition."

When no one answered at Callava's house, three of the soldiers entered and proceeded toward the only lighted room. They found Colonel Callava in bed, fully clothed.

"I will not quit this house alive," he said.

"Prime and load," the commander said to his soldiers.

Callava changed his mind.

The Spaniard, however, was a man of spirit. Hauled before Jackson, he battled the American in a two-hour screaming and ranting match. A Spanish officer, witnessing the event, described Don Andrew Jackson's behavior as "turbulent and violent actions, with disjointed reasonings, blows on the table, his mouth foaming and possessed of the furies."

The shouting ended when Don Andrew ordered the imprisonment of His Catholic Majesty's Royal Commissioner and Governor. Callava was escorted to the calaboose, a small, dirty, uncomfortable structure built by the Spaniards years ago.

As he entered the jail, Callava, struck with the absurdity of the evening, suddenly broke out into laughter. During his short stay he was supplied with cigars, claret and champagne. The Spaniards who witnessed the encounter performed imitations of "Don Andrew Jackson."

The next morning Jackson issued a writ for the Vidal papers. As soon as he received them, he released Callava from the calaboose.

In reporting the Callava incident to John Quincey Adams, Secretary of State, Jackson wrote:

"I did believe, and ever will believe, that just laws can make no distinction of privilege between the rich and poor, and that when men of high standing attempt to trample upon the rights of the weak, they are the fittest objects for example and punishment. In general, the great can protect themselves, but the poor and the humble require the arm and shield of the law."

This belief would be a guiding principle during his two terms as President.

After hearing the case, Jackson ruled in favor of the Vidal heirs. Meanwhile, Callava left the calaboose as quickly as possible and headed for Washington to protest his rough treatment. A few Congressmen considered an investigation, then thought better of it. Old Hickory was just too popular.

By this time Jackson felt he had seen enough of Florida. He didn't want the job, didn't like it, but at least he accomplished what he set out to do—"Americanize the Floridas." He served for just 11 weeks.

At his farewell dinner on October 4 he declared: "I have made no discrimination of persons. My house has been surrounded by no guards . . . all have had free admittance . . . when they required my aid for the protection of their rights."

Three days later a carriage drawn by four gray horses left Government House carrying the Jacksons away from Pensacola, bound for Nashville and the leisurely peaceful life of a Tennessee plantation. He had hoped to retire, but few would call two terms in the White House retirement.

The man was just too popular to stay hidden away at the Hermitage. The

American people saw him as a leader and they wanted him at the head of their government.

* * *

Jackson's life had been a hard one. Less than two weeks after his father died, Andrew Jackson was born on March 15, 1767, in the Waxhaws, a settlement on the border between the two Carolinas. At 13 he fought in the Revolutionary War, which claimed the lives of his brothers; by the war's end, his mother, too, had died, leaving him an orphan at 14.

After studying law in Salisbury, North Carolina, he was appointed attorney general of a part of western North Carolina that became Tennessee. In Nashville he made a great deal of money selling land he had bought for as little as 10 cents an acre to new settlers for as much as $3 an acre.

At 24 he married Mrs. Rachel Donelson Robards. Both she and Jackson believed she was divorced from her army officer husband, only to find they had wed before the decree became final. Thereafter even a hint of a slur directed toward Rachel brought out the dueling pistols.

Jackson was a busy man. He was elected to the U.S. House of Representatives and then to the Senate. He served also as a justice of the Tennessee Supreme Court.

It was his war record, however, that brought him the fame and adoration that led to the White House. In the War of 1812 the U.S. Government's resistance to Great Britain had been so feeble that British troops marched into Washington and burned the Capitol. Many lost faith in their new country. Jackson restored it with a resounding victory in the Battle of New Orleans.

In 1824 Jackson ran for president against the incumbent, John Quincy Adams, son of America's second president. Old Hickory led the large field in electoral votes but failed to win a majority. This threw the outcome of the election into the lap of the House of Representatives. There the vote went to Adams.

Four years later Jackson ran again against Adams. This time he scored a convincing victory both in the popular vote and the electoral vote. It had been a bitter campaign, which included attacks on Rachel as an "adultress." Only a little over a month after his election she died of a heart attack.

Jackson would go on to win reelection four years later by an even bigger margin. Upon leaving office, he was still so popular that his hand-picked successor, Martin Van Buren, also was elected president and his protege, James K. Polk, won election in 1844.

In the closing months of his presidency, Florida, a world he had hoped he had put behind him, claimed his attention again. In December of 1835 the Second Seminole War erupted in north Florida. He assigned Major General

Winfield Scott the task of conquering the Seminoles, but when Jackson left office in March of 1837 the fierce war was still raging and would for another five years.

He returned to the Hermitage where he lived out the rest of his days. On June 8, 1845, Old Hickory died at his home and was buried beside Rachel in the garden at the Hermitage.

His legacy is remembered in many ways. Florida's largest city bears his name, as does a small county in the Panhandle, the capital of Mississippi, and many other cities and counties around the nation. Even a bourbon is named after him. He is probably best known today as the face on the $20 bill. He undoubtedly would have preferred a smaller denomination.

CHAPTER 13

First Constitution

56 delegates met in St. Joe to draft territorial document

For Richard Fitzpatrick it was a long journey, from a South Florida county so sparsely settled its total population was only 314, to Florida's largest city, wild and wicked St. Joseph on the upper Gulf of Mexico. Travel by land was out of the question; in 1838 the Second Seminole War was raging across the peninsula. Fitzpatrick's boat had to sail north from the Keys across the Gulf to reach St. Joseph by December 3, the day he and 55 other elected delegates were scheduled to begin the enormous task of creating the territory of Florida's first constitution.

As the convention delegate from Dade, Fitzpatrick had to speak for a county which stretched from Indian Key to the Hillsboro River. He would also speak for himself, as the largest landowner in the county, motivated always by his uncompromising belief in the Old South's slave-holding, plantation-style society. For a little over $2,000 he had bought more than four square miles near the Miami River, then for $500 more he obtained the Frankee Lewis Donation, a square mile of land on the New River, near the Army's newly built Fort Lauderdale. His stake in South Florida was a large one.

In February, 1838, the territory's Legislative Council passed an act calling for a convention to meet "to adopt a bill of rights and constitution and all needful measures preparatory to the admission of Florida into the national Confederacy."

A powerful man in Florida politics, Fitzpatrick had represented Monroe County in 1834, 1835 and 1836. After he introduced legislation to split the Upper Keys and the lower southeastern mainland away from Monroe, he became the new county's delegate from 1837 through 1840. For each legislative session he had been chairman of at least one standing committee and in 1836 had been elected President of the Legislative Council, next to the Governor the most important post in the territory.

In the battle over the convention site, Fitzpatrick's influence loomed large.

Candidates for the convention included the capital, Tallahassee; St. Augustine; Pensacola; Mineral Springs on the banks of the Suwannee River; the site of the Seminole War Battle of Withlacoochee; and the eventual winner, St. Joseph.

Wrote the *Apalachicola Gazette:* "The selection of St. Joseph resulted from a log-rolling compromise between the East and the West. Says Fizzy to Peter, 'scratch my back and I'll tickle your elbow.' The proposition suited the fancy of both parties. So Peter scratched the Banks and Fizzy tickled the Town."

Fizzy was Fitzpatrick, a pro-bank delegate, while Peter Gautier, Jr. was the publisher of the *St. Joseph Times,* chairman of the site selection committee, an ardent booster of his home town and a promoter all the way.

Only three years old, St. Joseph had grown rapidly into a town of 4,000 by 1838. The town's founders had formerly lived in nearby Apalachicola as squatters. When the land company began charging exorbitant prices for lots, they moved out in vast numbers and started the town of St. Joseph, just 28 miles to the east on St. Joseph Bay.

The town's founders called themselves the Saints but St. Joseph actually went in the other direction, quickly developing a reputation as a sinful city. In one account it was described as "the richest and wickedest city in the southeast." Another writer called it a "town of wickedness and licentiousness, of moneyed men and pretty women." St. Joe had a race track, gambling casinos, saloons, taverns, even a theater. It was also one of Florida's first railroad towns.

The town took the convention seriously. It had to. It was so new it lacked many niceties the convention would need. New hotels went up quickly, bearing such intellectualized names as the Byron, Pickwick and Shakespeare. A stage coach line was established, and more passenger boats began to serve the area. Work began immediately on a convention hall.

St. Joseph was ready by December 3 when 46 of the delegates responded to the roll call at noon. Only three of the delegates were natives of Florida; four were foreign born. The delegation included mostly lawyers and planters but also two newspaper editors, three doctors, an innkeeper, a merchant, a fisherman and a sea captain.

The meeting was opened with prayer by the Reverend Peter Gautier, father of the enterprising promoter. Delegates then set about naming the convention's officers. Nominated as president were William P. Duval, territorial governor for 12 years, and Robert Raymond Reid, of St. Johns County, who would later be elected governor. Reid won by one vote, but promptly a problem arose. He had cast Hillsborough County's proxie vote for himself, only to learn that the Hillsborough election had been challenged. He resigned

Diorama at Constitution Convention State Museum at Port St. Joe. (Florida State Archives)

but was immediately reelected. As presiding officer, Reid sat beneath a picture of George Washington.

Meanwhile, a delegate from Hillsborough showed up. He was not, however, the one the county had elected. Mr. Right did not arrive until December 17.

The nonelected delegate was a former associate of Fitzpatrick's, one William M. Cooley. Cooley had come to the New River in 1824. As a squatter, he had established a starch mill and a small, prosperous farm. Six years later Fitzpatrick had bought the Lewis property and converted it into a southern-style plantation, complete with black slaves. He obtained a justice of the peace appointment for Cooley, who had in turn reciprocated by turning out healthy majorities for Fizzy in territorial elections.

On January 6, 1836, Cooley was attempting to salvage a shipwreck near the Hillsboro Inlet when a group of Indians attacked, killing his wife and children and their tutor. After the Cooley Massacre, the New River Settlement was deserted. Fitzpatrick lost some 50–60 slaves, who ran away with the Indians. The Seminole War would shatter his dream of a plantation society in south Florida, similar to the one in which he had grown up at his family's country home near Columbia, South Carolina.

The work of the convention was divided among 18 committees, which drafted articles on such important subjects as a bill of rights; executive, legislative and judicial departments; suffrage; militia; census; taxation and revenue; education; slavery; and banks. Drafting of most of the articles proved fairly simple since delegates used the constitutions of various southern states, particularly Alabama, as models. One of the convention's problems was absenteeism. In early December an Indian scare cut into attendance. Still, all in all, the delegates worked hard, toiling even on Christmas Day.

The one big problem area was banking. Following the Panic of 1837, antibank sentiment ran strong through the country. Three Florida banks were operating under territorial faith bonds. This meant the territory was liable in the event of bank failure. Since these banks mostly benefited the wealthy planters buying land and slaves, smaller farmers and businessmen were none too happy with the cozy arrangement.

Believing that the controversy could be resolved, Fitzpatrick proposed that the Union Bank of Florida be adopted as the State Bank of Florida, with increased government regulation and a decreased use of faith bonds to benefit privately owned banks. Amendments, however, created a banking article that Fitzpatrick regarded as downright antibanking.

Angry at the antibank protectors of the public's funds, he proposed to "relinquish any mileage or pay due him as a member of the Convention, if other members would do the same." A Key West delegate countered by moving "that each member who shall vote aye, shall be considered as having relinquished his claim to pay."

On January 11, 1839, the delegates assembled for their final vote. Fifty-five of them voted for the new constitution. Only one delegate, Richard Fitzpatick, voted against it.

Florida's first constitution—known now as the Constitution of 1838 even though it was not completed until 1839—provided for a four-year term without reelection for the governor. Members of the House of Representatives would be elected for one-year terms, senators for two. The Bill of Rights contained 27 clauses, in many cases guaranteeing rights already protected by the U.S. Constitution. The vote, as would be expected in 1839, would be the right only of free white males, 21 or older, who had lived in Florida for two years.

Antibank sentiment was so strong that the constitution prohibited bankers from holding public office while employed by a bank. Strong feelings about separation of church and state led to a provision denying ministers of the Gospel the right to elected office.

The constitution frowned on dueling. Fighting in one or even challenging someone to a duel disqualified a citizen from running for office.

In August, 1839, the citizens of the territory voted on whether to accept or reject the constitution. The vote was surprisingly close: 2065 to 1961 in favor of the document. Six years later, on March 3, 1945, Florida became the 27th state, thus requiring a state constitution.

What happened later to the first constitution so proudly signed by the delegates, to Fitzpatrick who refused to sign it and to the go-getter town of St. Joseph? Sometime after 1845 the first constitution of Florida simply disappeared. Fitzpatrick, born to the wealthy planter class, died a poor man in Matamoras, Texas, in 1865. But he never cashed his $444 expense warrant from the Convention.

St. Joseph ran into the roughest time of all. First, the town was hit with a yellow fever epidemic, next a fire burned down every house in the deserted town. Then in 1844 a hurricane and tidal wave destroyed what little was left. Once Florida's biggest town, it vanished in less than a decade.

CHAPTER 14

Milton's Paradise Lost

State's Civil War governor committed suicide

John Milton, the fifth governor of Florida, bore a distinguished name, that of the celebrated English poet who wrote the epic *Paradise Lost.*

Governor Milton, a direct descendant of the poet's family, lost what he too thought was a paradise—antebellum Florida, where the planter class was free to raise cotton on vast plantations with slave labor. Milton himself owned 52 of the state's 60,000 slaves.

As his Confederate world crumbled about him, Milton committed an act that makes him unique among Florida governors. Eight days before Gen. Robert E. Lee surrendered at Appomattox, Virginia, John Milton killed himself.

A native Georgian, Milton was born into a Deep South world of cotton, slaves and plantations—a world immortalized by Margaret Mitchell in *Gone With the Wind.* He was a graduate of the University of Georgia and practiced law in New Orleans and Mobile. He also served as commander of a company of Alabama militia in the Second Seminole War.

In 1845 Milton bought "Sylvania," an impressive plantation near Marianna. He eventually accumulated more than 7,000 acres in the heart of the state's best cotton country.

A stocky man with a square, fleshy face, Milton proved to be a fiery orator when he entered Florida politics in 1848. By 1860 his eloquence had taken him to the steps of the state capitol in Tallahassee. After 23 ballots, he won the secessionist Democrats' nomination for governor. As a staunch advocate of state's rights, he went on to win the election in October.

By the time Milton took the oath of office a year later, Florida had seceded from the Union, joined the Confederate States of America and gone to war against the United States of America.

Over the next four years, Milton's face took on the somber look of a man who was learning the horrors of civil war the hard way. His major concerns were the state's lack of money and manpower. The treasury was broke and Florida's population of 70,000—excluding slaves—consisted mostly of small farmers scattered around a huge state.

"I shall enter upon the duties of governor with a heavy heart and fearful apprehension," he said in his inaugural address in 1861.

When the South pulled nearly all of Florida's soldiers into the bloody Battle of Shiloh in Tennessee in 1862, Milton wrote: "The effect of this order is to abandon middle, east and southern Florida to the mercy and abuse of the Lincoln government."

He was right. Union troops moved swiftly to occupy Pensacola and Cedar Key on the Gulf Coast and Fernandina, Jacksonville and St. Augustine on the Atlantic.

Soon, Florida had become a haven for deserters from the Confederate army. One of those deserters, William Strickland, headed a group called the "Union Rangers of Taylor County," later known as the "Florida Royals." These men took a secret oath of allegiance to the United States. Another group of deserters, who were also sympathetic to the U.S., learned about Milton's travel plans and plotted his capture. However, Milton got word of their intentions and remained close to Tallahassee, where he could be protected.

The morale of Florida's fighting men was given a boost in February, 1864, when Union forces, some 5,500 strong, moved westward from Jacksonville to fight the Battle of Olustee. Near Lake City, about 100 miles east of the state capital, an equal force of Confederates took a strong defensive position near a large cypress swamp. The South, inflicting heavy losses, forced the Union troops back to Jacksonville.

It was the only major battle fought in Florida, but its outcome had little effect. The Civil War was going badly throughout the South, though most Floridians, isolated from the rest of the country, did not realize it at the time. One who did was John Milton. War profiteers and blockade runners constantly hindered his efforts to keep the Confederate army supplied with food and weapons.

"The floodgates of all species of villainy seemed to be unhinged," the governor lamented.

He was obsessed with fear of freed slaves. He believed the Union wanted to make Florida "a waste, a howling wilderness, or to colonize it with Negroes." The news grew even worse. General Sherman was making his devastating March to the Sea through Milton's native Georgia. In Virginia, General Lee was struggling to hold Richmond, the Confederate capital.

A momentary break in the curtain of gloom came in March, 1865. Fourteen Union vessels unloaded a thousand troops near St. Marks on the Gulf and

Governor John Milton (Florida State Archives)

moved up the St. Marks River to capture Tallahassee, the only state capital still in Confederate hands.

On the night of March 4, locomotive whistles called Tallahassee to action. Reserves, militia, cavalry, civilians, seminarians and farmers with squirrel guns converged on Natural Bridge, south of the capital, determined to halt the Union forces.

Firing from behind trees, Indian-style, Florida's motley army of defenders surprised and confused the enemy, and forced Union soldiers to retreat after suffering heavy losses.

But the governor knew that the victory, though an admirable effort, was futile. In his last message to the state legislature, he said, "Death would be better than reunion."

On April 1, 1865, Milton called for his horses and carriage. Along with his wife and son, Major William Henry Milton, the governor set out from Tallahassee for his plantation in Marianna.

Arriving in town, they rode past the blackened ruins of the Marianna church. At Sylvania, no servants greeted them. But one of Milton's daughters, who was already at the plantation, set about preparing a homecoming dinner for her father. He never got to eat it.

John Milton went to his room, took out a pistol, and shot himself in the head. Florida's Civil War governor died instantly.

CHAPTER 15

Stealing the County Seat

Palm Beach "muscle" too much for outmaneuvered Miami

To take the county seat of Dade County away from Miami today would be impossible. A century ago it was merely difficult, involving only a winning election strategy, a grasp of how rough frontier politics could be, the good sense to enlist some armed men in your cause, and a fearless boatman who knew how to navigate an Indian canoe through the meandering Snake Creek and into the Everglades in the dead of night. Here's what happened.

In 1888 Dade County stretched from the Upper Keys to the Stuart area, a huge county containing 7,200 square miles but only 726 residents. The biggest settlements were along the shores of Biscayne Bay and Lake Worth.

After the election of 1888, E. N. "Cap" Dimick, who would later become the first mayor of Palm Beach, and other leading north-county Democrats noticed that the "lake people" cast far more votes than the "bay people." So, they asked themselves, why is the county seat in a rented room in Miami? Irritating the populace further, the county's landlord, J. W. Ewan, the "Duke of Dade," had announced he was tripling the county's rent from $5 a month to $15.

As their compromise candidate for the county seat, Dimick and his colleagues agreed on the little unincorporated village of Juno on the north shores of Lake Worth. Since Juno would soon become the southern terminus of a short-haul railroad already under construction, it would be relatively easy to reach from the north by railroad and from the south by boat. To sweeten the choice still further, Albert M. Field, a county commissioner, agreed to donate an acre of his Juno land for the county's first courthouse.

With the site settled, the lake people petitioned for a vote on moving the county seat. On February 19, 1889, the voters went to the polls. Juno polled a heavy vote, and the lake residents also elected some of their own to important county posts, such as A. F. Quimby as county clerk and Allen E. Heyser as county judge.

Totals in the north county looked large enough to win comfortably, but there was always the danger of some sleight-of-hand in Miami, where the ballots would be certified. The Juno group took precautions by engaging the services of three brawny souls who would be described today as "muscle." Leading this sturdy and well-armed trio was one Patrick Lennon, an Irishman chased out of the British Isles for his efforts at chasing England out of Ireland. A member of the Fenians, an early ancestor of today's IRA, he was a brawler of note—and at the same time a respected owner of waterfront land in the Palm Beach area.

The trio of toughs accompanied three "proper" county officials, the newly elected county clerk and judge and county commissioner James Porter, from Lake Worth. Since no roads connected the lake and bay areas, the men had to walk some 70 miles down the beach to deliver the election results.

When the votes were counted for the entire county, the Juno location had won handily, 107 to 80. And that's when the trouble started. Miamians declared they would use force to keep the county's records from leaving their town.

E. L. White, a county commissioner from Lemon City, spoke in a more conciliatory vein: "Gentlemen, I am opposed to moving the records just as much as anyone, and I certainly hate to see them go, but Lake Worth and the north end of the county have won in a fair fight by an honest vote of the majority of the citizens of the county. We have got to take our medicine, however much we dislike it, and let the records go."

"Never," shouted one hothead.

"Not on your life," cried another.

The Miamians had the numbers, but the Lake Worth officials had the edge in guns. At least for the time being.

By late afternoon some of the noisier Miamians had left, threatening to return the next morning well-armed. One man promised to bring in a jug of Dutch Courage whiskey to keep the Biscayne partisans inflamed. They were not concerned that the crew from the north would try to smuggle the records out after dark. They figured that the record books were simply too heavy to be transported to Juno on foot, and no boat would dare venture into the ocean in such stormy weather.

Before returning to the county office at 8 p.m., Quimby had used the dinner break to good advantage. Mingling with the crowd, he had learned that he and his group could expect violence the next day. The answer, he figured, was to leave that night. And he had a plan. Venturing up the Miami River, he had borrowed an Indian dugout canoe, big enough to hold all the records.

"I have the canoe at the dock now," he told his north-county colleagues. "I am for loading the records into that canoe and starting for the New River at once, by way of the Glades. I know the way and can take her through without a hitch."

Quimby picked Pat Lennon and Commissioner Porter to go with him. The other members of the contingent would wait till the winds subsided, then walk up to the Fort Lauderdale House of Refuge, where they would rendezvous.

But, Quimby added, there just might be a complication: "There is one more thing I want to call your attention to, and it's a situation I am just a little bit afraid of. In going up the bay, we will have to keep near the west shore in order to reach bottom with our poles. Some of these fellows might see us passing and open fire on us. In that case we would have to surrender the records or get killed."

Help came from an unexpected source, a young real-estate man named Fred Morse. A Bostonian who had come to South Florida for his health, Morse was a descendant of a distinguished American family that included the inventor of the telegraph.

Said Morse: "I can eliminate friend Quimby's fears on that score by towing the canoe to the head of the bay with my sharpie (a long, narrow shallow-draft boat)."

From there, Morse explained, they could enter Snake Creek and follow it into the Everglades. By now it was 10 o'clock, and so dark and stormy that no one was around to watch them load the records into the canoe. At midnight Morse's sharpie delivered them to Snake Creek.

Poling and paddling, the men set out in the darkness. Fortunately, Quimby knew the creek, but even he admitted that this trip was different: "I never was through here before when I expected to be chased by an armed mob."

Even tough Pat Lennon, who came from a land without snakes, was nervous as they moved through the tortuous channel. The name of the waterway didn't help any. Was it called Snake Creek because it was so crooked, or, as some said, because of a huge snake observed by one of its first explorers?

Far to the east they saw the sun rise as they floated out of Snake Creek and into the vast wilderness of the Everglades. The going would be easier now in the shallow waters where poles could replace paddles. Soon they reached the headwaters of the New River, where a swift current could help them on their way to the coast. At three in the afternoon they arrived at the barrier island where the Fort Lauderdale House of Refuge stood, near today's Bahia Mar.

Loaded down with bulky record books, the men struggled across a half-mile of sandy soil. Charles Coman, the keeper of the House of Refuge, helped them, and by 4 p.m. the job was finished. The men sat down with Coman to recount their adventures of the previous day and night. It was good to relax with a pot of coffee, far from the threat of Miami guns and clubs.

Statue of E.N. "Cap" Dimick, first mayor of Palm Beach. (Stuart McIver)

Then one of the men glanced down the beach and saw three men coming up the shore from the south. They were walking rapidly. The invaders had to be Miami toughs!

There seemed to be only one answer. Move the records to the attic and get ready to shoot it out. They hadn't struggled through Snake Creek and the Everglades to give up now.

Quimby armed himself with an iron crossbar from one of the cots at the refuge. Lennon and Commissioner Porter, armed with guns, stationed themselves near the stairs to the attic. Said Porter, "I can shoot as well with my left as my right . . . no man shall come up here as long as I have a cartridge left and can pull a trigger."

They were even in numbers, three against three. But the north-county boys held a stronger position.

From the attic they heard the pounding of bare feet on the porch floor. They could not make out the words that Coman spoke to the intruders, but his tone was sharp and businesslike.

There were a few quiet words in answer, then loud laughter from Coman:

"It's all right, fellows. Put up your guns and come down. These are your own men on their way home, the fellows you left behind in Miami last night!"

Quimby remained at the House of Refuge to guard the records while the rest of the group returned to the lake country. A boat was sent to Fort Lauderdale to pick up the county records.

The contract to build the county's first courthouse was awarded to C. C. Haight of Lake Worth for $1,495. The two-story building, measuring 30 by 35 feet, contained an office, two jury rooms and a courtroom on the second floor. When not in use for county business, it was rented as a church, lodge hall or ballroom for $5 a night.

Laying the cornerstone for the partially finished courthouse was the greatest day Juno had ever known. On April 19, 1890, the Jupiter and Lake Worth Railroad, better known as the "Celestial Railroad," ran a special train to Juno for the occasion.

The scene was captured on film by photographer C. A. Lane, who sold many a print to north-county households.

Juno enjoyed its brief days of glory. The southeast coast's leading newspaper, *The Tropical Sun,* moved to the county seat. Attorney C. C. Chillingworth, who opened an office there, recalled it as "an unincorporated village that . . . had about seven dwelling houses, two boarding houses, one newspaper building, one very small railroad station and a store building on the dock near the water's edge." And, of course, one courthouse painted white.

Trials at the courthouse reflected the pioneer spirit. One night when a jury was pondering a murder case, the baying of a deerhound could be heard nearby. A sheriff's deputy took the jury with him to chase the deer. For the next two days, the judge, jury and court and county officials dined on venison. The prisoner received a life sentence.

Miamians, angered at the long trip to the new county seat, kept pecking away at Juno. In 1891 the state legislature had to pass an act declaring that the vote in 1889 had been a fair one and the new county seat was "in all respects legally located."

Even so, Juno's greatness was shortlived. The railroad, which had brought it glory, in the end took it away.

From the north a man named Henry Flagler was moving down the coast with his railroad and hotel empire. He tried to buy the Celestial Railroad, but the asking price was too high. He decided to build his own track instead.

Flagler's Florida East Coast Railway bypassed Juno and in 1894 reached a new town he had created called West Palm Beach. Two years later the railway moved triumphantly to the shores of Biscayne Bay. Settlers along the bay incorporated the city of Miami. It grew so fast that in 1899 Miami once again became the county seat of Dade County.

The records, smuggled out of Miami in a dugout canoe, had become so voluminous that a railroad box car was needed to take them back. The jail cells were placed on a barge and towed to Miami by steamer with the prisoners inside.

Almost overnight, Juno became a ghost town. The Celestial's rolling stock was sold at auction. The newspaper and the lawyers moved to West Palm Beach. In 1907 a forest fire swept into Juno, burning all the buildings that remained.

CHAPTER 16

Commodore vs. Tycoon

Little boats gave way to big boats as Munroe battled Flagler

A cold-water sailor from Staten Island, New York, found his Garden of Eden when he sailed into Biscayne Bay in September of 1877. Two decades later a tempting apple called progress contaminated the tropical Paradise he had found in Coconut Grove.

A lover of the simple life, close to nature, Commodore Ralph Middleton Munroe brought to Florida a vast array of talents to serve him well in his new world. He was a boat designer, an architect, a photographer and a natural scientist whose writings appeared in scientific journals.

Munroe was a man of respect in the primitive yet elitist society of 19th-century Coconut Grove. Unfortunately for him, he was fated to collide with a well-nigh unstoppable force named Henry Morrison Flagler.

Flagler could flatten his opponents with the wallop of a speeding freight train. And why not? He was a builder of railroads.

Nineteenth-century progress often took the form of iron tracks leading into small towns or settlements and quickly transforming them into hustling, bustling cities. Flagler's iron tracks already reached from North Florida down to the ritzy winter resort of Palm Beach. Next stop, Biscayne Bay, Munroe Country—but also Julia Tuttle Country.

Julia Tuttle, a major Miami landowner, was pushing The Man hard to bring his rails on into her domain. In 1894–95, hard freezes in North Florida dealt her a winning hand. The damage so devastating to the state's citrus crop stopped short of Biscayne Bay. The time had come, she felt, to step up the pressure on Flagler. Munroe, on her side at first, even gave her a pep talk:

"Go to Flagler in person. Take with you all the evidence possible as to the country not having had any destructive freeze in very many years. I can furnish you copies of my photographs and substantiate the time of making the exposure and the location. Catch him after a good dinner and give him one of your attractive talks. The pictures will do the rest."

Flagler sent one of his top men, James E. Ingraham, to Miami to check out her claims. Even more convincing than Munroe's pictures were fresh orange blossoms, undamaged by the terrible freeze that had wrecked Florida's citrus industry. Flagler agreed to come down to see for himself.

In 1895 several hundred settlers were scattered along Biscayne Bay. Just south of the Miami River dwelled a colony of fishermen, farmers, Bohemians and an intelligentsia that included the Commodore, America's most popular author of books for boys, and a couple of European counts. They called their idyllic community Coconut Grove.

Flagler's river steamer landed at the pier for the Biscayne Bay Manufacturing Company, a pineapple cannery run by Munroe. The Commodore lived in a comfortable, airy, high-roofed bungalow of his own design. Always a man of the sea, he built his home from timber salvaged from shipwrecks and gave it a maritime name—the Barnacle. The royal palms on Munroe's lushly landscaped property caught the eye of the tycoon.

"I am contemplating building a large hotel in Miami," he told the Commodore. "It will be called the Royal Palm. I'd like to buy your palms and transplant them."

"Not for sale," Munroe replied. At Palm Beach Flagler had already built the world's largest resort hotel, the Royal Poinciana. Maybe the Commodore was fearful the Royal Palm would be even bigger, creating irreversible pressures on his Eden. Later, in his memoirs he wrote: "I imagine that a pretty big price could have been gotten for them but I turned down his suggestion."

A bigger disagreement loomed ahead. Happy boosters were practically drooling at the thought of the railroad's impact on property values when Munroe tossed in a surprise.

"I hope that you will settle upon Miami as the site of your city and leave Coconut Grove entirely alone," Munroe told Flagler. A day of developer talk had convinced the Commodore he wanted no part of a railroad in his unspoiled world. His fellow Groveites did not agree. "Coconut Grove . . . nearly flew off the handle, and I became the object of some little censure," he wrote.

The stage was set now for a lifetime of discord between two of South Florida's most important leaders—the all-powerful robber baron and the child of nature.

Flagler and his partner John D. Rockefeller had managed to dominate an emerging oil industry with their enormous Standard Oil of Ohio, operating today as Exxon. With one world conquered, Flagler turned his attention to a sparsely settled frontierland along the east coast of Florida. Before his death he would open it up to the outside world—all the way from St. Augustine to Key West—with a combination of railroads, luxury hotels and a string of developer towns and farming communities. He even threw in a steamship line.

Flagler saw the world from the executive suite, the Commodore from the tiller of a 35-foot sharpie sailing through the blue waters of his beloved Biscayne Bay.

A love of nature was bred into the bones of Ralph Middleton Munroe. As a boy he spent many a summer in Concord, Massachusetts, with his grandfather William Munroe, the first manufacturer of lead pencils in the United States. Granddad was a member of the Concord "Social Circle," which included such philosophers as Ralph Waldo Emerson and Henry David Thoreau, who eloquently preached the joys of the simple life.

At Coconut Grove Munroe lived in a world of boats. His neighbors sailed small seaworthy sharpies he had designed for the shallow waters of Biscayne Bay. Some of the boats were work boats, others were used simply for transportation in a land without roads for wagons or tracks for trains.

In 1887 his neighbor, Kirk Munroe (not related to Ralph) concluded there were enough boaters in the Grove to warrant a yacht club. Kirk, a nationally known author of books for boys, organized the Biscayne Bay Yacht Club and without hesitation designated Ralph as its founding Commodore. Fifteen boats competed in the club's first regatta on Washington's Birthday, February 22, 1887.

BBYC, the southernmost yacht club in the United States, continued for the next decade as a small, cozy, down-home group, small sailboats only—none of these big, noisy powerboats or luxury yachts.

This was about to change. As the Commodore had hoped, Flagler settled on Miami as the terminus of his railroad and the location of his huge hotel on the north side of the Miami River where it flows into the Bay. Ralph Munroe, however, was to find that there was no way the coming of Flagler could leave either Coconut Grove or the yacht club untouched.

After the arrival of Flagler's railroad in the spring of 1896, a bank and the city's first newspaper, the *Miami Metropolis,* promptly sprang up. Then on July 28 a total of 343 voters met to incorporate the city on the north side of the river. They wanted to name it Flagler. The tycoon liked Miami. Miami it was.

The city's first mayor was John B. Reilly, a Flagler employee. A "Flagler Gang" emerged to take control of city politics. Miami became Flagler's town.

On January 15, 1897, the tycoon opened his lemon-yellow Royal Palm: 350 rooms, two electric elevators, a swimming pool and an electric generator to provide lights for the hotel and the city.

Commodore Ralph Munroe at tiller of sailboat. (Historical Association of Southern Florida)

His Florida East Coast Railway would, of course, bring in most of the wealthy guests—"swells," as they were called by the locals. But Flagler was looking ahead to the kind of clientele who would arrive aboard large ocean-going, powered luxury yachts. He wanted Vanderbilts, Carnegies, du Ponts, Mellons.

The problem was, the bay was too shallow. But for Flagler, no problem. He simply allocated $20,000 to dredge the mouth of the Miami River to create a deeper channel.

For the BBYC the dredging was a disaster. Left near the channel were unsightly spoilbanks, one 30 feet high. Near the river, these reduced the navigable waters to the cuts themselves. Pilings along the new channel added an additional hazard for sailboats. To make matters worse, the new obstructions blocked part of the race course the yacht club used for its regattas.

"So the railroad came to Miami. . . ," wrote the Commodore. "Where were now the pleasant friendships of the early days? What now signified the quiet, wild beauty of the Miami River? Neither was 'profitable' and both vanished like smoke. That was the turning point, from quiescence to progress, from waiting to doing, from enjoying to making, from the old times to the new—and I have never quite made up my mind whether I am glad or sorry for the change!"

Despite his misgivings about the dizzying developments of 1896, Munroe approached the 1897 Washington's Birthday Regatta with his usual zest. Sailing a yacht he designed, the *Utilis,* he defeated his close friend, Kirk Munroe, in *Allapatta,* also designed by the Commodore, to win the 12-mile race in the 35-foot-and-under class.

Ralph's joy at winning was tempered promptly by a change in location for the party that traditionally followed each regatta. Instead of assembling at the Peacock Inn, Coconut Grove's homey hotel, BBYC members sailed across the river to the Flagler's fancy Royal Palm. As guests of Flagler, they attended a ball, lavishly decorated with colored lanterns and enlivened by a fireworks display.

Recognizing the promotional value of a yacht club on his hotel grounds, Flagler began pushing the idea of a club station on the Magic City waterfront. The Commodore was less than happy. He described the new city as a "rather sordid growing town, many miles from the sea beach and the best of the fishing."

Another significant trend was disturbing Munroe, who wrote: "The motor boat had also taken such hold that the interest in sailing races declined and a club picnic to Cape Florida was substituted for the annual regatta. . . ."

More and more captains of industry were joining the club. In 1909 BBYC added Walter Mellon, the famed Pittsburgh financier, and Max Fleischmann, a Cincinnati manufacturer whose products included Fleischmann's Yeast.

One of the big new houseboats on the bay was *Everglades,* a 120-footer owned by Colonel Robert M. Thompson, a BBYC member since 1905. The colonel, who made his fortune in copper, was widely rumored for a possible post in the cabinet of William Howard Taft, elected to the Presidency in 1908. He would later head the American Olympic Committee.

The Commodore, who fancied 35-foot sailboats, could see his world slipping away. Huge powered luxury yachts, too big to dock at the Coconut Grove clubhouse, shouldered aside the small, picturesque sharpies.

By 1909 the yacht club, which had started life with just 15 Grovites, sported a membership list of 100, liberally laced with the rich and famous and, more to the point, with such Flagler powerhouses as the tycoon himself, his two principal executives, Ingraham and J. E. Parrott, and Frederick Morse, who had handled the Flagler railroad's real estate interests. That year Flagler and his henchmen convinced members to open a second clubhouse on the grounds of his Royal Palm Hotel.

After 23 years, Ralph Munroe decided to step down as commodore. It was no longer his club and to him the changes were not for the better. Dispiritedly, he wrote of his club, "the displacement of sails by gasoline . . . caused it to degenerate into a 'chowder party.'"

Colonel Thompson, who didn't make it into President Taft's cabinet, earned a consolation prize. A winter resident only, he succeeded Munroe as commodore, a post he held for three undistinguished years. At least Munroe considered him undistinguished. In his 378-page *The Commodore's Story* he makes not a single reference to his successor.

Meanwhile the Flagler organization proceeded to complete the east coast canal to Miami—later to be known as the Intracoastal Waterway—and more and more big boats were reaching Biscayne Bay. By 1914 the club's biggest boat was almost the length of a football field, the 277-1/2 foot *Vanadis,* built in Glasgow, Scotland, for C.K.G. Billings, of New York City. A little over a decade later 13 of the club's yachts measured over a hundred feet in length.

Munroe's old foe, Flagler, died in 1913 but the booming growth he had started exploded in the mid-1920s, bringing more bad news to the Commodore. In September of 1925, at the height of the Great Land Boom, Miami gobbled up Coconut Grove. The unfriendly takeover reduced the once proud Eden to a new status as just one of many neighborhoods in the sprawling Magic City.

And as if to flex its muscles even more, the Flagler interests built a newer and fancier clubhouse, still on its hotel property. The club decided it was time to abandon its old Coconut Grove clubhouse and make Miami its headquarters.

The Commodore, gazing out across the bay from the front porch of the Barnacle, had watched his pristine wilderness change into the American Riviera, a booming winter resort crowded with people and automobiles. In the winter of 1926 he saw it all change again. The boom collapsed into the greatest real estate bust the country had ever seen. Then in September, the forces of nature struck Miami with a killer hurricane. Deadly winds of 125 miles an hour blew away Munroe's old boathouse, where the club had met for a time in the 1890s. The storm also destroyed Flagler's old wooden hotel. The newly built BBYC clubhouse survived.

The yacht club, however, barely survived the collapse of the Miami economy. By 1928 a club meeting drew just 11 members. Even the likes of a W. K. Vanderbilt dropped out. Unable to pay the rent to the Flagler organization, the club had to abandon its downtown Royal Palm location at the end of 1930.

On August 20, 1933, Commodore Munroe died at 82. In one sense he died happy. He lived just long enough to see the BBYC work its way back to its present location in Coconut Grove, less than a mile from the Barnacle.

CHAPTER 17

The Perot of Las Olas Isle

Fiery Tom Watson led Populist challenge to major parties in early 20th century

In 1904 Populist Tom Watson, friend of the farmer and the laborer, foe of Wall Street and the railroads, ran for president on the People's Party ticket.

Nationwide, he received 117,183 votes, not an overly impressive figure when measured against the 7,628,834 votes for incumbent President Teddy Roosevelt, 5,084,491 for his Democratic challenger, Alton Parker, and 402,400 for Eugene Debs, the Socialist candidate.

After his failure to dent the lock of the two major parties on the presidency, Watson did what any self-respecting "man of the people" would do. He bought Fort Lauderdale Beach.

At 49 Watson was a wealthy man, a legendary courtroom lawyer, an editor and publisher of note, a popular lecturer and author of a bestselling book on France, biographies of Thomas Jefferson and Napoleon and one novel. With some 9,000 acres of cotton plantations, he was believed to be the largest landowner in Georgia. He also owned a mansion, Hickory Hill, near the Savannah River, and Mountain Top, another home in Virginia.

In Fort Lauderdale Watson paid $10,250 for 28 acres of waterfront property, including a hunting and fishing lodge which would later become the Las Olas Inn. In *Tom Watson's Magazine,* one of the two magazines he published, he wrote of his new winter home, Las Olas Isle:

"Sit here on the wall of the boathouse and gaze southward. A lovelier stretch of water the world does not hold. . . . A fringe of forest bounding the view southward, a thread of brilliant blue marking the spear-thrust which the ocean makes into the brown bosom of the river, the tossing foam which shows where the billows from the sea charge home upon the distant beach; and over all the mellow radiance of a sunny afternoon."

He sounds mellow when writing about Las Olas. But there was very little mellow about Tom Watson, an intense, belligerant crusader to the very end. Small and red-headed, he was quick with his fists and on one occasion shot another lawyer in the hand. And Fort Lauderdale would not be spared the turmoil that swirled around him throughout his 66 years.

Watson was born in Thomson, Georgia, five years before the Civil War. As a child he had wandered through battlefields with his mother, searching for his father, twice wounded in the fighting. The end of the war plunged the affluent Watson family into a world of poverty.

Tom grew up in the turbulence of the Reconstruction era, when former slaves were struggling to find their place in a hostile society still smarting under occupation by federal troops. His was a world in which the farmer was trapped in the quicksand of low farm prices and harsh terms from lenders. It was a world controlled by big-money interests from outside the state. It was a world ripe for rebellion, ripe for angry men like Tom Watson to fan its flames.

After studying law at Mercer University, a Baptist college in Macon, Watson, just 20 at the time, opened a law office in his home town. For his first year his earnings totaled $212. His gift for oratory, however, quickly asserted itself in courtrooms along the Savannah River Valley.

In 1878 the 22-year-old Watson married Georgia Durham of Thomson. Nearly three decades later he was still writing love poems to her. In one sense their marriage was marred with tragedy; they outlived all three of their children, one of whom died in infancy.

At 26 Watson entered politics, running as a Democrat for a seat in the Georgia legislature. Tom won the black votes by backing free schools for Negroes and attacking Georgia's system of leasing convict labor, mostly former slaves, to private contractors. He won by 392 votes.

His championing of the poor and dispossessd, both black and white, brought him powerful enemies within the party. He served only one term, but in 1890 he was elected to the U.S. Congress by tapping into an emerging political force.

Farmers in the west and the south were uniting to fight back against intolerable working conditions. By 1890 the Farmers' Alliance in Georgia alone could boast over 2,000 lodges with a membership of 100,000. In 1891 the Alliance combined with the Knights of Labor to form the Populist, or People's Party.

The Populist Party advocated widespread political reform to help the farmer and the laborer. Soon after taking office, Democrat Tom Watson switched parties. He became head of the Georgia Populists.

In Washington he introduced bills so radical at the time they brought forth the outcry of "communism." Oddly enough, many of them would later become law, particularly in the administrations of Theodore Roosevelt, Woodrow Wilson and Franklin D. Roosevelt. He called for a graduated income tax, an eight-hour workday, government insurance on bank deposits and

Thomas E. Watson (Broward County Historical Commission)

subtreasuries which would later evolve into the Federal Reserve Bank. None of these passed in his time. The legislation for which he is most famous was the establishment of RFD—rural free delivery of mail.

Because of his attack on monopolies, professional strike-breakers, high railroad rates and credit policies he attracted an army of enemies—many of them wealthy out-of-state interests. Insurance and railroad companies in New York contributed $40,000 to block his reelection bid.

It proved to be a bloody election. The Democrats nominated Major James Conquest Cross Black, a respectable, conservative lawyer from Augusta, to oppose Watson. Taunted by a Black supporter who called him a deserter from the Democratic Party, Tom beat the man up on the train.

One of Watson's most effective supporters was a young black preacher, H. S. Doyle, who made 63 speeches for his candidate. Near the end of the campaign, Doyle, under threat of lynching, fled to Watson's home in Thomson.

The candidate sent out horsemen to round up support. All night long armed farmers poured into Thomson, some 2,000 all told.

At a courthouse rally the next day both Doyle and Watson spoke. Said the candidate: "We are determined in this free country that the humblest white or black man that wants to talk our doctrine shall do it, and the man doesn't live who shall touch a hair of his head, without fighting every man in the People's Party."

Later Doyle said: "After that Mr. Watson was held almost as a savior by the Negroes."

Not everyone agreed. Stunned by the spectacle of white farmers protecting blacks, one paper declared, "Watson has gone mad." Another wrote that "the direful teachings of Thomas E. Watson" threatened the entire South with "anarchy and communism." The Democrats brought in wagonloads of voters from just across the river in South Carolina, plying them with whiskey and cash payments. Votes cast in Augusta totalled more than twice the number of registered voters.

Black, of course, had more votes, but Watson, figuring, correctly, that the election was a fraud, went back to Congress anyway. Eventually, Congress got around to reviewing his case and ruled that he had indeed lost. Watson took the defeat hard.

By the election of 1896 the Democrats had adopted so many of the ideas of the Populists that his party was willing to accept the Democratic nominee, William Jennings Bryan, as its candidate for president. Watson was named as the People's Party's vice-presidential candidate.

If Bryan had won, an awkward situation would have arisen since he also had a Democratic vice-presidential running mate. The problem never arose. William McKinley, the Republican candidate, won.

After the 1896 fiasco, an increasingly embittered Watson concentrated on his law practice and began a successful writing career. In 1898 the Macmillan Company contracted with him for a two-volume history of France. The two volumes sold 50,000 copies, then went through several later editions.

He followed *The Story of France* with biographies of Napoleon and Jefferson and in 1904 saw his only novel, *Bethany,* published by D. Appleton and Company.

That same year Watson came out in support of newspaper publisher William Randolph Hearst, a Democrat, as a candidate he could back. Hearst returned the favor by offering Tom a high-paying job as editor of one of his New York papers.

Watson did not even bother to attend the People's Party convention in Springfield, Illinois. He had indicated he didn't want the nomination as president. He got it anyway, by acclimation.

The Populist candidate had no illusions about his chances. The movement was fading fast, a victim of changing times. He campaigned vigorously anyway, drawing and delighting large crowds in a particularly bland election.

The result was as he expected, a small vote of little more than 100,000.

The election behind him, he turned his attention to Florida. When he arrived in 1905 in a sparsely settled community called Fort Lauderdale, he found an attractive real estate opportunity awaiting him.

In the 1890s two Chicagoans, Hugh Taylor Birch and John MacGregor Adams, owned three miles of beach property, lying north of the Fort Lauderdale House of Refuge, a haven for shipwrecked sailors located on the site of today's Bahia Mar Marina. In 1902 Birch and Adams split the property between them, Adams keeping the land south of today's Bonnett House.

Adams built a hunting lodge on his land but died two years later. His widow sold it in 1905 to the Watsons for $10,250; Georgia Watson's name is on the deed.

By now Watson was becoming more reclusive. His nearest neighbor on the beach was the keeper of the House of Refuge. Occasionally he came out of his shell. In 1906 he dined at the White House, the guest of President Roosevelt.

It was clear by 1908 when he made his last run for the presidency that endless political defeats had left him a warped, bitter man. From a staunch supporter of the rights of blacks, a man who personally blocked a lynching, he had became a total bigot, lashing out at Negroes, Jews and Catholics.

In trying to understand the strange mood swings of the man, a *New York Times* editor wrote: "For much in (his) career . . . the most plausible and charitable explanation is a certain mental instability, an overexcitability of temperament, even the presence of actual delusions, such as the hallucination of persecution."

Declaring himself the only candidate "standing squarely for *White Supremacy,*" he ran as a Populist in 1908 against Republican William Howard Taft, who won with 7,628,834 votes. Democrat William Jennings Bryan had nearly 6.5 million and even the Socialist candidate, Eugene V. Debs, saw his totals again exceed 400,000. Against these opponents, Watson garnered a pathetic 29,146 votes.

That year he found something he could support: Governor Napoleon Bonaparte Broward's program to drain the Everglades. In his new publication, *Watson's Jeffersonian Magazine,* he wrote a lengthy piece on the drainage project. It was reprinted in *The Weekly Miami Metropolis,* which introduced it by describing Watson as "one of the acknowledged great men of the country."

Watson cheered the governor on, agreeing that converting the vast wetlands into productive farm land was a noble venture. That the Populist did not like the Glades was indicated by his story:

". . . the Everglades of Florida are desolate reaches of sawgrass marsh dotted here and there by thickets of myrtle bushes and by occasional 'islands' of dismal cypress from whose ghostly limbs trail long streamers of gray moss. Stealthly rivulets wind and twist beneath the waving grass. . . ."

He described it further as a "God-forsaken realm . . . a world of death and desolation—a world which once had been alive, perhaps, but which had been smitten, ages ago, with a curse whose blight sunk deeper as time and its own stealthy streams ran on forever."

At Las Olas Isle he continued to work on such books as his biography of Andrew Jackson and his account of the Battle of Waterloo. The year 1908, however, was not without problems at his Las Olas estate.

On the west side of his Las Olas property Watson had dredged a cove to make it navigable for small boats. One day in the winter of 1911, a wealthy New York stockbroker named Waldo Clement wandered into the cove. He assumed the tidal cove was public water for fishing. Watson assured him otherwise, belting him with an oar.

The next time Clement came to the cove he was carrying a rifle. It did him little good. Watson took it away from him and gave it to the sheriff. Clement swore out a warrant for Watson's arrest, but again it did little good. The courts backed Watson.

In 1911 a huge land sale was conducted in Fort Lauderdale, aimed at selling small farms in the Everglades, a piece of the landscape which he again blasted in the *Jeffersonian:* "The Everglades is the best country in the whole world in which to raise alligators, rattlesnakes, mosquitoes and malaria."

Watson still spent most of the year in Georgia. On the morning of April 27,

1913, the body of Mary Phagin, a 14-year-old girl, had been found in the basement of an Atlanta pencil factory. Mary, a Gentile, had been murdered.

The superintendent of the factory was Leo Frank, a Jew and a northerner. The case against him was insubstantial, but he was quickly railroaded through the courts and sentenced to hang.

The case became a national scandal, but the state took no action other than to delay the execution. Finally a date was set for the hanging, just one day after the end of the term of Governor John Slaton, a popular official elected to office by a huge majority. One of his last acts in office was to commute the sentence to life imprisonment.

The next day a mob of 5,000 marched on the governor's mansion. Sixteen soldiers were injured defending Slaton, who was then forced to leave the state.

Watson's paper was filled with sensationalized stories about the case, condoning lynching and vigilante justice. The "*Jeffs*" sold so fast that circulation rose from 25,000 to 87,000.

On August 12, 1915, Watson wrote: "THE NEXT JEW WHO DOES WHAT FRANK DID, IS GOING TO GET EXACTLY THE SAME THING THAT WE GIVE TO NEGRO RAPISTS."

Four nights later, 25 armed men entered the state penitentiary, seized Frank, drove 175 miles, then hanged him from a tree in Marietta, near Atlanta.

Tom Watson seemed almost to be foaming at the mouth. Next he called for the reactivation of the Ku Klux Klan. On a summer night late in 1915, a bizarre torchlit ceremony on the top of Stone Mountain launched the new Ku Klux Klan.

Watson was already deep into an antiCatholic crusade, which included the publication of such offensive stories as "The Roman Catholic Hierarchy: The Deadliest Menace to Our Liberties and Our Civilization." He brought his anti-Catholicism to Fort Lauderdale in his final year on Las Olas Isle.

In July of 1915 school superintendent R. E. Hall had hired a Miss Murphy to teach second grade in Fort Lauderdale. She had taught in public schools in Nebraska and Colorado.

Watson immediately raised an objection to her. The reason? She was a Roman Catholic.

A month later a meeting to settle the issue was called by Robert Reed, president of the Board of Trade, H. V. Colver, editor of the *Fort Lauderdale Herald,* and Col. George W. Matthews, editor of the *Fort Lauderdale Sentinel,* a close friend of Watson's.

After a lengthy hearing residents of the young town were asked to vote. One hundred and eighty-one of the 188 residents voted against Miss Murphy.

Tom Watson's Fort Lauderdale home, until it was sold and converted into Las Olas Inn. (Fort Lauderdale Historical Society)

By now Watson was ready to leave Fort Lauderdale. The caretaker of his estate, decribing it in a letter as the "prettiest place in all the world—the natural scenery and tropical groth(sic) is simply a dream," declared it "could be sold for $50,000."

The politician did even better. He sold the property for $55,000 to D. C. Alexander. The new owner would convert Watson's hunting lodge into the Las Olas Inn and the waterfront into Fort Lauderdale Beach. The palm grove would be used by the noted film director D. W. Griffith as a South Seas island jungle in his film, "The Idol Dancer."

The last years of Watson's life were tragic, particularly 1917, the year the United States entered World War I. Watson's attacks in the *Jeffersonian* on the U.S. draft program ran afoul of the espionage act. The post office took away his mailing privileges. As he put it, the war had "killed my *Jeffersonian*."

Within a week his only living daughter died. Devastated, he turned to drugs and alcohol. In January he returned to Florida, to Jupiter where he had bought property. John Durham Watson, his last remaining child, came to visit him. He too died unexpectedly, of convulsions, in his father's arms.

A Negro servant found Watson wandering on the beach, out of his mind. For the next nine hours he talked constantly, repeating old speeches from the glory years of the 1890s when Populism was in bloom.

Somehow Watson recovered. After the war, he acquired a small weekly paper, then in 1920 won election to the U.S. Senate. In the campaign a scuffle in a Buford, Georgia, hotel landed Watson in jail overnight.

To *The Nation* his election was a victory "of the sinister forces on intolerance, superstition, prejudice, religious jingoism, and mobism."

Though probably the smallest man in the Senate, he challenged three senators to fights. Watson blistered the reactionary administration of President Warren Harding, directing his most extreme rantings at Harding's secretary of commerce, one Herbert Hoover. The ravings did not last long. In September of 1922 the tough old Populist, worn out from his long battles with asthma, died in Washington of a cerebral hemorrhage. He was 66.

At his funeral at Hickory Hill nearly 10,000 of his followers attended. The Ku Klux Klan sent a cross of roses, eight feet high.

In Fort Lauderdale, Watson's old friend, Colonel Matthews, ran a long front-page story in *The Sentinel* and commented, "He was one of Georgia's most distinguished sons in politics and literature."

CHAPTER 18

Key West Kingfish

Julius Stone turned America's poorest city into a tourist Mecca

In July of 1968 the *Key West Citizen* ran a short announcement of the death of one Julius F. Stone, Jr. In his late 60s, he had died peacefully in his sleep nearly a year earlier in Double Bay, New South Wales, Australia. Many who read the story had never heard of him. They should have.

He invented modern Key West.

But many others did remember him. What they thought of him depended on what period of his multicolored, many-splendored life their memories touched. Did they recall a shady lawyer who left behind a trail of well-bilked clients or did they remember the powerful government official who turned the poorest town in America into a tourist Mecca?

If a time machine could take a traveler back into the man's past, widely differing Stones would step forward, depending on when and where the contraption touched down.

January, 1960. A bad time for Julius. Debts had engulfed the attorney, and, many believed, the law was starting to close in on him for too much shuffling around of clients' money and investments. He decided the time had come to slip away to the home he had built in Cuba.

But before he could start a new life in Cuba he had to sell his house in Key West, the "Southernmost," which he had bought from the novelist Thelma Strabel author of *Reap the Wild Wind.* Working secretly from Cuba with the Old Island Realty Company and the U.S. Consul in Havana, he managed to sell the house for $45,000. The trick would be to slip back into Key West, complete the transaction and then return to Cuba without letting his army of creditors know he was back in town with a wallet full of money.

He flew into Key West International Airport in a small plane. One story has it that he never left the plane. The deed was exchanged for a sum of money, whereupon he flew away. Angry creditors didn't even know he was in town.

Another story, however, says the plane developed engine trouble, forcing him to watch just one more sunset and to stay overnight at a motel. The next morning Stone, well fortified with a large infusion of money, slipped out of town for the last time. He left memories, a ruined reputation, huge debts and a glorious island city that was a monument to his brilliant imagination.

The following year the Internal Revenue Service filed a $125,251 lien against Stone for income taxes owed from 1955 to 1959. But Stone was long gone. He stayed in Cuba until Castro made it too unpleasant for Americans. After that people reported seeing him in Jamaica, Nassau, and the Bahamian out islands. Then he faded out of the picture until the story of his death in Australia reached Key West.

June, 1926, Cambridge, Massachusetts. A different Stone. Stone the scientist. That year a 25-year-old Julius Stone received a Ph.D. from Harvard University in organic chemistry. His thesis: "The Reaction between Alpha, Beta Unsaturated Alephatic Nitro Compounds and the Grignard Reagent."

July 2, 1934. Deep in the Depression the Key West city council and the Monroe County commission adopted identical resolutions, closing down the city government. The politicians surrendered "to the Governor (David L. Sholtz) all legal powers conferred upon the officers of the city of Key West by law in order that he may administer the affairs of the city of Key West in such a way as he may deem proper."

The action was drastic, but the city fathers had their reasons. Key West, once Florida's largest city, was broke, more than $5 million in debt, its tax base shattered. The city didn't even have enough money to pay its employees. Eighty per cent of its residents were on welfare.

The problem had been a long time coming. Cigar manufacturing had meant 11,000 jobs in 1910. Now the cigar makers had gone to Tampa, the sponge divers to Tarpon Springs. The Navy, a Key West fixture since 1822, abandoned its Key West base. The Coast Guard moved its headquarters. Mallory Steamship Lines no longer listed Key West as a port-of-call, and the railroad was in bankruptcy. From a high of 26,000 in 1910 the population had dropped to 12,000.

The fall had been a steep one. From the richest city per capita in America in the 1880s Key West by 1934 had become the poorest. Per capita income was down to $7 a month.

What do you do when a city hands you a government? Governor Sholtz's first move was to declare the entire island on welfare relief. This had the effect of getting Key West off a struggling state's hands and into the embrace of the newly formed Federal Emergency Relief Administration (FERA), one of President Franklin D. Roosevelt's bold New Deal programs. FERA's goal was to restore morale among some 5.5 million unemployed workers nationwide by paying them in cash for labor on public works projects. The agency's director for the southeastern states was Julius Stone, Jr.

Stone, it turned out, had not pursued nitro compounds. Instead he had switched his energies to two of his wealthy family's manufacturing corporations, one in his hometown of Columbus, Ohio, and the other in Tonawanda, New York. His biggest earnings, however, came from the stock market, a bounty that left him when the 1929 stock market crash wrecked his personal fortune.

He went to work for Harry Hopkins, who was running the New York state welfare program when FDR was governor of New York. Stone proved to be a skilled administrator. When Roosevelt was elected president in 1932, Hopkins became one of the stars of the New Deal and Stone soon found himself appointed to FERA.

Sholtz asked Stone to handle the Key West problem personally. Something about the assignment appealed to Stone. Maybe it was the lure of unlimited power, or maybe the challenge of reviving America's *numero uno* poverty pocket. Stone had *carte blanche* authority to change or amend the city charter, to hire or fire relief workers and to use roughly a million dollars worth of FERA funds just about any way he wanted. Legally, it was a questionable arrangement, but something had to be done. The new head man in Key West liked it that way.

"With a scratch of my pen I started this work in Key West and with a scratch of my pen I can stop it—just like that!"

It wasn't always easy. On August 25 a small plane in which he was traveling with a party of New Dealers crashed in Biscayne Bay. Stone and the others escaped without a scratch but had to wade to shore.

Stone brought with him a staff of eleven: engineers, architects, city planners, a lawyer and a public relations writer. The writer went to work immediately. The Key West "state of civil emergency" story ran in many of the nation's principal newspapers. But more than press agentry was needed. When the "monarch of all he surveyed" gazed out over his kingdom, he saw abandoned cigar factories and navy buildings, collapsing piers and ruined houses. He also saw garbage, everywhere, in the streets, in vacant lots.

Stone set about organizing more than 10,000 recipients of relief into the "Key West Volunteer Corps." He told them: "Your city is bankrupt, your streets are littered and filthy, your homes are rundown and your industry gone. We will begin by cleaning up. Then we will rebuild."

More than a thousand volunteers formed a line three city blocks long to work free for an average of 30 hours a week to clean up the city. Within a few weeks the number grew to 4,000 volunteers. One volunteer was a 102-year-old man.

Plain clothes attendees at a Key West masquerade party were Julius Stone, third from left, and Harry Hopkins, head of the United States Works Progress Administration, (WPA). (Monroe County Library)

Cleanup was the first goal. But where do you put weeks of accumulated garbage? Stone had no environmental guidelines to hamper him. He had the volunteers dump the stuff in the ocean.

As the cleanup moved ahead, Stone pondered the options before him. At a cost of two-and-a-half million dollars he could provide relief, including food and medical care for the needy, for a five-year period. But that would build nothing for the long run. After five years the problem would be the same. No jobs, no tax base, no hope.

The second option was to stop all grants to Key West, evacuate the island and relocate three thousand families, probably to Tampa. That would have cost seven-and-a-half million, but even worse, Stone realized, it would have sent the ruggedly individualistic Conchs reaching for hunting rifles, oyster knives, broken bottles, and any other weapons they could have laid their hands on.

The third way would be to find some way to rehabilitate Key West. Stone needed a bold scheme that would give the Conchs a way to make a living over the long haul.

Stone had heard the trade winds rustling the coconut palms and the sounds of the sea splashing against the island. He had watched the sun rise over the ocean, then watched it set in brilliant orange splendor in the Gulf of Mexico. He marveled at the bougainvillea in bloom. He saw Key West as an island of "fantastic plants, Spanish limes, sapodillas, anemones, dates, pomegranates and coco palms . . . sun-streamed, shuttered, balconied houses, the aroma of ardent tropical flowers and the salty sea air."

Why not, he thought, transfer this old, rundown, cigar, sponge, salvage wreck of a town into what it was meant to be all along—a tourist resort? A touch of the tropics in a temperate zone, Caribbean climate and mood, waters of unsurpassed beauty and a distinctive architecture lurking behind the old, unpainted houses, many of them unoccupied. Maybe a warmer version of Bermuda.

Best of all, Stone figured that playing the tourist card would cost only about a million dollars, substantially less than either of the other two options.

Stone put his volunteers to work repairing and painting the conch houses, inside and out. This would improve the look of the city. And at a time when the island's biggest hotel, the Casa Marina, was in receivership, the conch houses would provide lodgings for the thousands of tourists he was sure would soon come flocking to the island.

He even figured out a way to make the renovation pay for itself. The owners would retain title to the houses but the Key West Administration would rent them and apply the rent money to the cost of renovating them. The owners could only begin receiving the rent money after costs were paid off. FERA guidelines didn't allow any such free-wheeling deals, but that didn't slow Stone down.

"I got away with it," Stone said years later to *The New Yorker* magazine, "because we were so far off no one knew what we were doing . . . also because I chose a time when Hopkins was on a long vacation."

In five furious months, from July to mid-December, Stone had his volunteers renovate more than 200 guest houses, build thatched huts on the beach, paint and clean up restaurants, bars and nightclubs and remodel the once elegant Casa Marina Hotel so it could reopen. He had them landscape the main thoroughfares and plant coconut palms. Outhouses were demolished and work was begun on a municipal sewer system. With a $30,000 appropriation, FERA began construction of the Key West Aquarium on Mallory Square. Work resumed on the highway to link Key West with the mainland. Repairs were pushed ahead on the Key West airport and an airline was subsidized to provide air transportation for tourists.

Anyone looking for a stuffed-shirt bureaucrat would not find one in Stone. To keep his Bermuda dream alive he began wearing Bermuda shorts to work.

First order in putting bankrupt Key West back on its feet was cleaning up the city. (Florida State Archives)

He wanted others to follow suit. He felt it would give the island a tropical feel. One day one of his volunteers showed up in his drawers. His explanation: "If Julius Stone can come to work in his underwear, so can I."

He was always a flashy dresser. A later newspaper story described his outfit as "red linen shirt, mustard yellow jacket and light taupe trousers."

Stone brought in a dozen artists from the WPA Federal Arts Project. Their paintings and watercolors were used on postcards and in tourism brochures to bring more people to Key West, where they could see the actual pictures in bars and restaurants.

The press was fascinated with the Key West experiment. "The New Deal in miniature," the respected writer and commentator Elmer Davis called it in a *Harper's Magazine* article. "The experiment . . . gave life there a fourth-dimensional flavor. Words are poor tools to convey the feeling created by the experiment and the atmosphere of continuous intellectual excitement and surcharged intensity. . . . Nothing quite like it will ever be seen again."

Stone certainly had the island humming, but not all was as positive he would have the world believe. Critics were not slow in speaking up.

"Key West Has Its Kingfish" read the headline over a story in the conservative *Florida Grower,* based in Orlando. "FERA rule is the rule of fear," it proclaimed. "No American city is more completely ruled by one man than is this small island city. . . . Mr. Stone admits he is the big boss and can do just about as he pleases down there."

In a series of United Press articles, Harry Ferguson called Stone "the king of a tight little empire. . . . Call it a dictatorship, a 'kingdom within a republic' or anything you choose."

After he found out that two nightclubs were redecorated with FERA funds, Ferguson wrote: "Nowhere else in the United States is the FERA encouraging wine, women and song." *The Sarasota Tribune* picked up on the theme, referring to a new government department called "NCER—Night Club Emergency Relief."

One of Stone's most outspoken critics in Key West was the author Ernest Hemingway, who made the island his home after 1931. One of his characters in *To Have and Have Not* sees an unattractive woman and says, "Anyone would have to be a writer or a F.E.R.A. man to have a wife like that." Another character complains that Conchs cannot eat "working here in Key West for six and a half a week." Hemingway, one of the few islanders not on relief, had solved his income problem another way. He married a wealthy woman.

Hemingway, who called Stone "that Jew administrator" in a letter, may have opposed him simply because the writer was strongly anti-New Deal. Some felt it may have been opposition to change in an island that he liked or it may have been an ego clash—one powerful figure resenting the invasion of his domain by another.

Some critics equated Stone's rule with socialism. Others claimed that residents signed up so quickly because they confused "volunteer labor with forced labor."

Two years after it began, the Key West state of emergency was lifted. The city could begin governing itself again. Stone was reassigned to other "trouble-shooting" jobs in the southeast. He left behind a city emerging rapidly as a resort. Within a year the island's hotels showed an 85 percent increase in guests, passenger travel into the city increased 42 1/2 percent and one restaurant reported a rise of 84 percent in business. Unemployment was reduced by two-thirds. The rich cultural life of today's Key West is another of Stone's legacies. The characteristic architecture of the island was brought back to life, uncovered and preserved by the volunteers. Artists wielded their brushes. Little theater and choral groups were formed and classes were held in folk dancing and painting.

Stone summarized it best: "Last year, hopelessness and resignation ruled; now hope and confidence are on the throne."

In 1937 Stone left government service to study law at Harvard. He returned to Key West in 1940 to begin a new career, no longer the Kingfish who made the rules but now a lawyer, investor and real estate broker who was supposed to play by the rules.

Autumn, 1941. World War II was raging in Europe and Asia when Harry Hopkins contacted Stone again. President Roosevelt, now in this third term, was looking ahead to his retirement. He remembered his visit in 1924 to a small island called Channel Key, near Long Key. The President made a rough sketch of a hurricane-proof fishing camp he wanted to build.

As a friend, and a real estate broker, Stone checked out Channel Key for Hopkins. He wrote that it could be bought for $3,500; filling and bulkheading would cost another $18,000. President Roosevelt and Hopkins were still talking about Channel Key when the Japanese attacked Pearl Harbor. There would be no Keys fishing camp for FDR—and no more brushes with the seat of power for Julius Stone.

February, 1951. Julius Stone began to dread each knock on the door of the Key West house where he lived with his beautiful wife Lee and their daughter Julia.

"Would you settle a bet, sir? Is this really the southernmost house in the U.S.A?"

"Yes, it is. Excuse us. We'd like to finish our lunch."

Julius Stone, who made Key West a tourist destination, was paying the price.

BATTLEGROUND FLORIDA

The Second Seminole War, known at the time as the Florida War, was the longest and costliest of all the United States Government's Indian wars, extending from December of 1835 to 1842. It turned the state into a battleground from North Florida to the Middle Keys. Most people, if they think of the Seminole War at all, think of Osceola. Outside of Florida few have even heard of the greatest of all the Indian leaders, the unconquerable Sam Jones. But Florida was a battleground before the Seminole War. Slaves fled here in the 1700s and fought for their freedom, and again in the Civil War freed slaves served in Florida with Union troops.

CHAPTER 19

Underground Railroad

Fort Mose was first free black community in United States

Before the Civil War black slaves escaped their bondage in the South by fleeing north into Canada. Abolitionists hid them from slave-catchers and helped them along to the next stops on their dangerous, secretive escape route. It bore the name "underground railroad."

Now it turns out that an underground railroad was in place more than a century earlier. It led not north, from Dixie's plantations through the farmlands and towns of Pennsylvania and Ohio, but south from the Carolina Lowcountry into La Florida, the domain of the Spanish.

Somehow word reached the slaves through a primitive grapevine that freedom awaited them at St. Augustine—if they could make it alive through some 400 perilous miles of slave plantations and hostile Indian country.

In 1687 the first African slaves from Carolina—eight men, three women and a three-year-old child—arrived at Spanish Florida, already known as a kinder and gentler land where slaves were concerned. A year later their former British owners in Charleston tried to reclaim them.

The Spanish governor said no. They were usefully employed, they had converted to Catholicism, and some had married. In 1693 Charles II of Spain freed the slaves and made La Florida an official sanctuary, encouraging runaways from the British colonies to come to St. Augustine "so that by their example and by my liberality others will do the same."

Thus began the Florida version of the underground railroad. By 1738 some 38 black families had reached St. Augustine. These became the founding residents of the first free black town in what would later become the United States.

One of those residents would emerge as a leader of remarkable ability, skill and character.

* * *

Fourteen years before Fort Mose was formed a 20-year-old slave from the Mandingo tribe in West Africa made it into St. Augustine with nine other slaves who had fled the Carolina Lowcountry. The journey of just 400 miles had taken three years. They hid out in swamps and forests to evade the slaveholders and slavecatchers, then joined forces with the Yamassee Indians to fight the colonists.

Even at 20, the Mandingo had emerged as a military leader of considerable talents. His leadership skills, however, were not enough to save him from being sold into slavery again, double-crossed by an Indian named Mad Dog. His cause was not helped by the Spanish governor's loose interpretation of the Crown's edict on fugitive slaves.

The young African was bought by the royal treasurer of St. Augustine, one Don Francisco Menendez Marques, part of whose name he would adopt. Two years after his arrival at St. Augustine, the Mandingo, Francisco Menendez, was appointed by the governor to command a slave militia.

Within two years Menendez found himself at the head of his troups helping defend St. Augustine against British colonial invaders led by Colonel John Palmer.

Five years later the crown issued an edict, commending the militia for their bravery in the battle and decreeing that after four more years of royal service they would be free. Captain Menendez continued to petition the governor and the auxiliary bishop of Cuba, who toured the province in 1735, to free them immediately in accordance with the crown's promise of sanctuary.

When Manuel de Montiano was appointed governor in 1737, Captain Mendendez again submitted his petition. The new governor ordered an investigation. The Yamassee cacique, Jorge, testified about the brave deeds of Francisco and three other slaves in the wars against the Carolina colonists. He related how Mad Dog, whom he characterized as an "infidel," had sold the slaves improperly and criticized the Spaniards who had bought the fugitives.

The governor reviewed the case, then granted all the petitioners unconditional freedom on March 15, 1738. He decided this would be the time to establish a town for them two miles north of St. Augustine at the head of Mose Creek, a tributary of the North River, near trails to the north and the west.

The governor designated the town Gracia Real de Santa Teresa de Mose, combining the creek's name, with a reference to the King of Spain, "Gracia Real," and the name of the patron saint of Spain, Teresa of Aviles. Naturally, people just called it Mose (pronounced Moh-say).

It was felt, too, that a fort would provide a frontline defense against invaders from the newly created colony of Georgia. Who would fight harder than ex-slaves to preserve their freedom?

Spain's policy toward runaway slaves grew from a mixture of motives.

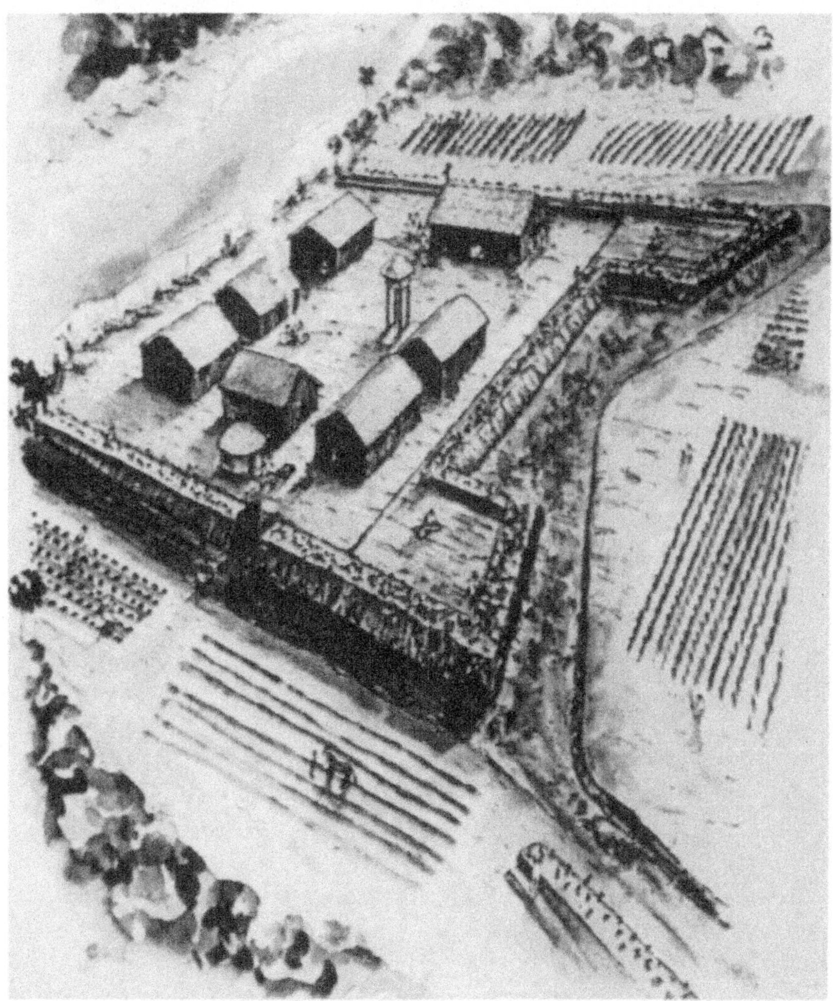

Artist's rendering of Fort Mose

Whereas British law regarded them only as chattel property without rights, both the Spanish Crown and the Catholic Church saw them as human beings invested with a number of rights, among them pathways that could lead to their freedom. In addition Spain appreciated the destabilizing effects of sanctuary on a slaveholding society in which slaves outnumbered whites by nearly two to one. At the same time fugitive slaves promised both military and civilian manpower to thinly populated St. Augustine. The capital of Spanish Florida had only 1500 residents.

No one understood the Florida policy better than the freedmen. In a declaration to the king they vowed to be "the most cruel enemies of the English,"

Fort Mose soldier

ready and willing to risk their lives and spill their "last drop of blood in defense of the Great Crown of Spain and the Holy Faith." One of the conditions of their freedom was conversion to the Catholic faith.

Their first job as freedmen was to build their own town. Their homes were primitive thatched huts, located just south of their four-cornered stone fort, roughly 20 yards square. It was built to accommodate about two dozen soldiers, armed with muskets, two cannon and six catapults. Around Fort Mose the free blacks dug a moat three feet deep and four feet wide, containing not water but a ferocious plant known as Spanish bayonet.

Fertile land around the fort promised food crops in the future, and a saltwater stream running through the area offered fish and shellfish. The governor provided the freedmen with corn, biscuits and beef from his meager government stores. The people of Mose lived in poverty—but they lived free.

As captain of militia, Menendez was the town's boss. Governor Montiana, in fact, referred to the freedmen as Francisco's "subjects."

The founding population of Mose grew sharply in the fall of 1738. Twenty-three more black men, women and children arrived at St. Augustine. They had fled from Port Royal, near today's town of Beaufort, South Carolina.

The only white resident of Mose was a student priest, Don Joseph de Leon, a Franciscan whose duty it was to instruct the freedmen in the Catholic faith and "good customs."

The freedmen didn't have to wait long for Mose's first testing in battle. In 1740 tensions over British smuggling in the New World led to a small-scale war between England and Spain.

It bore the unlikely name of the War of Jenkin's Ear. A British sailor, one Jenkins, showed members of Parliament what he claimed was one of his ears, cruelly sliced off, he said, by Spaniards who had captured him. The strange event did not cause the war, just its bizarre name.

In January James Oglethorpe, governor of the new Georgia colony, invaded Florida. He captured two Spanish forts on the St. Johns River, then moved against St. Augustine in May.

Fort Mose was not big enough to defend against the invaders. The Spanish pulled the free blacks back into St. Augustine, protected by its fortress, Castillo de San Marcos.

The Georgians laid siege to the capital, but retained only a small force to prevent small Spanish parties from venturing forth to forage for food. Their orders were to range back and forth as a "flying party," staying on the move. Confusion in the command led to their camping instead at Mose.

Governor Montiano ordered a surprise attack. Striking in the dark of night the Spaniards and the free blacks routed the British with heavy losses. Among the casualties was Colonel Palmer, who had attacked St. Augustine more than a decade earlier.

The only defeat for the Georgians in the War of Jenkin's Ear, the Battle of Fort Mose contributed to their failure to capture Florida. The British would wait another 23 years to take over the Spanish province.

After the battle the Florida governor wrote a special commendation of

Francisco Menendez. He praised the valor displayed by the captain in the battle that drove the British from St. Augustine. He commended him for the role he and his troops played in driving the enemy away from the walls of Castillo de San Marcos and for dangerous reconnaissance missions against the British and their Indian allies.

Furthermore, he declared that Menendez had "distinguished himself in the establishment, and cultivation of Mose, to improve that settlement, doing all he could so that the rest of his subjects, following his example, would apply themselves to work and learn good customs."

How well the captain had learned the ways of the society that had wrenched him from his African home was shown in his response to the governor's kind words.

"Why don't you start paying me for the service I am rendering the Crown?" he suggested in two petitions to the governor.

A man who always used his time well, Menendez, apparently, had learned to read and write Spanish while in the service of the royal treasurer. His petition called for a salary based on the "loyalty, zeal and love I have always demonstrated in the royal service, in the encounters with the enemies, as well as in the effort and care with which I have worked to repair two bastions on the defense line of this plaza, being pleased to do it, although it advanced my poverty, and I have been continually at arms, and assisted in the maintenance of the bastions, without the least royal expense, despite the scarcity in which this presidio always exists, especially in this occasion."

He declared: "my sole object was to defend the Holy Evangel and sovereignty of the Crown," and closed by stating he hoped to receive "all the consolation of the royal support . . . which Christianity requires and your vassals desire."

The captain's plea was eloquent but there is no indication the Spaniards ever paid him for his services.They should have paid him. Two years later the Spaniards mounted an invasion of Georgia, again utilizing the free black militia as an important part of their fighting force. Unfortunately Menendez was not there to command the blacks. The previous year he had embarked on a disastrous quest for material gain.

In July of 1742 British and Spanish forces clashed on St. Simon's Island, off the Georgia coast. So many Spaniards were killed that the crushing defeat became known as the Battle of Bloody Marsh.

Could Captain Menendez have made a difference? He might have helped make the battle less of a debacle, but he wasn't there. Since his devotion to the Spanish cause had reduced him to poverty, he embarked on a venture that he hoped would bring funds to care for himself, his wife, Ana Maria de Escovar, and their four children.

Menendez became a pirate aboard a ship commissioned by Spain to operate out of the port of St. Augustine. Spain hoped that the capture of British ships would provide supplies and prizes to help the impoverished province of Florida. The corsairs aboard these ships would, of course, share in the proceeds.

In July, 1741, the British ship *Revenge* captured a Spanish privateer. Aboard was a black named "Signior Capitano Francisco." He was further identified as "Capt. of a Comp'y of Indians, Mollattos, and Negroes that was att the Retaking of Fort (Mose) att St. Augus'ne. . . ."

Still bristling at the mutilation and castration of wounded British prisoners after the Battle of Fort Mose, Francisco's captors tied him to a gun and ordered the ship's doctor to pretend to castrate him.

Menendez "frankly owned" that he was captain of the company that retook Mose but he denied ordering the atrocities. These, he said, were performed by Florida Indians who were part of the Spanish defense force.

He told them he had taken a commission as a privateer in hopes of getting to Havana and then on to Spain to collect a reward for his bravery in the defense of St. Augustine. The British questioned captured mulattoes and whites who had been in the battle. They backed up Menendez's story.

At that point they withdrew the castration threat. But to show a measure of disapproval, they gave him 200 lashes, then "pickled him and left him to the Doctor to take Care of his Sore Arse."

In August *Revenge* landed at New Providence, in the Bahamas. The ship's commander, Benjamin Norton, argued before the Admiralty Court that all the blacks should be returned to slavery.

In his argument he described Menendez as ". . . this Francisco that Cursed Seed of Cain, Crust from the foundation of the world, who has the Impudence to Come into this Court and plead that he is free. Slavery is too Good for such a Savage, nay all the Cruelty invented by man . . . the torments of the World to Come will not suffice."

The verdict of the court: Capitano Francisco to be sold as a slave, "according to the Laws of the plantation."

The end of Francisco Menendez? Not hardly. In time he made his way back to St. Augustine. Just when and how is not clear. An eloquent, persuasive man, he might have appealed the verdict successfully, he might have escaped or the Spanish might have concluded that so valuable a man was worth their paying a ransom.

At any rate, he was back at the head of the free blacks when Fort Mose was rebuilt in 1752. In the 1740 battle it had been wrecked so badly the Spanish decided to bring the free blacks back into St. Augustine.

Integration proved a happier way of life for the free Negroes. They earned their wages by working on government projects or by serving as crew on ships and privateers. They helped track escaped prisoners and forage for food for the city. In the spring they rounded up wild cattle and wild horses. Some worked as artisans.

Racial restrictions were minimal in a frontier settlement so small that everyone knew everyone else. Prejudice, however, was still a factor. As ex-slaves they remained at the bottom of the social order, trapped in continuing poverty. In St. Augustine's marginal economy the free blacks were seen by some of the poorer whites as threats for scarce jobs.

At Mose the free blacks built 22 shelters to serve as their homes. Within the new fort they built a church and a house for the Franciscan priest. The only known census of Mose, in 1759, showed 22 households with a population of 67 persons.

The blacks at Mose spoke Spanish and other European languages, Indian dialects and languages brought from west Africa. Religious observances often combined their African beliefs with the Catholicism on which their freedom was based. Catholic feast days were celebrated with traditional African costumes, music and instruments.

Mose survived until 1763, when military defeat at the hands of the British wrested Florida from Spanish hands. When the Spaniards evacuated St. Augustine, the free blacks left Fort Mose and sailed away with them to Cuba.

The people of Mose, founders of the first free black town in the future United States, became homesteaders in the rough frontier lands at Matanzas, Cuba. There they continued to live in crushing poverty, just as they had at Mose—but at least they were free.

Capitano Menendez once again rose to the top. He worked his way out of Matanzas and into Havana, where opportunity awaited him.

In the years after 1763 Mose was never again a town, although sometimes a fort until it was leveled in 1812. Except for occasional references in scholarly publications, by and large the historic town was forgotten until the 1960s.

The civil rights movement brought it back to life. In St. Augustine, cross burnings, violence and the arrest of Martin Luther King, Jr., drew a sharp contrast with the ancient city's important contribution two and a half centuries earlier.

Then in 1968 a retired armanents worker from Maryland, one Jack Williams, found an old map in a little-known book that revealed the fort's location. He bought the property, then tried to get the state to excavate the site, which lies behind the Ponce de Leon Resort Hotel, just east of U.S. 1.

In Tallahassee the lead was seized by Representative Bill Clark, a former history teacher from Lauderdale Lakes. For nine years Representative Clark, backed by his fellow members of the Black Caucus, supported the project, coming up with appropriations to dig at the site and part of the time pitching in himself with a shovel.

The exploration involved digs led by Kathleen Deagan, curator of anthropology at the Florida State Museum at the University of Florida campus, and searches in Spanish records by Jane Landers, a doctoral student at the University of Florida.

"I would like to see it become a tourist attraction," said Clark. "There's a great deal of racial pride involved. But it's American history in the sense it shows an important aspect of one of her peoples—that blacks were never content to be slaves. The blacks at Fort Mose were our first freedom fighters."

CHAPTER 20

Osceola's Head

Doctor decapitated leader of Indians in Charleston prison

Osceola was already a dying man when he boarded the *SS Poinsett,* bound for a prison cell at Fort Moultrie, Charleston, South Carolina. As the ship sailed away from St. Augustine, the great Seminole warrior looked back for the last time at the Florida he loved.

Osceola's valiant resistance to the U.S. Army had won the admiration of Americans everywhere, many of whom were bitterly opposed to the "Florida War," as the Second Seminole War was called at the time. Osceola's popularity had soared even higher when the infamous Major General Thomas S. Jesup treacherously seized him under a flag of truce and imprisoned him at Fort Marion, today known as the Castillo de San Marcos National Monument in St. Augustine.

Public outrage, however, wasn't enough to free the charismatic Seminole war leader. On January 1, 1838, the *Poinsett* delivered him to the Fort Moultrie prison cell where he would live out the few weeks that remained of his life. During that time, he would be visited by many admirers, including the painters and writers who would immortalize him.

Osceola, already weakened by malaria, failed rapidly in prison. Confinement proved deadly to his free spirit, and Dr. Frederick Weedon, with whom he had become friendly during his incarceration in St. Augustine, was unable to do much to help him. Weedon was the brother-in-law of Wiley Thompson, the Indian agent shot dead by Osceola at the start of the war in December of 1835, and that killing may explain the macabre deed later committed by the doctor.

When George Catlin, a noted painter of Indians, arrived at the fort, Dr. Weedon told him that Osceola had only a few weeks to live. Catlin moved quickly to complete two memorable paintings of the Seminole leader.

As he painted, he talked to Osceola and other Seminoles captured with him. Wrote Catlin: "they had taken great pains to give me an account of the war and the mode in which they were captured, of which they complain bitterly. I am fully convinced from all I have seen and learned from the lips of Osceola, and from the chiefs who are around him, that he is a most extraordinary man, and one entitled to a better fate."

Catlin went on to describe his appearance: "In his face he is good-looking, with rather an effeminate smile; but of so peculiar a character that the world may be ransacked over without finding another just like it. In his manners and all his movements in company, he is polite and gentlemanly. . . . I painted him precisely in the costume in which he stood for his picture, even to a string and a trinket. He wore three ostrich feathers on his head and a turban made of a varicolored cotton shawl, and his dress was chiefly of calicoes, with a handsome bead sash or belt around his waist, and his rifle in his hand."

On the day Catlin finished his second painting, Osceola was seized with an attack of quinsy, a severe abscessed inflammation of the tonsils. Catlin and the officers of the post stayed up most of the night keeping watch over the dying man. Wrapped in a blanket, Osceola lay before the fire with his head in the lap of Morning Dew, one of two wives with him at the prison.

On the morning of January 30, Osceola realized he was dying. Too weak to speak, he signaled Dr. Weedon that he wished his chiefs and the officers at the post to join him. His wives prepared him in full dress. He shook hands with all present, his chiefs, the officers, the doctor, his wives and his two small daughters.

"He made a signal for them to lower him down upon his bed," wrote Dr. Weedon, "and he then slowly drew from his war-belt his scalping knife, which he firmly grasped in his right hand, laying it across the other on his breast, and in a moment smiled away his last breath without a struggle or groan."

One account says that officers and chiefs alike wept at the death of a man revered even by his enemies. He was just 33.

Osceola was buried near the main entrance to Fort Moultrie. A marble slab, supplied by a Charleston resident, says simply:

Osceola
Patriot and Warrior
Died at Fort Moultrie
January 30, 1838

Before the burial, however, Dr. Weedon suddenly plunged into the Twilight Zone. He cut off Osceola's head.

Later, he used it to punish his small sons when they misbehaved. He would hang the head from the bedstead where they slept.

The head was subsequently given to the doctor's son-in-law. Continuing

Osceola (Florida State Archives)

the weirdness, he sent it to the founder of the New York University Medical School and the New York Academy of Medicine. The head was lost during a fire in 1866.

Today, Dr. Weedon is a forgotten man, as is General Jesup, but the name Osceola lives on. Not only is it one of the most popular names among the Indians themselves, it enjoys enormous popularity as a place name. Around the United States, 20 towns, three counties, two townships, one borough, two lakes, two mountains, a state park and a national forest all bear the name of the great Seminole warrior who died a century and a half ago.

CHAPTER 21

No Surrender

Sam Jones was the Indian U.S. Army Couldn't Defeat

The soldiers at Fort King knew the old man as a fish peddler. From his village in nearby Silver Springs he showed up at sunrise each day with his wares, tasty freshwater largemouth bass. There was nothing to indicate the old man was a leader, a respected medicine man of the proud, independent Miccosukee tribe. To the soldiers, he was a harmless, eccentric and very old Indian, already, it was thought, in his late 70s, or possibly his early 80s. With a mixture of derision and affection, they joked about him. Connecting him with a bawdy ballad of the time, they gave him an Americanized name and sang:

"It was Sam Jones the Fisherman
"Was bound to Sandy Hook. . . ."

Before the Second Seminole War was over, the affection was long gone and the derision had turned into a combination of hatred, fear, frustration and grudging respect.

And Sam Jones the Fisherman had become Sam Jones Be Damned, the immovable object to the white man's goal of ridding Florida of every breathing Indian.

Between 1835 and 1842 the U.S. Army, Navy and Marine Corps poured some 50,000 fighting men into the narrow peninsula against a loose confederation of Florida tribes, including the Seminoles, Miccosukees, Alachuas, Tallahassees and Creeks. Opposing them were roughly 1,700 Indian warriors. Plus Sam Jones, an ancient medicine man who could not be talked to, reasoned with, captured, bribed, outsmarted or killed.

They fought on the banks of the Withlacoochee River, at Lake Monroe, in the Wahoo Swamp, at Lake Okeechobee, at the Loxahatchee River, on the islands in the Everglades, at the Caloosahatchee River, in the Big Cypress Swamp. When a weary Brigadier General William Jenkins Worth, who would leave his name to Lake Worth, declared the unpopular war at an end in the summer of '42, he had to stop short of claiming victory. There was no peace treaty, no formal surrender by the hostiles. Nor had the government's objective been met. Of the five thousand Indians who had called Florida home at the start of the war, roughly three hundred Indians stubbornly refused to migrate to Arkansas.

Sam Jones spoke for them:

"In Florida I was born. In Florida I will die. In Florida my bones will bleach."

Florida Indians trace back to Sam Jones and his tiny, battered, impoverished band held together by their devotion to the most indomitable spirit that ever walked the sands of Florida. If there had been no Sam Jones, there might be no significant Indian presence in the state today.

* * *

Even the name of Sam Jones is shrouded in confusion. Various accounts list his Indian name as Arpeika, Arpiaka, Aripeka, Abiaca, Appayakka, Apiaka, Apeioka, Appiaca and Opiacca. Some whites called him Old Yakky.

Just where he was born is unclear, probably in the Tallahassee area, near Lake Miccosukee, the ancient home of his tribe. When he was born is just as hard to pinpoint, possibly as early as 1750. He could already have been in his late 60s when the First Seminole War broke out in 1818. Very little is known about Sam Jones prior to the Second Seminole War. In 1828 the historian James Lee Williams, who lived in Palatka, on the St. Johns River, encountered him on one of the islands in the Everglades just west of a settlement of whites on New River. Accounts of the signing of the Treaty of Payne's Landing on the Oklawaha in 1832 described him as already so old that Chief John Hicks took his place at the ceremony.

Bad feelings prevailed between the Indians and the United States, which had acquired Florida from Spain in 1819. Slaveholding interests pressed for strong measures against the Florida Indians, who for years had offered safe haven for runaway slaves. The treaty offered payment to the Indians to move to Arkansas, provided they approved their new land after an inspection trip. The treaty produced little except worsening relations. The Seminoles felt they had been tricked, the white man felt the Indians were stalling.

In 1835 in April, the Big Spring Moon, the Indian agent Wiley Thompson applied heavy pressure at Fort King to force the Indians to sign another paper. Five leaders, including Sam Jones, refused to sign. Thompson then declared the Fort King Five would no longer be recognized as chiefs. Sam, accounts of the meeting say, stamped his feet and gnashed his teeth. The following month,

Blackberry Moon, Thompson committed a rash blunder. When talks went badly with Osceola, he had the fiery leader seized and placed in chains, an unforgiveable act in the eyes of Osceola.

Later that year the Indians concluded they had no choice but to strike the hated white man before the start of Indian removal. In late December, Big Winter Moon, the Indians of Florida launched a widespread, coordinated strike. Five east coast sugar plantations were destroyed on Christmas Day. Three days later warriors attacked the detachment of Captain Francis Dade en route to Fort King from Fort Brooke in the Tampa Bay area. Over a hundred soldiers were killed. Just one man escaped. That same day Osceola shot and killed Wiley Thompson. A little over a week later a band of Creeks attacked the home of William Cooley on New River, killing four and driving away a community of more than 50 people. The war was on.

Sam Jones was considered an effective medicine man. He planned war parties and raids, then fired a gun to start the attack. He exhorted his band into action with incantations and midnight chants and mixed magical potions, using roots, barks, snakes and animal skins. There was a lot of the con man in Sam. When roughly half of the horses of Major William Lauderdale's mounted Tennessee Volunteers died en route to New River, Sam claimed that the equine deaths resulted from his spells.

An 1837 account in the *Army & Navy Chronicle* described Sam: "He is represented as being a well-set, neatly-formed and perfectly-finished small man, with 'locks' white as the driven snow—aged and venerable, yet active as a hind, and as Intrepid as a Lion, struggling for the home of his childhood and the graves of his forefathers."

* * *

What made Sammy run? What kind of juices kept this old man going in the face of doom? It surely wasn't abstemious living. Even in his late 70s he had a pretty young wife, much admired by some of the soldiers at Fort Lauderdale, less admired by one of the army's officers who referred to her as a "bitch" in an official report. Jones also had a reputation as a heavy boozer. Perhaps it was sheer meanness that kept him charged up. He would rather die in the woods, a fellow chief once said, than shake hands with a white man. He was just as rough with his own people.

Near Jupiter in the spring of 1838 a subchief and five other Indians were captured by Major General Thomas S. Jesup. They agreed to find Sam and tell him the odds against him were so overwhelming that the fight had become pointless. Surrender was not a message Sam wanted to hear.

The six Indians never returned to give Jesup Sam's answer. To their great misfortune they found Jones near Fort Lauderdale. He heard their story, then gave orders to shoot them all dead. Yielding to the white man was as bad as being a white man.

One observer felt that Sam's resistance stemmed from the death of a brother early in the war. Or maybe it was patriotism in its purest sense. He simply loved his native land too much to leave it.

Whatever the forces that fueled the fierce fires burning inside this old man, they certainly had the power to generate incredible motion. He was all over the state, an amazing performance for a man who had to carry with him a "family" of warriors, women, children, and old people, though none as old as he. He was said to have been the oldest man in Florida.

Furthermore, most of the time Jones and his people had to travel on foot around a very large state. Sometimes horses and dugout canoes were available.

Early in the war Sam was reported near Silver Springs, then on to Tampa for a midnight raid. Later he was reported near today's Sanford, then west of Cocoa Beach. Next he camped at the spot where the Kissimmee River flowed into Lake Okeechobee. He spent Christmas Day, 1937, fighting Colonel Zachary Taylor.

The old Indian moved on to the islands at the south end of Lake Okeechobee, then east to the Jupiter area. He set up camp west of Fort Lauderdale on the Seven Islands of Sam Jones, which he had visited in the 1820s. Driven out for awhile, he came back to burn down Fort Lauderdale. He was reported south of Miami, then near the west coast in the Big Cypress Swamp. He came back to the New River, on to the Loxahatchee, and once more back to the Big Cypress. Sam Jones was a traveling man.

* * *

In the Florida War, as it was called at the time, most of the early clashes were won by the Seminoles, but at a price. Superior in numbers, equipment, firepower and food supply, the U.S. Army could afford casualties. The Indians could not. Forced from their ancestral towns, farms, grazing lands and hunting and fishing grounds, the Indians soon found that the real victims were their families, their wives and children and the old people of the tribe, worn down by constant flight and worsening food shortages. Some retreated farther south. Others were induced to migrate to Arkansas, among them the hereditary chief, the fat and lazy Micanopy. While awaiting passage to the west, the Indians were held in a Tampa detention camp.

As early as 1837 in March, Little Spring Moon to the Indians, General Jesup was optimistic enough to write: "I now for the first time have allowed myself to believe the War at an end."

Three months later Jesup's glowing optimisim was gone. From St. Augustine he wrote: "The war must be one of extermination. There is no alternative. The body of this nation have resolved to die on the ground rather than emigrate."

What caused the change in Jesup? Mostly, Sam Jones.

When Micanopy caved in to the general's demands, the Indians promptly replaced him with the most intractable of all the hostiles—Sam Jones. The first sign that Jesup's troubles were starting all over again was a report that the Indians might raid the Tampa camp. An untroubled Jesup took few precautions.

One Blackberry Moon night three of the most dangerous of all the Indians—Osceola, Wildcat and Sam Jones—slipped quietly into camp with 200 warriors. Micanopy was given an ultimatum: either walk out of camp immediately or be killed on the spot. The deposed chief, 250 pounds on a five-foot-six-inch frame, walked. When dawn broke, 700 Indians had been spirited out of camp.

* * *

As central Florida became a battleground, the Seminoles began moving their families farther south, breaking their ties to their farms and grazing lands. By December, 1837, some two thousand had gathered near the area where the oxbows of the Kissimmee River reached the huge lake the Indians called Okeechobee. Protecting that group were roughly 380 warriors under the command of three major leaders—Alligator, Wildcat and Sam Jones.

Colonel Zachary Taylor, commanding U.S. forces numbering about 800, prepared to attack the Indians at a large hammock near the northeast shore of the lake. On Christmas morning Taylor struck. Two and a half hours later the U.S. Army broke through the right side of the Indians' line. The Seminoles, alarmed at the threat to their families, retreated to the south shore of the lake, leaving the victory to Colonel Taylor.

It had been a costly battle, however, for both sides. Twenty-six of Taylor's soldiers had been killed and 112 wounded. The Indians, who could ill afford casualties, counted 12 of their braves killed and 14 wounded. The Army's victory brought Colonel Taylor a prompt promotion to brigadier general. He would go on to greater feats in the Mexican War and in 1848 would win the presidency. But Jones, who was more than 30 years older than "Old Rough and Ready," would outlive the president by more than a decade.

The Indians kept moving south, settling for awhile in the islands in the

U.S. sailors and marines followed the Seminoles into the Everglades. (U.S. Navy)

Everglades, just west of the newly activated Fort Lauderdale. When the sutler William Tucker came up from his Miami River base to sell military supplies to the new fort, he found it abuzz with activity. Lieutenant Colonel James Bankhead was organizing a joint Army-Navy strike on Pine Island, the largest of the Seven Islands of Sam Jones.

Major William Lauderdale, who had built the primitive frontier fort on the north bank of the New River, commanded a hundred mounted Tennessee volunteers, while Lieutenant Leven Powell, U.S. Navy, led 150 sailors and soldiers in shallow draft boats.

The second day out, Bankhead's men left their boat, the *Isis,* to plow ahead in waist-deep water, battling thick, cutting Everglades sawgrass up to their armpits. By 5 P.M. the soldiers were five hundred yards from Pine Island. Bankhead sent a small company ahead with a flag of truce. The Indians fired at the flag and started whooping.

"Believing that all the Indians . . . were on this island, with their women and children, I anticipated a complete victory, and made with all haste my arrangements to attack them," Colonel Bankhead's official report read.

"With all haste" proved to be too slow to catch the ancient Jones. Bankhead dispatched Powell's sailors to the west side of the island, sent seven companies of soldiers to the east side, then advanced straight at the hammock from the north. Darkness halted them. When sunrise came, the Indians had vanished into the Everglades.

The old man had eluded them again. Still, they had driven him away, and, considering the supplies and provisions he had been forced to abandon, the Army counted it a victory. At least the New River country was safe again. In Blackberry Moon the military deactivated the fort and reassigned its troops elsewhere.

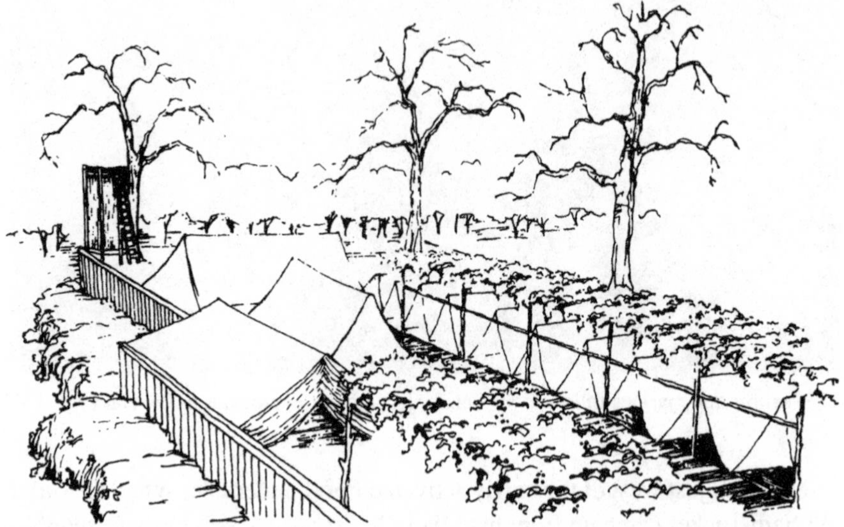

Dr. Ellis Hughes's sketch of the second Fort Lauderdale in 1939. (Broward County Historical Commission)

But Sam Jones was still around. His Indians promptly burned Fort Lauderdale to the ground. New River was theirs again.

* * *

That fall in September, Little Chestnut Moon, a gale wrecked the French brig *Courier de Tampico* near New River Inlet. Sam Jones and his band descended upon the survivors. Then, when he learned they were French, he spared their lives.

"I only kill Americans," he explained.

Sam Jones proved it when the brig *Aloma,* bound from Maine to the West Indies, wrecked near the French ship. Two Americans escaped by hiding in the mangroves. All the others were massacred except for one man—a Dutchman.

Nearly 20 ships were wrecked off the reefs that stormy fall. Few crewmen or passengers escaped Sam's bloodthirsty band.

The Army responded by reactivating Fort Lauderdale. A second fort, little more than a camp, was built on the river, two miles east of the original, and a third, a stronger and more permanent fort, was constructed on the beach, just north of the inlet.

By late spring an uneasy peace prevailed. At a parley at Fort King, at which

Sam was represented by Chitto-Tustenuggee, an agreement was reached, allowing the Indians to remain in Florida on the southwest coast. Major General Alexander Macomb proclaimed the war at an end on May 20, 1839. Even Sam Jones, who came into Fort Lauderdale to hear the terms, said he liked them and would order his people to comply.

That summer the peace was shattered. Indians under the fierce chieftain Chekika attacked a Caloosahatchee River trading post, killing 14 civilians and soldiers under the command of one of the most effective of all Indian fighters, Lieutenant Colonel William S. Harney. The colonel escaped wearing only his drawers.

Did the Chekika raid mean the war had resumed? Not at all, said Sam Jones: "I shall never raise my hand against the white man for I am an old man and what can an old man like me do?"

Chitto went so far as to extend a "friendly" invitation to the fort's commander, Christopher Tompkins, to bring his entire force out to the site of the old fort to watch an Indian ball game and dance. The more insistent Chitto became, the warier Lieutenant Tompkins grew. Instead of the entire command he sent two privates, Edward Hopkins and Tom Boyce, and a black interpreter, George. They left at dusk, carrying a gallon of whiskey as a gift to the Indians. They were simply to carry a message that the others would not be coming that evening.

The three of them paddled up the river to the site. As they shook hands with the Indians, a feeling of uneasiness gripped them. They saw no Indian women, no children, only armed warriors.

"Have the officers come?" asked an Indian. When another answered, "Yes," a third cried out, "Now for it."

Terrified, George looked around and saw two rifles aimed straight at their party. Behind one was Chitto's brother, Behind the other was Sponge, the son of Sam Jones.

The three men plunged into the river, just ahead of heavy gunfire. George swam up the river and hid among the branches. In the distance he could hear the voice of Sam Jones and then a chilling remark by Chitto: "Why didn't you wait till we got them clear up into the camp? We might then have sliced them up to our taste."

Lieutenant Tompkins waited for his men to return. As darkness set in, he grew even more worried. Finally, he felt he could wait no longer. In the hours after midnight he led a search party up the river, a terrifying venture for the men. Near the old fort they heard a faint voice: "Here I am." It was Hopkins, lying in the water. "I am wounded and they have killed George and Boyce." Six hours later Hopkins died from a bullet wound in the stomach.

Colonel W.S. Harney (Florida State Archives)

After daylight, they found the body of Boyce. He had not been wounded but rather had drowned. Later in the day they found George—frightened, exhausted but otherwise unhurt.

* * *

The indomitable Indian fighter Colonel Harney set his sights on Chekika and Sam Jones. In Big Winter Moon, 1840, he tracked the fierce Chekika to his wilderness island, deep in the Everglades. Overwhelmed by numbers, Chekika extended his hand in surrender. One of Harney's men shot him dead. Two other Indians who were captured were hanged on the island. To the Seminoles, death by hanging is a particularly demeaning way to die, as Harney well knew.

A furious Sam Jones reacted with rage: "We give them a decent death. We shoot them, or quietly beat their brains out with a pine knot, never hanging them like dogs."

Harney had succeeded in his search for Chekika, a war chief in his prime. With Sam Jones, a medicine man now believed by some to be drifting into senility, he had no such luck.

Harney assembled an impressive force to track the old medicine man, 90 sailors, 60 marines, 70 soldiers and 20 dragoons. Harney left Fort Dallas on the Miami River on New Year's Eve, 1840. They moved only at night, hoping to surprise Jones.

After three hard nights of slogging through the Glades, the men reached Chitto's camp, just south of New River. It was deserted. But Harney was lucky. On a nearby island he captured five Indians who told him Sam and a hundred warriors were headed for a cypress swamp north of the river. There he planned to brace for a last showdown.

When Harney reached the swamp, there was no sign of Sam. Harney's command then crossed the Everglades, emerging on the west coast. A force of close to 250 men had chased Sam for 20 days without finding a trace.

In the summer of 1841 a joint Army, Navy and Marine force tried another sweep, but again they failed. A report was received that Sam had quarreled with another important chief, the Prophet, and had moved out of the Big Cypress. But where?

Word came that he had been seen at the headwaters of the Loxahatchee, west of Fort Jupiter. Worn out from endless pursuits through the swamps, Harney's men took six days of slogging through swamps to get from the New River to the Loxahatchee. Again, no Sam Jones.

By the winter of 1842 a note of despair was creeping into some of the official reports. Wrote Major Thomas Childs: "It is not necessary for me to say how much I regret that these successive efforts to find the hiding place of Jones and his band have been in vain. I cannot, however, but view with admiration the cheerfulness with which every new movement given the most distant chance to success is embraced by officers and soldiers and the zeal & perseverance with which they are carried out, so long as there's a hope of meeting the long-sought obstacle to the termination of the war."

Even bad verse was written about the elusiveness of one "Sam Jones! Sam Jones! thou great unwhipped. . . ." It read in part:

"The war is ended past a doubt—
"Sam Jones has just come in!
"But hark! next day the tune we change
"And sing a counter-strain;
"'The war's not ended,' for behold!
"Sam Jones is out again!"

In the summer of 1842, in August, Big Ripening Moon, General Worth, military commander for Florida, declared the war was over. Of a nation that had numbered nearly 5,000 people seven years earlier about 300 Indians still remained in Florida, less than a hundred of them warriors. Close to 4,000 had been deported to Arkansas.

* * *

Once the war broke out, Sam Jones generally avoided any contact with the white man. He attended few parleys and managed to stay away from artists. The only known sketch of Jones was made unbeknownst to him by an amateur, Ellis Hughes, a Baltimore doctor stationed at Fort Lauderdale. During the lull in the fighting in 1839, Hughes asked Jones: "You're an honest man. What did you go to war for?"

"It was all about the emigration," Sam replied. "I never consented to it and there is no use to talk any more at all about it."

A sailor who served in war was destined to become a famous author of dime novels in later years. Edward Zane Carroll Judson, who wrote under the name Ned Buntline, had chased Jones back and forth across the Glades. In a novel he wrote nearly four decades after the war ended he makes the hero of his *The White Wizard, or The Great Prophet of the Seminoles* a man named Arpiaka. Ironically, he is not an Indian, but rather a white man adopted by the Seminoles—an action Sam Jones would have blocked violently.

Betty Sue Cummings, in her perceptive 1984 novel, *Say These Names—Remember Them,* used Sam Jones as a highly sympathetic character, far kinder than his usual image of cruel leader.

"I didn't make up much," she said. "I went on the assumption that they were defending themselves and their homes. The fierceness that people speak of is perfectly logical when you see it in that light. They were defending their homes."

* * *

With the Florida War behind them, Sam and his band lived quietly somewhere back in the Big Cypress Swamp. Sampson Forrester, a black who had lived with the Indians in the last years of the war, described Sam's camp:

The only known picture of Sam Jones was a sketch at Fort Lauderdale by Army doctor Ellis Hughes in 1839. (Broward County Historical Commission)

"In the center of the swamp is the council ground. South of this, within two miles, is the village of Sam Jones, Otulke Thlocke (the Prophet) lives within two miles of him. . . . No trail whatever is visible outside the swamp, as such would guide their pursuers. Within the swamp are many pine islands upon which the villages are located. They are susceptible of cultivation. . . . The Indians rely principally upon their crops, which, though small, add much to their comfort. Corn, pumpkins, beans, wild potatoes, and cabbage palmetto afford subsistence. The scarcity of powder deprives them partially of game; though bears and turkeys are frequently killed with arrows."

The quiet was shattered in the summer of 1849. An outlaw band of five Indians attacked an isolated trading post near Charlotte Harbor. Two white men were killed. Would it start a third Seminole War?

Chief Billy Bowlegs and the old medicine man decided the crimes of outlaws would not be worth another war. They promised General David E. Twiggs that they would surrender the perpetrators within 30 days. When the general arrived at the site of the trading post a month later, he found that Bowlegs and Sam Jones had been waiting for him for nine days. They handed over three of the five wanted men. They also presented him with the hand of a fourth, who, they said, had been killed trying to escape. The fifth outlaw they were still pursuing.

Apparently, Sam Jones had mellowed. Now he was willing to deal and to negotiate with the hated white man. Perhaps he was just getting too old to fight any more, or maybe he saw all too clearly that right was hardly on the side of five outlaw Indians.

Still, the tension between white and Indian wouldn't go away. In 1855 the festering Third Seminole War finally broke out. More Indians were captured and sent west. Again, Sam Jones, deep in the Big Cypress, avoided capture. Perhaps by now the Army wasn't trying very hard to find him. He was now well over a hundred and hardly a threat to anyone.

Sam's band was down to five very old men, a few women and children, and 12 warriors. His followers refused to emigrate and abandon their venerable chief. Another war was declared over in the late spring of 1858.

But Sam hadn't forgotten the riches to be seized when ships foundered on the Florida reef. A year after the war ended his band showed up on the Atlantic Coast to work the wreck of a slave ship off Jupiter Inlet. The slaver carried both whiskey and ammunition.

Two years later America was plunged into a war bigger by far than the three Seminole Wars. The State of Florida sought officially to woo Sam to the Confederate side, but rumors began to circulate in the fall of 1862 that Jones had been persuaded by the Union forces to attack white settlers on the Peace River.

Jacob Summerlin, the west coast cattle king, had visited Jones at his camp. He reported all was quiet. The following year the state sent its Indian agent, Henry Prosens, out to see if Seminoles could be recruited to fight in the Civil War.

Prosens finally met with Jones, but he had no luck in reaching any agreement with him. "I don't think," Prosens reported, "they would respect an agent sent to negotiate a Treaty with them, while the war lasts and they are surrounded by Yankees."

The Indian agent reported that Jones's camp contained about 70 people. Very few of the males were young enough to fight. Prosens also found the Indians, deep in the swamp, surprisingly well informed about the progress of the war.

By now Sam had seen it all. When he was a boy in north Florida, English colonists farther north were fighting the French and Indian War. He was an adult when the American Revolution was fought. He lived through three Seminole wars and was still alive when the Civil War began. He always kept a low profile in contrast to the better-known Osceola. Only the little Pasco County town of Aripeka bears his name although a joker in the 1930s placed the legend on a Florida map, informing the unwary about the nonexistent "Ruins of Sam Jones Old Town."

Sometime during the Civil War Sam Jones finally wore out. While North and South fought out their bloody differences, word went out to Florida's

Indians that Jones was dying. His impending death was of no great concern to the U.S. military, involved by this time in a far bigger and bloodier conflict than any of the Seminole Wars. To the Indians, however, who owed their survival in Florida to the relentless will of Sam Jones, it was another matter. From all over south Florida, Miccosukees and Seminoles made their pilgrimage to the Big Cypress to pay homage to their dying leader.

The old man who had tormented the United States military for more than two decades died quietly beneath the sabal palms in a hammock in the Big Cypress. He was thought to be about 113 years old. Only the Indians know where his bleached bones lie.

CHAPTER 22

Too Rough, Too Ready

Zachary Taylor harsher toward Missouri Volunteers than Seminoles

By Civil War standards, it was little more than a skirmish, a fight between 800 soldiers and 380 Indians that left more than 30 dead. History, for the most part, has forgotten it.

But the clash waged more than a century and a half ago on the northern shores of Lake Okeechobee was the biggest battle in the longest and costliest of wars between whites and Native Americans—the Second Seminole War of 1835–1842. It was followed by a controversy that embroiled the American commander, future president Zachary Taylor, and resulted in a congressional inquiry.

In October of 1837, 600 Missouri volunteers under the command of Colonel Richard Gentry left their home state for Florida. The punishing trip was complicated by an outbreak of yellow fever. When they reached Tampa, they were down to 220 men, and most of their horses were dead or ailing.

Colonel Zachary Taylor, "Old Rough and Ready," commanding a brigade consisting of the 1st, 4th and 6th infantries, was regular Army. He had no use for volunteers. Gentry and his volunteers had the bad luck to be placed under his command.

On December 19, Taylor and his force set out to attack a concentration of some 2,000 Indians on the north shore of Lake Okeechobee. Roughly 380 were warriors under the command of three major Indian leaders: Sam Jones, Alligator and Coacoochee.

The Indians waited for Taylor in a large hammock near the lake shore. In front of the dense cypress hammock lay a swamp deep in mud, water and sawgrass five feet tall. The Seminoles had cut back the sawgrass just in front of the hammock to give them a clear field of fire. They had staked out a strong defensive position, but the U.S. troops held more than a two-to-one edge in manpower.

When Taylor called for suggestions, Gentry spoke up for a flanking attack.

General Richard Gentry (Broward County Historical Commission)

He reasoned that a frontal assault would offer too good a target for the Indians. Even though it was a sound military plan, Taylor ridiculed it, apparently because it came from a citizen soldier rather than from an Army regular. He ordered Gentry and the Missouri Volunteers to attack the Indians head-on through the swamp. The 6th and 4th Infantries were to follow. Taylor's 1st Infantry was held in reserve—at the rear.

On Christmas Day, 1837, the Missouri Volunteers marched forward into the sawgrass and into a withering fire. Gentry, leading his men, was struck in the chest in the first volley. He kept going. The Seminoles, firing from cover, concentrated on hitting the officers. Just as they reached higher ground Gentry was hit again, this time in the abdomen. His son, Harrison, the regimental sergeant-major, immediately behind him, was also severely wounded.

The 6th Infantry followed the ranks of the Missourians and suffered heavy losses, especially among the officers. When the 4th Infantry began to move forward, the Army's numbers began to tell. Lieutenant Colonel William S. Foster finally penetrated the right side of the Indians' line. After more than two hours of fierce fighting, the soldiers prevailed.

Who had won? Since the Indians left the field, the victory is usually awarded to Taylor. But the cost was high.

From a study of documents, Wesley Coleman, field consultant for the Archeological and Historical Conservancy of Florida, tabulated the casualties. In the two-and-a-half-hour battle, 26 soldiers were killed and 112 were wounded. Two of the wounded, including Colonel Gentry, died shortly after the battle. Twelve Indians were killed and 14 wounded.

As Gentry lay dying, he said to Taylor: "I depend on you to do my brave men full justice in your official report."

Instead, Taylor's report asserted that the Missouri Volunteers had retired in disorder and could not be reformed. Missourians were furious. Taylor was condemned in resolutions in the state legislature and attacked on the floor of the Senate by the powerful Missouri senator Thomas Hart Benton.

The hurt has still not gone away. Descendants of Colonel Gentry, one of the founders of Columbia, the city where the University of Missouri is located, published a book on the 100th anniversary of the battle entitled *Full Justice,* presenting the case against Taylor.

Zachary Taylor went on from the battle at Lake Okeechobee to the presidency following his election in November, 1848. He served less than two years. He died on July 9, 1850, after eating a bowl of cherries and drinking cold milk after sitting for hours in a hot sun.

Some thought he might have been poisoned. A Florida author, Clara Rising, of Holder, thought so and convinced authorities to exhume his body from its grave in Louisville, Kentucky, in June of 1991 to test her theory. She believed he might have been murdered by pro-slavery interests. The medical findings were that he had died of natural causes.

Speculation about his "murder" generally ended with the medical examiner's report. If, however, arsenic had been found in his remains, a closer look at the motive for the murder might have pointed not just at the pro-slavery faction but also at the descendants of the Missouri Volunteers and the much-wronged Colonel Gentry.

CHAPTER 23

Major Lauderdale's Fort

Obscure Tennessee soldier left his name to famous resort city

In the third year of the Army's bloody war with the Seminoles, Major William Lauderdale led his Tennessee Volunteers deep into south Florida. Late in the afternoon of March 5, 1838, they arrived at the New River. A heavy rain beating down on the major dampened, even drenched, what would prove to be a momentous arrival. Worse yet, the downpour could only aggravate the respiratory ills that continued to plague him in the final year of his life.

The next day dawned clearer. What a sight emerged for the eyes of the major, a battle-seasoned fighting man in his 50s who had seen service in the War of 1812 and the First Seminole War. Looking south from the stream's high northern bank, he saw a river 60 yards wide and four fathoms deep, clear and sparkling. Palms, pines, pond apple trees and tropical hardwoods lined its banks. A scene of primitive beauty, but also a scene of danger, of death that could burst at any moment from the lush undergrowth.

Along the river the major and Lieutenants Robert Anderson and Frederick Searies found an abandoned plantation, the ruins of "Cooley's Patch," William Cooley's thriving farm and starch mill that had anchored a settlement of nearly 60 people. On January 6, 1836, early in the Florida War, Indians had struck. They killed Cooley's wife, his three children and their tutor. By the next dawn every resident had fled from New River Settlement.

Just an eighth of a mile west of Cooley's Patch, they found the location they were looking for. Sitting high above the water, it commanded a clear view of the river's southern and northern forks. Seminoles paddling in from the Everglades by either branch would have to float past them.

Lauderdale chose this as the site for the Army's New River fort. Five days later the troops, numbering 223, had cleared the area, hacked down trees and assembled them into a 30–foot square, two-tiered blockhouse. Not until early April would they finish the 60–by-50–foot log picket fence around the blockhouse.

On March 16, 1838, General Thomas S. Jesup, commander of the Army of the South, issued Special Order No. 74, decreeing: "The new post established on New River by the Tennessee Battalion of Volunteers and Company D, 3rd Artillery, will be called Fort Lauderdale."

It was an honor Major Lauderdale was not to enjoy for long. Two months later his weakened lungs finally gave out. On his way back to his Tennessee home he died, an obscure soldier in an obscure war, never dreaming that one day his wilderness fort would lend its name to a world-famous, semitropical resort city.

Hostile Indians, led by the fierce medicine man Sam Jones, lived near the New River, an area where the coontie plant grew in profusion. Starch made from coontie was an important source of food for the Seminoles, a source severly threatened by the new fort on the river.

With his chief Indian guide, Billy Benefactor, Lauderdale scouted the unknown land to the west. They found a deserted Indian village across from the fort in the forks of the river. Farther to the west they came upon a vast, shallow, freshwater marsh, in some ways like a lake, in some ways like a river, dotted with small islands on which tropical hardwoods grew. The Indians called it "grassy waters." The white man would come to know it as the Everglades. Near the source of the north fork of the New River he found Pine Island, the northernmost and largest of the Seven Islands of Sam Jones.

When General Jesup heard that Sam Jones and two other Seminole war leaders, Wildcat and Alligator, were hiding on Pine Island with possibly as many as 100 warriors, he named Lieutenant Colonel James Bankhead to take over command of the new fort and mount a major military thrust into the Everglades.

Assuming command on March 18, Colonel Bankhead prepared to lead a large-scale operation against Pine Island. More than 500 military men, including Major Lauderdale and 100 of his Volunteers, moved out from the fort on March 22.

A sutler (military supplier) named William Tucker wrote to his brother that day, one of the earliest known appearances of Fort Lauderdale as a dateline:

"Today about 500 men left our Camp an are still out in search of Wild Cat Alligator & Sam Jones, who was until a day or two about Eight miles distant. They have left & these 500 men are on their trail in search of them- Tomorrow we shall expect to hear of a battle."

The battle he heard of amounted to very little. Gunfire was exchanged as the Americans advanced on Pine Island late in the afternoon. The next morning all the Indians had vanished. One soldier suffered a finger wound in the Battle of Pine Island.

Major Lauderdale and his Volunteers, their job done, left the fort on April

Statue of Major William Lauderdale (Stuart McIver)

2 to return to Tennessee. The major never made it back to his plantation, dying in an Army barracks in Baton Rouge, Louisiana, on May 11, 1838.

Even before his death the fort he had built was abandoned. Believing the Indians had been driven out of the New River area, the military deactivated the fort and left. They guessed wrong. Sam Jones and his band returned to burn Fort Lauderdale.

Once again in charge of New River, the Seminoles began salvaging shipwrecks along the coast, but they overdid it. By slaughtering any American survivors who made it to shore, they forced the Army to return.

The following winter a second Fort Lauderdale, a temporary fort, was built on the north side of the river on high ground, a mile and a quarter closer to the ocean. It was occupied on Valentine's Day, 1839.

A log stockade about eight to ten feet high surrounded the fort. At its southeast corner stood a two-story log blockhouse and at its southwest a watchtower with an observation platform. Tents were erected within the fort.

During the spring the troops were busy building a third fort on a thin strip of land between the ocean and New River Sound, a site better suited to protecting Americans cast ashore by shipwrecks. In late September the third fort, a rectangular enclosure with blockhouses at three of its four corners, was finished.

Life was hardly easy at any of the three forts. Between 1839 and 1842, the year the seven-year war ended, 14 Third Artillery soldiers died—five from battle wounds, three from diarrhea, three from unknown diseases, one from fever and two from drowning.

A journal kept by Lieutenant Ellis Hughes, the post surgeon, gives the best account of life at the second and third forts. Isolation, insects, heat, disease, boredom and the uncertain danger of fighting a fierce, elusive foe combined to create severe morale and discipline problems. Steamboats calling at Fort Lauderdale helped ease the pain. Food was adequate, and such niceties as books and tobacco were available, along with a variety of alcoholic beverages, including wine, beer, porter, champagne, brandy and rum. Hughes dipped into these so often that he was forced to resign his commission after facing eight different charges, most of them associated with drunkenness, insubordination and generally bad conduct. Among the charges were assertions that he was seen too often "cheek by jowl" with enlisted men, one of whom was observed sitting on his lap. His interests ranged much farther, however. One plaintive entry in his journal cries out, "I want a girl."

Some of the soldiers who served at Fort Lauderdale went on to achieve a measure of fame. Robert Anderson, who helped Major Lauderdale select the fort site, moved into the history books as the Union commander of Fort Sumter when it was fired on to trigger the start of the Civil War.

During the Third Seminole War, Captain Abner Doubleday built a military road from the Biscayne Bay area to New River. Later he would become famous as the "father of baseball," a claim that is now generally discredited.

Joseph E. Johnston fought at Pine Island. Later he would command the last Confederate army in the Civil War. He surrendered at Durham, North Carolina, to General William Tecumseh Sherman, who had served as a lieutenant in the Third Artillery at the third fort.

William Lauderdale, however, remains a shadowy figure. It is not even clear when he was born, although his birthplace is known—the Fincastle community in Virginia. His lineage traces back to the noble Scottish family of Maitland in the Edinburgh area. Major Lauderdale served with distinction with General Andrew Jackson, who called him "a sterling soldier and patriot." When not soldiering, he was a man of substance, a plantation owner and a slave-holder near Nashville. He married twice and at his death 150 years ago left behind five children. He also left behind his name.

CHAPTER 24

Florida's Biggest Battle

54th Massachusetts, of "Glory" fame, fought in bloody Civil War clash

"On the double." The order came straight from Brigadier General Truman Seymour. By midafternoon on a clear, cool winter day, the commander of the Union army could clearly see the Battle of Olustee had turned into a rout for his troops.

Six miles to the east, over 500 fighting men, guarding supplies at the Florida Atlantic & Gulf Central Railroad station, got the message. Quickly, the soldiers leaped into action, charging west through the north Florida pinewoods.

"Faster, faster," came the command. To lighten their loads they dropped haversacks, blankets, knapsacks—anything nonessential. Now the sounds of the battle were reaching their ears: the sharp crack of rifles, the boom of cannons.

Hundreds of wounded lay about. Dispirited stragglers and regiments in retreat called out discouraging words: "We're badly whipped!" "You'll all get killed!"

Then, from a disabled battery moving to the rear, they heard the words of their already famous battle cry: "Three cheers for Massachusetts and seven dollars a month!"

Seven dollars a month, the starting pay for the battle-toughened 54th Massachusetts Infantry, the Civil War's first regiment of free Negroes. It was less than the $13 paid to white soldiers.

The 54th had led the valiant, though doomed, assault on Fort Wagner, South Carolina, a charge, as it turned out, to glory. "Glory," in fact, would be the name of a motion picture about the 54th a century and a quarter later. Part of the film was shot at Olustee.

At Olustee, however, the 54th was not looking ahead to future fame. The Volunteers, commanded by Colonel E. N. Hallowell, faced a brutal task—to slow down a relentless Confederate advance long enough to let the rest of Seymour's disintegrating command begin their retreat back to Jacksonville.

About four o'clock they took up their position on the left flank of a tired and battered Union army. The Volunteers, armed with Enfield rifles, gained a brief respite when the Confederates ran low on ammunition. The break didn't last long.

The 54th held the line as dusk drew near. By early evening, most of the Yanks had left the battlefield. Only then could the black regiment fall back. Even with the 54th's holding action, Union casualties were staggering. Without the 54th the battle, the biggest ever fought in Florida, could have been a disaster.

When the Union army left the field on February 20, 1864, there were no spectators around to cheer the victorious Southerners. It was a battle fought in the real world. Union casualties, killed, wounded and missing, totaled 1,861 out of a command of 5,500 men. The South, which fought with a force of 5,200, had a casualty total of 946.

At an annual Battle of Olustee reenactment a packed house of Civil War buffs, mostly staunch Southerners, belted out Rebel Yells when the Yankees finally fled back into the pines. They had cheered earlier when a uniformed band from Athens, Georgia, had played "Dixie" in front of the bleachers.

Olustee, hardly a pivotal battle, has become one of the biggest annual reenactments in the southeast. It started modestly in 1976 in the Gator Bowl in Jacksonville, not a bad locale since some have observed that reenactments show many parallels to football games.

The reenactment craze grew out of the Civil War Centennial in the 1960s and gained new vigor in recent years because of the hit movie "Glory" and the Ken Burns series *The Civil War* on public televison. Today some 30,000 reenactors recreate battles from the Civil War, the American Revolution, the War of 1812, the French and Indian War, the Florida Seminole Wars and assorted smaller conflagrations that happened on American soil. In addition, they take part in living history demonstrations, acting out less violent scenes from America's past.

* * *

The Union's crushing defeat in the Battle of Olustee, despite its edge in manpower, can be attributed largely to blunders by the insubordinate General Seymour. The previous year he had commanded the assault on Fort Wagner. Of the 54th, which suffered dreadful casualties in leading the charge, he said: "Well, I guess we will . . . put those damned niggers from Massachusetts in the advance. We may as well get rid of them one time as another."

A bearded Alvin Batiste, 71, was an enthusiastic representative of the 54th Massachusetts Infantry Volunteers at a reenactment of the Battle of Olustee. (Stuart McIver)

In early February of 1864 Union troops from Hilton Head, South Carolina, took over Jacksonville and began raids on a number of settlements, among them Gainesville.

The Confederate commander of the District of East Florida, Brigadier General Joseph Finegan, had only about 1,500 troops to defend his vast territory. The Irish-born general called for reinforcements from the regional commander, the flamboyant General Pierre Gustave Toutant Beauregard.

On February 9 a strong Union force occupied the town of Baldwin, west of Jacksonville, and the following day moved on to Barber's Plantation, a large farm and ranch owned by Moses Barber, a most unlucky man. Driven from his holdings by the Union, he retreated to the Gainesville area. In less than a decade he would find most of his family wiped out in the Barber-Mizell range war.

At Barber's, Seymour chose to ignore the orders of his superior, Major General Quincy Adams Gillmore, who told him to return to Baldwin. On February 14 the two generals met again in Jacksonville. Gillmore's orders were to make no advances west of Barber's without his consent.

Seymour, however, came up with ideas of his own. He decided to march west to the Suwannee River to destroy an important railroad bridge. A fellow officer had once said of him: "Seymour's a devil of a fellow for dash."

At seven o'clock the morning of February 20, he defied orders by marching west from Barber's with a force of some 5,500 men. That morning he was told that a large Confederate force had assembled east of Lake City. He didn't believe it, so he ignored the information.

The information, as it turned out, was correct. Beauregard had sent reinforcements. Furthermore, the Confederates had used their knowledge of the landscape to set up defenses where wetlands would pinch in the dry land area over which the North could advance. The Olustee area lies just south of that part of the Okefenokee Swamp that reaches down into Florida.

Union troops had already marched more than 30 miles when they collided with the Johnny Rebs. Skirmishing, begun in midafternoon, quickly accelerated into a major battle.

Seymour, restricted by the terrain, sent his troops forward in numbers too small to handle the superior Southern forces. The Union collapse began when the 7th New Hampshire Regiment suddenly fell apart. Some men started running to the rear, others simply milled about in confusion.

Later it was learned that Colonel Joseph Abbott, of Manchester, New Hampshire, had given an incorrect order, which created a chaotic positioning of his troops. Abbott was a political appointee, who would later become a carpetbagger and U.S. Senator from North Carolina. Nearly a third of Abbott's fighting men were killed, wounded or captured.

Union forces suffered defeat at the Battle of Olustee, the largest Civil War battle in Florida. (Florida State Archives)

The disintegration of the New Hampshire 7th was far from the end of the battle. Heavy fighting brought severe casualties on both sides. Shortages of ammunition slowed down the Confederate advance, but by late afternoon Seymour realized the day was lost.

At this point the commanding general sent forward his last reserves, Colonel James Montgomery's Brigade, consisting of the 35th United States Colored Troops and the 54th Massachusetts Colored Infantry.

Montgomery, portrayed as a villainous character in "Glory," was a "jayhawker," a member of the anti-slavery guerillas who fought in Kansas and Missouri just before the Civil War. A slave owner at one time, he later became an abolitionist and an associate of John Brown. He had a virulent hatred of Southern landowners but he could also be harsh to blacks, perhaps a carryover from his days as a slaveholder.

The North has been criticized for sacrificing blacks unnecessarily to save its white troops. The charge seems unwarranted since the black units remained in the rear until desperately needed. Furthermore, the casualties for the 54th were lower than those of the rest of the Army—83 killed, wounded or missing out of a force of 500.

A more serious accusation is the recurring charge that Confederate troops throughout the war were killing wounded blacks as they lay helpless on the battlefields. From a report by Brigadier General John P. Hatch USA:

"Soon after the battle of Olustee, in Florida, a list of wounded and prisoners in the hands of the enemy was forwarded to our lines by the commander of the rebel army. The very small number of colored prisoners attracted immediate attention, as it was well known that the number left wounded on the field was large. It is now known that most of the wounded colored men were murdered on the field."

To the South, a black soldier was seen as a slave who had rebelled, a crime punishable by death. The Confederacy simply refused to recognize the blacks as soldiers protected by the rules of war.

The Battle of Olustee had little effect on the outcome of war as northern armies steadily ground down the South's resistance. It had, however, an effect on the future of General Seymour. He had defied the orders of his superior, ignored accurate information given to him, marched his troops 35 miles in one day and then thrown them into battle against a well-entrenched enemy. Seymour was promptly relieved of his command. A few months later he was captured during fighting in the wilderness in Virginia.

An amusing aftermath to the bloody battle was the dunking of Union rifles after the war. Occupation troops taking a meal at Lake City's Hotel Blanche stacked their weapons outside the dining room. Unreconstructed rebels gathered the guns and dumped them in Lake DeSoto a block away.

The story took on a legendary cast, often told but not necessarily believed. Then in 1982 the lake was drained. In the mud lay 16 trapdoor Springfield rifles. They are now on display at the Lake City Public Library.

ON THE MOVE

Florida is a big state, three coasts and 58,560 square miles. Getting around Florida has always called for ingenuity. Automobiles raced on the beach for speed records and trains raced on iron rails for mail contracts. Froghunters whooshed through the Everglades in airboats and family cars dared to cross the Glades on a road called Alligator Alley. Those who were really in a hurry used the airlanes above the swamps and the beaches.

CHAPTER 25

Speeders on the Sands

Early auto racers hit the beach at Ormond-Daytona Beach

The wide beach was packed so hard by rain and tide that some of the Ormond Beach Hotel's wealthy guests figured it would be a good surface for a bicycle race. One winter's day in 1902 they decided to try it.

James Hathaway, a guest from Somerville, Massachusetts, strolled down to the beach to watch. When the race was over, he noticed something unusual about the tire tracks in the sand. There weren't any.

If the beach is that hard, he mused, why couldn't you drive a car on it? At a time when only about 10,000 cars a year were sold in the United States, he was one of the few who owned an auto. Hathaway drove his little Stanley Steamer onto the beach. He found his answer. The sands were ideal for that new-fangled machine that was just beginning to catch on in America.

So, he thought, why not an automobile race on the sands at Ormond Beach?

In 1902 most Americans had heard about the automobile but only a minority had ever even seen one. Most of the world's auto racing at the time was held in France, where roads were better and cars more numerous. Eight years earlier, 19 cars, departing from Paris, competed in the first organized race. The winner averaged 11.6 miles an hour.

In the United States a few races had been held in the New York, Chicago and Detroit areas. The problem was dirt—dirt tracks and dirt roads. A racing driver, wheezing and coughing, soon found himself blinded by the dust. Some races were even held on frozen lakes—anything to get away from the dust.

At Ormond Beach and adjoining Daytona Beach there would be no problem with blinding dust or slippery ice that might crack. The sands, dampened down each day by a kindly tide and baked by a Florida sun, provided the perfect racing surface, hard as paving and free of upkeep.

In 1888 John Anderson and Joseph D. Price had chased the resident bear population off the barrier island and built the Ormond Hotel. Oil, railroad and hotel magnate Henry Flagler later bought the property and renamed it the Ormond Beach Hotel. Flagler's Standard Oil partner, John D. Rockefeller, stayed at the hotel for awhile, then concluded Flagler was overcharging him. So he built his home, the Casements, across the street.

Anderson and Price, who now managed Flagler's hotel, liked Hathaway's idea. Auto racing would encourage the use of the bossman's product, gasoline, and at the same time would help promote the hotel.

Put together quickly, the first speed trials, set for April of 1902, drew only three entries: two auto racers, Ransom Olds and Alexander Winton, and the irrepressible Oscar Hedstrom, who would race his Indian motorcycle.

The small turnout was understandable. Cars and motorcycles had to be shipped as freight to Ormond Beach via Flagler's railroad. There simply were no roads to the area.

One year, Olds tried another approach. He shipped his car by train to Jacksonville, then transferred it to a St. Johns River steamboat to Palatka, figuring he could drive it through the rough sandy terrain the rest of the way. The steamboat captain gave him a problem. Afraid of carrying gasoline on his boat, he insisted that Olds drain his gas tank. This could create problems. Olds had no assurance he could obtain any more gasoline at Ormond Beach. But, playing on the fact that very few Americans had ever seen a car, he made a big display of draining the tank, only the tank he drained was the water tank.

Olds had built the first mass-produced automobile in America, his curved-dash Oldsmobile. By 1902 he was selling over 2,000 cars a year at approximately $600 apiece. The following year his sales soared to 3,750, roughly a one-third market share. Many regard him as the father of the American automobile industry.

The Michigan manufacturer called his racing car the Pirate. It has been described as "a spidery, cantilever contraption with a horizontal, water-cooled, single-cylinder engine; no body-work; and a sulky-type seat equipped with stirrups."

Olds would face a formidable foe in the Scottish-born Winton. A Cleveland manufacturer, he had made a name for himself in racing circles. In a race at Grosse Point, Michigan, he had driven a mile in one minute 12.4 seconds, which was a world's record for about an hour. His record was broken the same day in a New York race.

Starting out as a bicycle repairman, Winton built his first gasoline-powered auto in 1896 and two years later had collected a hefty $1000 for the first automobile ever sold in the United States. He would compete at Ormond Beach in Bullet No. 1, a racer with wooden wheels and a big roasting pan of a hood covering his motor.

The Olds Pirate built and driven by Ransom Olds reached 57 m.p.h. on the sands at Ormond Beach by the late 1890s. (Florida State Archives)

As the entrants prepared for the first Florida automobile race, the three dreamers who put it together could have had no notion of the awesome forces they were about to unleash. For the next three decades the sands, particularly at Daytona, would roar with the thunder of mighty engines revved to the limit by the world's most daring speed demons.

On that April day in 1902, however, the event was low key. The first racing car to test the sands was Olds' Pirate. The course was just one mile long. The racers, allowed a "flying start," were timed only for the stretch between the mile markers. Olds' time was 57 miles per hour, a respectable time but well below the world's record of 77.13 held by a French driver.

Winton followed Olds to the race course, started his engine, then raced his hardest to beat the Pirate's time. Surprisingly, he too was clocked at exactly 57 mph.

Hedstrom, shooting for a record for motorcycles, had trouble developing much speed. Still, the speed trials were judged a success. At least the auto racing world now knew where Ormond Beach was.

For the "official" races the following March, the American Automobile Association for the first time agreed to sponsor an auto racing event. The field might have been a large one if the Jacksonville Automobile Club, fearful of the publicity for the Ormond Beach/Daytona Beach area, hadn't refused to back the races. Some suspected them of sending a telegram announcing that the event had been canceled.

Even so race drivers and newspaper reporters joined the guests to crowd the hotel for the three-day event. Spectators by the hundreds arrived, mostly in horse- or mule-drawn wagons or bicycles. A few actually drove automobiles. A "worthy audience for a distant and sparsely peopled land," said *Motor Age*.

The course for the big 1903 race was a five-mile stretch extending from Granada Avenue in Ormond south into Daytona's sands. Telegraph wires were strung and a French-designed timing apparatus was set up.

The feature of the event was the renewed rivalry between Olds and Winton. This time, however, it would be a different kind of competition. Olds had replaced himself with driver H. T. Thomas at the wheel of Pirate. And Winton had brought two cars, Bullets No. 1 and 2.

The second Bullet developed clutch problems, but Winton's mechanics showed ingenuity. They dismantled a barrel and used the iron hoops to make replacement parts.

In warmup runs the drivers found that their solid racing tires failed to gain enough traction. Winton solved the problem by cutting notches in his tires.

With a run of 53.9 mph Olds' Pirate fell below his 57 of the previous year. Winton, on his second trip to the sands, increased his speed to 68.9 m.p.h., still well short of a world's record. Both times were well ahead of that of founder Hathaway, who entered the race with his Stanley Steamer. His speed was just under 18 mph.

Oscar Hedstrom came up with a good performance on his Indian motorcycle: 56.9 mph.

The success of the 1903 races led to the formation of the Florida East Coast Automobile Association. Its membership would include such names as Vanderbilt and Astor. The group built a clubhouse on the beach at Daytona and made plans for an even bigger event set for the last week of January, 1904. Flagler ran special trains to bring racing enthusiasts to the Ormond-Daytona races.

Hotels and boardinghouses throughout the area were filled. The Ormond Hotel housed such celebrities as William K. Vanderbilt, actress Irene Bentley and the renowned New York architect Stanford White. Two years later White would be shot dead by Harry Kendall Thaw, with whom he shared the affections of Evelyn Nesbit, in a popular night club in one of New York's most famous murder cases. It would become the subject of books and movies.

To drive his Bullet No. 2, Winton had hired one of the rising stars of U.S. racing, the cigar-chewing daredevil Barney Oldfield. In a field that included European cars and drivers, Barney won his event with a speed of 83.75 mph.

The high point of the races, however, was the appearance on the sands of Vanderbilt and his 90-horsepower, four-cylinder Mercedes, built in Germany. In 76-degree January weather Vanderbilt adjusted his goggles and then proceeded to give the Florida sands their first world's record. Vanderbilt's time was 92.30 mph.

Hedstrom was back again in the motorcycle races. His time was good but he was beaten by Glenn Curtiss, who set a world's ten-mile record with a speed of 53.4 m.p.h. Curtiss later became an aircraft builder, built the first Everglades airboat and developed the Dade County cities of Hialeah, Miami Springs and Opa-locka.

From the sandy sidelines one would-be racer watched ruefully. His car had been damaged in transit and he lacked the funds to replace its defective axle or to pay for a room at the ritzy Ormond Beach Hotel. He made do by living in a tent and eating cheese and crackers. The young man was Henry Ford.

Ford didn't like to race but he knew a good showing in competition would help sales for his struggling company. In 1901 at the Detroit Fairgrounds Henry had outgunned Winton and Vanderbilt in a 25-mile race to win $1,000 and a cut-glass bowl. As he climbed out of his car, he muttered: "Boy, I'll never do that again! I was scared to death."

Ford had to take the wheel again for a race across the frozen ice at Lake St. Clair in Michigan. He was terrified, but once more he got the job done. His time in his Arrow racing car was 91.37 mph, a world's record.

Soon Ford would be able to concentrate on building cars. Within a decade his assembly lines would revolutionize the automobile industry.

The 1904 races were not without mishaps. A. R. Parrington, chairman of the American Automobile Association's racing board, tried driving on the beach at night. A strong wind blew out the lamps of his Peerless. He steered his car into the Atlantic.

The following year the races suffered the first fatality. Frank Croker, son of Richard Croker, the boss of New York's Tammany Hall political machine, was killed during a test run when he swerved to avoid a motorcycle.

But by this time the momentum had built. The races were attracting even more top international cars and drivers, including people like the Chevrolet Brothers, Louis and Gaston, and the Italian Vincenzo Lancia, driving a Fiat.

1906 was a triumphant year for American cars and drivers. On January 26 Fred Marriott became the first American to drive an American-built car, the Rocket, to a world's record on the Ormond-Daytona sands. His record speed was 127.6 mph. The first man to drive two miles a minute, Marriott achieved his amazing time in a car not known for its speed: the Stanley Steamer powered not by the more common gasoline-burning engine but by a steam engine. The special red auto the bearded Stanley twins had designed for Marriott looked like an upside-down canoe with four bicycle wheels. This was not surprising since the car's body was built of wood and canvas by the Roberts Canoe Factory of Riverside, Massachusetts. It was even steered by a tiller.

Barney Oldfield drove the Blitzen Benz to a new world's record of 131.72 m.p.h. at Daytona Beach in 1910. (Florida State Archives)

The following year Marriott made another try with the Rocket. He wasn't so lucky this time. In a practice run Marriott hit a depression in the sands and sailed through the air like a kite for a hundred feet. Within a month he had recovered from his injuries, but the car broke apart and scattered along the beach.

J. C. Robinson, an enterprising young pioneer from a nearby town, saw the accident. Later he and a friend bought a length of plumber's pipe, cut it into small pieces and sold it as souvenirs of the wrecked Stanley Rocket.

In the years that followed, world's records were set by Oldfield, Wild Bob Burman and Ralph DePalma who moved the speed up close to 150 mph. After that, racing at Daytona went into a slump until a tall, slender, red-haired Englishman named Major H.O.D. Segrave arrived in January, 1927, with his 1000-horsepower, flame-red, streamlined Sunbeam. His goal was to break the 200-mph barrier. The record at the time was 174.95, held by a fellow Briton, Captain Malcolm Campbell.

On March 27 a crowd of 15,000 gathered to watch as the major pulled on his white helmet, climbed into his Sunbeam and proceeded to drive his car at an incredible 203.792 mph.

Segrave's great performance drew stiff competition the following year. On hand to challenge his record were Campbell, in his famous racing car, Blue-

By 1935 Sir Malcolm Campbell's "Bluebird" had reached speeds of more than 275 m.p.h. at Daytona Beach. (Florida State Archives)

bird; the daredevil Frank Lockhart, in a 16-cylinder Stutz Blackhawk, and J. M. White, in a Triplex, powered by three 500-horsepower Liberty motors.

In spite of trouble with the bumpy sands, Campbell regained the record with a run of 206.95 mph. He didn't hold it for long. White engaged a 27-year-old dirt track driver named Ray Keech to drive Triplex, a somewhat patched-together vehicle in sharp contrast to the sophisticated, streamlined British cars.

Keech, despite a severe scalding from a broken hose, drove the Triplex to another record of 207.55, just two months after Campbell's record run.

Lockhart's racing career ended on the sands at Daytona. In February he had wrecked the Blackhawk and had nearly drowned when pinned down under water. He survived, and the car was rebuilt for another try in April. This time he blew a tire and this crash killed him—but not before he had set a new record of 198.27 mph for Class D cars.

The Triplex, too, would meet a tragic end the following year. For his driver White had picked Lee Bible, a popular mechanic and racer who ran a repair garage in Daytona. Near the the north end of the measured mile, a Pathe News cameraman, Charles Traub, was filming Bible's run when black smoke suddenly shot out of the car's exhaust pipe. As the car veered out of control, Traub ran for the protection of the sand dunes. He never made it. The car hit him, then crashed, also killing its driver.

Ironically, his camera continued to run. The last reel he ever shot, the deadly wreck of the Triplex, was shown at the Vivian Theatre in Daytona Beach.

In England, Segrave and Campbell were both knighted for their racing feats. Segrave never returned to Florida; he was killed in an accident in a speedboat on an English lake.

Sir Malcolm, obsessed by his goal of a 300 mph run, kept coming back to Daytona, setting new world's records in 1932 and again in 1933. Two years later he brought over his latest Bluebird, a 30-foot auto weighing five tons. It was powered by a 2,500-horsepower Rolls Royce V-12 supercharged engine. Its specially built tires cost $1,800 apiece. The Bluebird burned three gallons a minute.

On March 7, 1935, Sir Malcolm, who already held the world's record with a 272-mph run, made his last Daytona try for the elusive 300-mph goal. He missed, but he moved the world's record just a little higher, to 276.816.

By now the day of the Daytona sands was winding down. The superb North Florida beach had been fine for bicycle races and had even served well in the early days of automobile racing. But long before Campbell's last run, racers knew the beach would no longer work. It was not level enough, and tidal action changed it from day to day. High-speed runs had just become too dangerous.

Sir Malcolm Campbell shipped Bluebird to the Bonneville Salt Flats in Utah. There he reached the record he couldn't achieve in Florida: 301.13 mph.

For Ormond Beach and Daytona Beach it had been a glorious run, starting with Olds and Winton on through to Oldfield and Vanderbilt and finally culminating with Campbell.

The day of speed, however, was not quite over. Stock cars still raced on the beach. After World War II Bill France, a driver from Washington, came to Daytona, where he organized NASCAR—the National Association of Stock Car Auto Racing. Why not, he thought, build a modern, two-and-a-half mile race track for stock cars in the land where speed was born? In 1959 his Daytona Beach Motor Speedway Corporation opened the Daytona International Speedway.

The opening day's race resulted in a dead heat after 500 grueling miles, just as the first time trials on the beach 56 years earlier had ended in a tie. In 1903 the one-mile event had just been declared all even and that was that.

By 1959 the camera was in use to settle these matters. This time the race was so close that track officials took three days to declare a winner, and even today the argument continues. Did Lee Petty get the nod because he was the stock car circuit's most popular driver? The winning time was 135.52, faster than Winton and Olds, slower than Campbell.

CHAPTER 26

Railroad Days

Nineteenth-century trains opened up America's last frontier

The prize was a big one. To the swiftest railroad between Savannah, Georgia, and Jacksonville, Florida, would go a fat U.S. mail contract. In 1901 the United States Post Office decided these matters by a simple, direct method—a race.

Engineer Ned Leake faced an all but impossible task. The Seaboard Air Line, his foe, traveled a direct, coast-hugging route that measured 31.8 miles less than the 149-mile course he would have to follow for the Plant System's Savannah, Florida & Western. Leake knew he would have to coax every bit of power from steam engine 107, a big, coal-burning 10-wheeler like the one Casey Jones drove to his doom the year before. Leake didn't want to join Casey as an American legend. He just wanted to win the mail contract for Plant.

On February 28, each train, hauling four carloads of mail, chugged away from Savannah. For the first 12 miles south the two tracks ran parallel. With 31.8 miles to make up, Leake drove his engine hard—too hard. He took the early lead. Then his engine developed a hot driving box and slowed almost to a crawl just before the western turnoff to Waycross, Georgia, a major railroad junction. Hooting and jeering, a cocky Seaboard crew steamed past Plant's creeping crawler.

Engine 107 limped eight more miles into Flemington, arriving just ahead of a northbound Plant freight train out of Tampa. Its engineer was the veteran railroader Albert Hodge, small and wiry, a man who could spur an engine on like a jockey in a stakes race.

The two Plant crews huddled, then agreed to a switch. Hodge would couple his engine, No. 111, to the mail train and try to beat the Seaboard into Jacksonville. The odds were poor. Not only was the distance greater for the Plant entry, but overheating had already cost the train more than an hour.

Hodge edged his train out slowly, then moved quickly up to 60, 70, then 80

Travel and Recreation

*"Now is the Winter of our discontent
Made glorious Summer by—"*

A TRIP TO FLORIDA!

FROM

The Raw, Bleak, Bitter, Biting, Bone-piercing Discomforts of a Northern Winter, with its Drifting Snow, its Treacherous Ice, its Blinding Sleet, and Benumbing Slush; its Blizzards, its East Winds; its Sudden Changes;

TO

An Ideal Summer Climate, where Life is all Lived Out-of-doors, from Michaelmas to May-day; a Haven of Health; a Heaven of Rest—a Lounging-place for all Creation; Sea-bathing in Midwinter; Boating, Hunting, Fishing; Brilliant Social Pleasures; Finest Hotels Imaginable.

ALL THESE PLEASURES ARE REACHED BY

ORMOND, FLORIDA.
An actual photograph of the Bathing Beach in Midwinter.

SOUTHERN RAILWAY,

AND

Florida Central & Peninsular R. R.

Running a train *de luxe*, THE FLORIDA SHORT LINE LIMITED, which for safety, comfort and convenience is not excelled by anything that goes on wheels. It leaves New York via Pennsylvania Railroad at 3:20 p.m., and arrives at Jacksonville and St. Augustine early next evening.

THE SHORTEST ROUTE! THE QUICKEST TIME!

Between New York or Boston and St. Augustine ONLY ONE NIGHT.

A. O. MACDONELL, G. P. A.
Florida Central & Peninsular R. R., Jacksonville, Florida.
New York Office, 353 Broadway.

W. A. TURK, G. P. A.
Southern Railway, Washington, D. C.
New York Office, 271 Broadway.

For mutual advantage when you write to an advertiser please mention the Review of Reviews.

22

Magazine and newspaper ads beckoned travelers to leave winter behind and take the Southern Railway to Florida. (Florida State Archives) miles an hour through the rural Georgia countryside. Faster and faster he went. For a five-mile stretch near Satilla, Georgia, two Plant officials clocked the train at two minutes and thirty seconds—120 miles an hour. The old record had been 112.5 miles an hour, set in 1893 by a New York Central train, later honored by a U.S. postage stamp.

One of the clockers began sweating heavily as a curve loomed just ahead. He wondered if the engine was going to "take that curve or take to the woods."

The wheels shrieked like Georgia crows but the train held to the tracks and cruised on in to Waycross. The pit stop lasted just three minutes and the train was on its way again, angling southeast now toward Jacksonville along the eastern edge of the spooky Okefenokee Swamp.

Another curve ahead. "Charlie, don't you s'pose he's going to shut off?" asked an anxious young coal passer. Fireman Charlie Johnson replied: "Naw, he jus' going good now."

The train moved into the curve. S. S. McClellan, one of the clockers, recalled: "Hodge closed up the throttle about three notches and immediately changed his mind and pulled it out again five notches. We hit the curve. Uncle Jimmy grabbed me and I grabbed the hot iron pipes on the front of the boiler head. . . ."

Charlie Johnson was laughing, the coal passer was lying flat on the tender, McClellan was mopping his brow in relief. The train approached the St. Marys River, the border between Georgia and Florida, then roared across the trestle over the river and into the Sunshine State. At Callahan the train hit 120 again, its lonesome whistle cutting through the early morning air.

As Hodge eased his over-stressed train into the Jacksonville terminal, a crowd of railroaders cheered loudly. Hodge wasn't quite sure just why. Then he found out. The Seaboard crew, convinced they had nothing to worry about, had made it a business-as-usual run. They still hadn't arrived.

A tired Plant crew went to the station restaurant that morning, March 1, 1901, to enjoy a well-earned breakfast. Soon a Seaboard conductor walked in and asked: "Has that broken down Plant engine been heard from yet?"

He wondered why the crowd laughed.

* * *

Near the end of the 19th century two Henrys, Plant and Flagler, one for the west and one for the east coast, performed the large task of opening up America's last frontier, the thinly-populated, subtropical land called Florida. They were, however, far from the first of the state's eager railroaders. They were just more competent, better financed and certainly luckier. Their predecessors were demolished by such powerful forces as pestilence, natural disasters and war.

The early Florida railroads used wooden rails laid over wooden crossties as did the rest of the nation. By the time of the Civil War most of the state had converted to iron rails. The gauge, the distance between parallel rails, was a gremlin in railroading's primitive days. A number of different gauges were used, thus creating great difficulties at junctions where railroads of varying widths met. Most southern railroads used a five-foot gauge.

Florida's first railroad, completed early in the railroad era, ended in total disaster. The Lake Wimico and St. Joseph Canal and Rail Road Company, nearly eight miles in length, served the cotton trade in Florida's Panhandle starting in 1836. The problem was that St. Joseph, the wild and wicked town where it was based, was doomed. Its downfall started with an 1841 yellow fever epidemic which killed 75 percent of the town's inhabitants, which at one time had totaled 6,000. Then a forest fire swept into town, followed in 1844 by a tidal wave and a hurricane that blew away what remained of St. Joseph. Nothing was left for the railroad to serve.

On January 8, 1853, the Florida Internal Improvement Trust Fund authorized the Florida Railroad Company to build the first cross-state track, from Fernandina on the Atlantic to Cedar Key on the Gulf of Mexico. The president of the Florida Railroad was David Levy Yulee, Florida's first senator.

The problem the ambitious newcomer ran into was a big one—the Civil War. In January, 1862, Union troops landed at Cedar Key and destroyed the western terminus of the Florida Railroad. In March a federal force of 29 ships attacked Fernandina and demolished the eastern terminus. Completing the job, the Confederates removed many of the rails in the interior and used them for tracks in other areas.

The eastern end of the railroad continues in operation to this day as a spur. Its depot, rebuilt in 1899 following a destructive hurricane, survives today as the Fernandina Beach Chamber of Commerce.

* * *

It ran for only seven and a half miles, and less than seven years. Still in its brief lifetime the Jupiter & Lake Worth Railway reached legendary status, principally because of the catchy name it acquired. Operating between Jupiter, at the southern end of the Indian River, and Juno, on the north shore of Lake Worth, the little railroad connected two large bodies of water which supported steamboat traffic. Two stops along the way were named Venus, with a population of one man and two cats, and Mars.

Passengers and crew riding the Jacksonville, St. Augustine and Halifax River Railroad pose for a photograph in the 1880s. (Historical Association of Southern Florida)

A writer for *Harper's New Monthly Magazine* dubbed it the "Celestial Line," soon to become known as the "Celestial Railroad."

It began operations in 1889, as a tiny narrow-gauge branch of the Jacksonville, Tampa and Key West Railroad Company. The JT & KW carried passengers from Titusville south through its subsidiary, the Indian River Steamboat Company. At Jupiter they could board the Celestial. Then from Juno the railroad connected with the steamer Lake Worth, which could then take them to the small lakefront communities of Palm Beach and Hypoluxo.

The Celestial made two trips a day. Passengers paid 75 cents one way for a 30-minute train ride. In 1891 the line added a second passenger coach. It also owned three freight cars but never more than one engine and never a place to turn around. The train chugged forward to Juno, then backed up to Jupiter.

Service was poor, as were accommodations on the Indian River wharf and the Lake Worth docks. What kept the line in reasonably good favor was the personal popularity of its employees. Particularly well liked was Blus Rice, its jovial, chatty engineer.

Rice had a rare skill. He is said to have been able to toot "Dixie" on his train whistle, a remarkable feat, if he indeed did it, since the whistle had only one tone.

A mighty hunter, Rice "leased" his hunting dogs to passengers who alighted from the train along the right-of-way and hunted for awhile. They returned to the train later when the engineer tooted for them, perhaps whistling "Dixie."

Until 1893 the Celestial Railroad, the only game in town, was cruising along in solitary splendor. Juno had been named the county seat of Dade County, business was flourishing, and the town even had the only newspaper on the southeast coast of Florida, *The Tropical Sun.*

Then from the north a mighty force struck.

The Celestial was a primitive, down-home delight, blissfully tooting its way across palmetto scrub, carrying a car full of passengers and a couple of hound dogs for rent.

Henry Morrison Flagler saw the Lake Worth country as the American Riviera, the land where he would build his country's premier winter resort for the rich and famous. The hound dogs did not exactly fit that image.

The man who with John D. Rockefeller had created Standard Oil of Ohio wanted to buy the Celestial. Its owners, well aware of the vast fortune at Flagler's disposal, quoted an inflated price. He could have, of course, paid it, but he did not become one of America's richest men by allowing himself to be gouged.

HMF decided simply to bypass the Celestial and build his railroad to the west. Across Lake Worth from the little town of Palm Beach he would construct the terminus for his road. He had great plans for Palm Beach and he wasn't about to let the Celestial wreck them.

Instead he wrecked the Celestial. Too much competition plunged it into bankruptcy. In June, 1896, its rolling stock was sold at public auction in Jacksonville.

Another victim of the Flagler bypass was the town of Juno. It lost the Dade County seat to Miami and by the end of the 90s had become a ghost town.

Dora Doster Utz, of Jupiter, who played on the locomotive as a little girl, wrote years later about the end of the line:

"There was something sad about how quickly the little stops along the Celestial right-of-way were abandoned. The jungle and the underbrush were fast claiming the right-of-way and the sorrowful call of the mourning dove seemed to sound a requiem to its passing."

* * *

While the Celestial faithful were fending off fleas from hound dogs, rail passengers farther north were luxuriating in the comfort of Pullman Palace

Cars, and for the truly wealthy the ultimate travel experience had become available—the private car.

These privately owned cars, the domain of the Vanderbilts, the Rockefellers and the Flaglers, were hauled by various railroads, depending on where the owner wanted to go. For the short haul from Jacksonville to Palm Beach, the Florida East Coast Railway in Flagler's day charged $342, a little over $9,000 by today's standards.

Flagler's car, the Rambler, was built in 1886. Some 60 feet in length, it contained his master suite, a double bed and bathroom; a sitting and dining area, with seats that could be folded down as beds for four, and a kitchen. The Rambler was furnished with gilded wicker chairs, desks, fold-down tables, oak cupboards and marble sinks.

Private cars built in the 1890s were roughly 90 feet in length and decidedly more luxurious. Flagler's second car, Alicia, Car 90, had stained glass window panels and carved mahogany and satinwood woodwork.

The Rambler led him into the railroad business. When traveling to St. Augustine, his winter home, he had to leave his luxurious private car in Jacksonville, take a ferryboat across the St. Johns River, then ride a dinky narrow-gauge railway, the Jacksonville, St. Augustine and Halifax River Railroad, to the ancient city.

When he decided to build a luxury hotel, the Ponce de Leon, he realized that his natural prey, the owners of private cars, wouldn't put up with shoddy transportation. He solved the problem by buying the JSA & HR, converting it to standard gauge and building a bridge over the mighty St. Johns despite the misgivings of his engineers who were somewhat cowed by the depth of the river—90 feet in one area.

Flagler's restless, energetic nature needed new challenges. He found them in the hotel and railroad business. And like any good railroader, he soon was building up a head of steam. He bought small rail lines to Tocoi and East Palatka on the St. Johns and then a logging road to Daytona. He promptly converted them to standard gauge.

Just north of Daytona he acquired a small hotel, rebuilt it, added an 18-hole golf course and named his resort the Ormond Beach Hotel. It was so popular with the affluent that by 1890 Pullman cars filled with guests were flocking to the Ormond.

To the south, agricultural lands were opening up and Flagler saw an opportunity to haul citrus and winter vegetables from Florida to the markets in the north. Below Daytona he had to build new railroads, for which the state of Florida gave him 8,000 acres of land for each mile he added, a powerful inducement. He moved down to Titusville, then on to Rockledge on the western banks of the Indian River.

In 1893 he made a momentous decision. He committed himself to extending his railroad all the way to Lake Worth. There on a small barrier island called Palm Beach he would develop the most exclusive winter resort in the western hemisphere. The rich and famous would flock to his American Riviera, warmed by the tropical winds that rustled through the dense stands of the island's coconut palms.

On the west side of the lake he would lay out a town for the working stiffs who would build Palm Beach and work in his hotels and restaurants. He would call it Westpalmbeach, later opened up into three words.

Flagler saw the private cars of the Vanderbilts, Rockefellers and the Whitneys arriving at West Palm, bringing with them the cream of American society. They would stay at a great hotel he would build.

The man not only thought big, but delivered big. In February, 1894, HMF brought his Florida East Coast Railway into West Palm Beach and that same month opened the world's largest resort hotel, the Royal Poinciana. It could accommodate as many as 1,200 guests, at rates which ran as high as $100 a day, American plan, the equivalent of more than $2500 these days. Its dining room could seat 1,600 people. The Poinciana provided jobs for 1,400 employees.

Two years later the FEC reached a little trading post settlement called Fort Lauderdale and kept going to the Miami River, where the city of Miami would bloom. Along the route small farming towns sprang up—Boynton Beach, Linton, Boca Raton, Deerfield and Pompano—and ethnic colonies, the Japanese Yamato, Danish Dania and Swedish Hallandale.

In 1903, when he was 73, he made a decision so bold that only a man who was both old and rich could have made it. Many had dreamed of reaching the island port of Key West with a railroad, but the engineering obstacles were too great. Henry Plant had chosen to reach the island city by steamships, connecting to his railroad in Tampa.

Flagler authorized his chief engineer, William J. Krome, to analyze two possible routes, one from Homestead to Cape Sable and across Florida Bay to Key West, the other down through the string of coral islands known as the Florida Keys. The engineers recommended the Keys route.

The tycoon studied the reports, consulted with his people, then gave the order: "Go ahead. Go to Key West."

Flagler would later call it the toughest job he ever undertook: 156 miles of railroad reaching out into the Atlantic, hopping from island to island across deep, swift-flowing channels. Its cost was enormous, roughly a billion in today's dollars, seven years of Flagler's life, the toil and sweat of 20,000 laborers and a death toll in the hundreds.

Workers on Long Key pitched their tents beside the rails they laid during construction of Henry Flagler's railroad to Key West. (Historical Association of Southern Florida)

A Flagler train steams across the viaduct at Long Key. (Historical Association of Southern Florida)

At 10:43 a.m. January 22, 1912, Flagler and his wife Mary Lily arrived in Key West in Car 90. Ten thousand adults and a thousand children greeted him.

"Now I can die happy. My dream is fulfilled."

Later he was serenaded by a group of school children. In his moment of glory, the old campaigner's eyes filled with tears. "I can hear the children, but I cannot see them." Nearly blind now, Flagler was 82. A year later he was dead.

* * *

More than a decade after Flagler's death, southeast Florida welcomed its second railroad, the Seaboard. President S. Davies Warfield established an operating headquarters in Indiantown in 1926. From there the uncle of Wallis Warfield, who would become the Duchess of Windsor, proceeded to push his tracks on down to boomtime Miami.

The trouble was, the boom was dying.

The Seaboard, already committed, completed its construction and prepared for a large celebration in January of 1927. The Orange Blossom Special, carrying an assortment of Roosevelts, the Ringling Brothers, a du Pont, the architect Addison Mizner and the noted gambler Colonel E. R. Bradley, arrived in Fort Lauderdale on January 8. They were greeted by Mayor Jack Tidball but the welcome was a pallid one indeed when compared with what awaited them in the suburbs of Miami.

The famed aviation pioneer, Glenn Curtiss, had developed a new town which he called Opa-locka, a Seminole word; but Opa-locka was not a Seminole town. Inspired by The Arabian Nights, the town sported mosques, minarets, domes and arches and bore such street names as Aladdin, Ali Baba and Sinbad. Arabs on white horses and Oriental dancing girls greeted a dazed Warfield.

The Seaboard's day of glory was short-lived. The Florida land boom was already dead and soon the Great Depression would spread across the land. Both the Seaboard and Flagler's FEC would go into receivership. They would, however, recover and for many years would continue to transport sunshine-seeking tourists, citrus and winter vegetables, always to the sound of their beautiful, lonesome whistles in the night.

The wonderful old steam engines, so beloved by railroad buffs, would give way in the 1950s to honking diesel and a little later to the dish-rattling roar of jet planes overhead.

The great railroad era is gone in Florida, but many of the men who made it happen are still remembered in place names around the state. Florida has a Flagler County and a Flagler Beach, a Plant City, a Sanford and a Chipley. David Levy Yulee is remembered through the town of Yulee and the county of Levy. Indiantown honors the Duchess's uncle through a Warfield Boulevard and a Warfield Elementary School.

Is anything named after Albert "120 miles an hour" Hodge?

CHAPTER 27

Wings over Florida

State's pioneer flyers logged many hours and achievements

Five years had passed since Orville Wright's first flight at Kitty Hawk, and still no aircraft had violated Florida's blue virgin skies.

So the mayor of the little cow town of Kissimmee could be forgiven for thinking that his city attorney, P. A. Vans Agnew, was just joking when he said he was working on a new law that would restrict flights over Kissimmee. Sure, the mayor agreed, tongue in cheek, Kissimmee certainly needed a law to protect its precious air space from daredevil aviators!

So when, on July 17, 1908, Mayor T. M. Murphy opened the *Kissimmee Valley Gazette* he was startled to read the headline, AIRSHIP ORDINANCE SUGGESTED.

Vans Agnew's ordinance called for the regulation of any "flying machine or airship" traveling "upon any street or alley of the town within 10 feet of the surface" upward to a height of "20 miles in the sky."

Annual license fees were proposed: Helicopters, $150; airplanes, $100; dirigibles, $50. The ordinance would make it illegal to drop anything from air machines while over the town or to collide with telephone poles or public buildings.

Penalties would be severe: "Five hundred dollars or . . . imprisonment in the town calaboose for not more than 90 days."

For the next few days Mayor Murphy's life was made miserable as everyone razzed him about his new law. The joshing became so great that the mayor talked about moving to California.

But a few weeks later, as news of the little town's ordinance spread, Murphy suddenly found himself being hailed as a visionary with an uncanny grasp of the future. Letters poured in from all over the country and even from Europe. Editorials in the nation's newspapers wrote glowingly of Kissimmee as a "progressive and farsighted little city."

The U.S. War Department wrote for a copy of Kissimmee's air-space law.

And even great cities, such as London, Paris, Berlin and Amsterdam modeled their air-space regulations on the cow town's ordinance.

There was just one catch: The city council never passed the law.

Whether it was all a hoax, as some charged, or just "whimsical" good fun as Vans Agnew later admitted, the air-space ordinance thrust Florida into the "Air Age."

Just a few years later, the skies over the state would be filled with airplanes, and, in time, with helicopters and jets. Major international airports and airlines would sprout up, taking passengers nonstop to and from Europe, the Caribbean and Latin America. Florida aviation would produce memorable achievements and failures, and a few mysteries that remain unsolved to this day.

* * *

On New Year's morning, 1914, thousands of people lined the pier at the St. Petersburg yacht basin. They were staring at a huge boat with wings that was floating in the bay. It had arrived in pieces the day before by train from its manufacturer, Ted Benoist of St. Louis. Head mechanic Jay Dee Smith and chief pilot Tony Jannus had assembled it in less than an hour.

Now the crowd was about to witness the world's first scheduled commercial flight, an 18-mile trip from St. Petersburg to Tampa via the St. Petersburg-Tampa Airboat Line. The honor of riding beside Jannus in the two-seat flying craft was determined by auction. Former St. Petersburg mayor A. C. Pheil put in the winning bid of $400.

At 10:30 that morning, Jannus started the 75-horsepower motor and taxied across Tampa Bay. Slowly, the unusual vehicle rose into the air. Jannus flew it at an altitude of 50 feet at speeds between 50 and 60 miles per hour. When he saw 3,500 people waiting to greet the plane in Tampa, he took it up to 150 feet. The 18-mile trip took just over 23 minutes.

The return flight to St. Petersburg brought only $175 at auction, and thereafter the airfare for a one-way flight was $5.

During the three months of its existence, the world's first airline racked up its share of records: first passenger flight, first airfreight shipment and first female passenger—a Mae Peabody of Dubuque, Iowa.

Jannus, the world's first licensed pilot, later flew for the czar of Russia during World War I. But flying in those daredevil days was a dangerous game, and Jannus died in a crash over the Black Sea.

* * *

Pan American Airways, the first U.S. international air carrier, got its start in Key West.

Pilot Tony Jannus, at left, poses for world's first commercial flight—from St. Petersburg to Tampa in 1914. (Florida State Archives)

Juan Terry Trippe was a bright young Wall Street broker blessed with excellent connections from his days at Yale. But he found Wall Street a dull place and decided that the newfangled aviation industry promised much more excitement, as well as the opportunity for a potentially profitable business venture. Carrying the mail for the U.S. Post Office would be one of the keys to a successful airline, Trippe decided. Through a Yale connection, Trippe gained exclusive rights to fly mail to Cuba.

There was one catch: He had to have a plane ready to fly the mail from Key West to Havana by October 19, 1927, or forget the contract and a $25,000 bond he had posted with the U.S. government.

The Key West airstrip he had leased was not ready for his new Fokker F-7 to land or take off. His only alternative was acquiring a seaplane. After numerous phone calls, he finally located a Fairchild FC-2 under repair in Miami.

Trippe talked the owners into letting him charter the seaplane for $175 for just one mail run. So, a few minutes before sunset on October 18, pilot Cy Caldwell flew into Key West. Early the next morning the Florida East Coast Railway's Havana Special arrived with seven mail bags containing some 30,000 letters. The mail was delivered by truck to a wharf, then by Coast Guard cutter to the plane.

At 8 p.m. Caldwell took off for Cuba. An hour and 20 minutes later he landed in Havana Harbor near Morro Castle. The postmaster rowed out to

Pan American Airways flights from Miami opened up the Caribbean and South America. (Historical Association of Southern Florida)

pick up the mail. With that delivery, Pan American became the first U.S. international air carrier.

A week later the Key West landing strip was completed. On January 16, 1928, Pan Am began regular passenger service and the following September moved its base from Key West to Miami. From there the company extended its routes throughout the Caribbean and down the Atlantic coast of South America. By the late 1940s it was the world's largest airline.

Pan Am's Clippers, the mighty Sikorsky and Martin seaplanes that flew across the seas to South America, were based at Dinner Key in Coconut Grove. Biscayne Bay was their landing strip. The Clippers' fame spread even further thanks to the 1933 musical *Flying Down to Rio*. In time, of course, the movie became better known for the first-time pairing of dancing greats Fred Astaire and Ginger Rogers than for its spectacular aerial scenes.

* * *

Long before Pan Am's Clippers were flying to South America, A. B. "Pappy" Chalk's seaplanes were buzzing the Miami area. In 1919 Chalk

A.B. "Pappy" Chalk started his seaplane operation in 1919 with service between Miami and the Bahamas. (Historical Association of Southern Florida)

opened the Red Arrow Flying Service at Elser's Pier, near what is now Miami's Bayfront Park. It would become Chalk's Flying Service, then Chalk's International Airline. Later the property of Merv Griffin's Resorts International, Chalk's laid claim to the title of "the world's oldest airline." The claim is a little shaky because KLM Royal Dutch Airlines and Avianca of Colombia were founded about the same time.

Over the years Chalk's has primarily served Miami and the Bahamas, particularly Bimini. One of the airline's regular passengers was a noted fisherman who also liked to write novels—Ernest Hemingway.

In August 1933, Chalk was asked to stand by in Cuba in case Gerardo Machado, president of the tottering government, should have to flee. Machado eventually made his escape from Havana by boat and headed for the Bahamas. When he arrived in Nassau, Pappy Chalk picked him up and flew him to exile in Miami. The manifest of the flight, dated August 24, 1933 read simply: "G. Machado. Age 61. Occupation, retired."

* * *

Eastern Airlines also traces its roots to Miami. In 1928 a biplane piloted by Fritz Schwaemmle took off from a dirt airstrip west of downtown and headed for Jacksonville, carrying a small bag of mail. The carrier, Pitcairn Aviation, was the predecessor of the giant airline that would establish its operating headquarters in Miami in 1935. By that time the carrier had emerged as Eastern Airlines, headed by Capt. Eddie Rickenbacker, America's leading ace in World War I.

However, Eastern's most famous pilot was Captain Dick Merrill. In 48 years he logged eight million miles and 36,500 hours. Merrill was the first man to fly round-trip across the Atlantic, using a plane whose wings and rear fuselage were packed with pingpong balls. If the plane was forced down into the Atlantic, the ping-pong balls supposedly would provide enough buoyancy to keep it afloat.

When it comes to tales of aviation, south Florida has never lacked for mysteries. Amelia Earhart's ill-fated plan to fly around the world in 1937 started from Miami. On June 1, the first woman to fly solo across the Atlantic took off from Miami Municipal Airport in a Lockheed Electra with Captain Frederick Noonan as her co-pilot. Their proposed 27,000-mile flight was the first attempt ever made to circle the globe at the middle latitudes.

Their last radio message on July 2 stated that the plane was over the Pacific, that their position was in doubt and their fuel supply was dwindling. For 16 days, more than 100 Navy planes and 10 ships searched the area east of Howland Island before giving up. The plane's disappearance inspired countless books and articles and a movie starring Rosalind Russell. But all attempts to solve the mystery were futile.

Six years later an even bigger mystery unfolded at the Fort Lauderdale Naval Air Station, now better known as Fort Lauderdale-Hollywood International Airport. On December 5, 1945, three months after the end of World War II, five Navy TBM Avengers with 15 men on board took off on a training mission. The final message from flight leader Lt. Charles Taylor, from the vicinity of the Florida Keys, was: "We seem to be off course."

No trace of the five planes was ever found. A Martin PBM rescue plane with 13 aboard was sent from a naval base in Melbourne to search for them, and it too disappeared.

These mysterious events became the foundation for the legend of the Bermuda Triangle, sometimes called the Devil's Triangle, an area defined by three points: Bermuda, Puerto Rico and the Fort Lauderdale-Miami area. As was the case with Amelia Earhart, the Bermuda Triangle has spun off a cottage industry of books, articles and films, attributing the tragedies to magnetic fields and other natural or unnatural forces—even the Devil himself.

More than 80 years ago the mayor and the town of Kissimmee joked about the coming "Air Age." Had they known the changes it would bring to Florida, they might have laughed even harder.

CHAPTER 28

Who Invented the Airboat?

Was it a good ol' boy frog hunter or wealthy aviation manufacturer?

The Everglades frog hunter works at night in the cold and the wet, searching endlessly across a vast river of grass for a very small animal. When he finds him, he fixes the bullfrog in the beam of his small headlamp, then pierces his prey with a quick jab from his sharp frog gig.

Johnny Lamb was averaging 75 pounds of frog legs a night but it was a tough way to make a living in Depression-plagued Florida. Getting around the Glades was the problem. Too big and too wet for walking, too shallow for powered boating.

Over a midnight cup of coffee at a campsite called Chicago Island, west of Lake Worth, Lamb and his buddy, Russell Howard, were grousing about their problems. Poling a flat-bottomed boat was hard going. Trying to use an outboard motor was even worse. Weeds and muck clogged up propellers and cooling systems.

"How about a wind machine on the stern, not in the water?" mused Howard. If a propeller worked for an airplane, why not for a shallow-draft boat?

Later, probably sometime in 1933, they put together a 12-foot flat-bottomed boat, a 75-horsepower Star automotive engine, a secondhand aircraft propellor, a plywood rudder and an auto steering wheel. Part fish, part bird, part boat, part airplane: that was the airboat. Lamb called it "a Rube Goldberg contraption." They went on from there to refine their invention into a vehicle that gave them a big edge over the other frog hunters. They decided not to go through the red tape and expense of getting a patent for their airboat.

"We figured we'd be the only ones that would ever need one," recalled Lamb.

They were wrong. Other froggers wasted no time in building their own versions of what some called a "Whooshmobile," at least one with tragic results.

In a 1960 report, Frank J. Ligas, a Florida Game and Fresh Water Fish Commission biologist, reported:

"About 1935 Mr. Willard Yates was the first man known to use an airplane engine . . . a 65 h.p. engine. The airboat was still steered by ropes attached to the rudder like reins on a horse." Yates' engine was so powerful it caused his death. Engine supports came loose, and the whirling propellor blade mutilated him.

The Lamb/Howard airboat proved the sire from which mainstream airboats descended. Today more than 3,000 of them "whoosh" through the marshes and wetlands of Florida. They are used for sightseeing, hunting, fishing, law enforcement, weed control, even warfare. Airboats built in Palm Beach County were used in Vietnam.

Gladesmen take pride in their airboats. Many assemble the boats themselves, bolting and welding hulls, engines and propellors together, resourcefully cutting corners by tracking down used motors and props to keep their costs down. When boats break down deep in the Everglades, airboaters repair them on the spot. They have to; the Glades, a million acres of mosquitos, sawgrass, maidencane and small tree islands called hammocks, suffers a shortage of full-service garages.

One reason for the Gladesmen's pride in their boats is the deeply held belief that the airboat is peculiarly their thing, a gritty, common-sense, down-to-earth-and-water contraption born of Depression necessity. And it was invented by one of their own. Or was it?

Before World War I a giant of American aviation, Glenn Curtiss, had come to Miami for the winter. A speedster who once held the world's motorcycle speed record of 137 mph, Curtiss was a designer and inventor of international stature. In 1919 a Navy-Curtiss flying boat made the first flight across the Atlantic.

Curtiss loved to hunt in the Florida backwoods, usually with bow and arrow. As frog hunters knew, and Curtiss discovered, getting around in the Everglades was no easy matter.

Curtiss designed, probably on a tablecloth, a shallow-draft motorboat powered by an aircraft engine connected to an aero propellor mounted on the stern. Unlike the struggling frog hunters, Curtiss could afford the best of everything. By the end of World War I he was worth $32 million.

His boat was enclosed so that a half-dozen people could ride comfortably, protected from the wind. It bore no resemblance to the open-cockpit, bare-bones boat of the frog hunters.

Curtiss called his airboat *Scooter*. With it he could reach 50 mph. through

Glenn Curtiss's *Scooter,* the first airboat, was photographed in 1920 in Miami. (Historical Association of Southern Florida)

the grassy waters of the Glades. Later he designed a smaller airboat capable of 70 mph.

Curtiss engaged one of Miami's most talented photographers, Claude Matlack, to photograph this strange new craft. After Matlack's death the Historical Association of Southern Florida received a collection of 10,000 of his photos.

One of these shows *Scooter* being towed by another boat, apparently in Biscayne Bay. On the back of the picture Matlack had written the date: March 5, 1920.

Since the date of the Lamb/Howard airboat is placed at 1933 by a Florida Game and Fresh Water Fish Commision report, it appears that Curtiss was first with an airboat by at least 13 years. Like Lamb and Howard he did not follow up commercially with his new creation, concentrating instead on aviation and a new enthusiasm, land and community development.

Not long after he built the first airboat, Curtiss was swept up in the Florida Land Boom of the 1920s. He developed the cities of Hialeah and Miami Springs, then followed with the bizarre Arabian Nights community of Opa-locka.

Lieutenant Jimmy Sistrunk, a law enforcement officer with the Game and Fish Commission, once estimated that there are probably about 50 small companies manufacturing airboats in South Florida. Gladesmen swear by their airboats, conservationists swear at them. Many environmentalists feel that the roar of an airboat disrupts the world of the Everglades' rich and varied wildlife, particularly nesting birds. Airboats for the public are banned in Everglades National Park; they can be used only by park rangers.

"You can go a hundred in an airboat," says Lieutenant Sistrunk, "but any time you go past seventy you run the risk of being airborne."

CHAPTER 29

Alligator Alley

Cross-state highway cut through swamps, squabbles, insults

Nobody called it by its official, buttoned-down name, Everglades Parkway. To booster and blaster alike, it was simply "Alligator Alley."

Digging in against the turnpike mile after paved mile was the American Automobile Association's Peninsula Motor Club in Tampa. Even as late as 1968, when cars started rolling across its 78 nearly straight miles, AAA called on its members to boycott the two-lane toll road, labeled by the Associated Press "the most controversial road ever built in Florida." Other AAA epithets were much rougher, among them "killer road," "suicide lane," "tragic mistake," "gross abortion" and "throwback to horse-and-buggy days."

In addition to the automobile club, the road builders faced a varied gauntlet of obstacles—politicians, most of the state's daily newspapers, TV commentators, cottonmouth moccasins, gators, wild hogs, mosquitoes, sawgrass, swamp water, and soft, squishy, black muck.

In the mid-1970s the Alley was plagued with dive-bombing buzzards who crashed through the windshields of nine cars and trucks in an unexplained and ultimately self-defeating exercise. Even the Alley's name, gleefully adopted later by the State Road Department, was meant originally as a withering insult.

"Swamp pike," chairman Marvin Holloway called the proposed road at a 1963 meeting with AAA aides. One aide chimed in with "Alligator Lane" to describe the proposed road through the Everglades and the Big Cypress Swamp.

It took a skilled wordsmith like Hampton Dunn to come up with just the right phrase. Dunn, Peninsula public relations director at the time and later the prolific author of some 20 books on Florida history, called it "Alligator Alley."

And Alligator Alley it became.

Today the Alley has beem swallowed up by the interstate system and is now just a brief interval on I-75, which rambles nearly 1,500 miles from Miami to the Canadian border. Four-laning the Alley was the last stage of I-75, the last of Florida's primary interstates.

Hampton Dunn can rightly claim a measure of fame as the "father of Alligator Alley"—the name, that is, not the road. That honor, if that is the right word, belongs to a crusty old curmudgeon named Guy Stovall.

As early as 1941 Stovall was talking up a road across the central Everglades. At the south end of the Glades the Tamiami Trail, built in the late 1920s, connected Miami and Tampa via Naples and Fort Myers. At the northern end of the River of Grass a state highway, now known as State Road 80, extended from West Palm Beach to Fort Myers, just south of Lake Okeechobee.

In the early 1940s spending millions in public money to connect Fort Lauderdale (population, roughly 18,000) with Naples (less than 1,000 residents) seemed a case of overkill. What Stovall wanted was simply to open up the Everglades. Close to the Seminoles, who lived there, he had been dubbed Florida's "Ambassador of the Everglades" by Governor John Martin in the 1920s.

Something of a buzzsaw, Stovall kept doggedly after his favorite projects. Blustery and impatient with petty details, Stovall cut through to the heart of the matter. He had long ago learned that a case of whiskey was a natural enemy of red tape.

His background was a strange mixture. A native of Georgia, he had managed a power plant and had served as a small town police chief. He had worked to promote a privately owned toll road along the eastern shore of Lake Okeechobee and a well-paid baseball team at Okeechobee City. He had published and edited a weekly newspaper in Pahokee.

In his later years he worked as a right-of-way agent for the State Road Department (SRD). There he won renown for his relentless promotion of welcome stations and wayside parks to relieve the tedium of long drives. The Florida Legislature proclaimed him "Father of Florida's Wayside Parks." His favorite was the wayside park at Bahia Honda in the Florida Keys. After his retirement, Stovall, who lived in Hollywood, had even more time to push his projects.

In 1961 Big John Monahan, of Fort Lauderdale, State Road Board member for the nine-county southeastern district, was invited to attend a joint meeting of the Naples City and Collier County Commissions. Big John, six feet two, 235 pounds, had made a goodly amount of money in the laundry business and in banking. He was appointed to the State Road Board by Governor Farris Bryant after serving earlier on the Florida Turnpike Authority.

"I knew something was up as soon as I walked in," he said. "Guy Stovall was there. He was a nice guy but he could sure be a real pain in the neck."

Stovall showed the commissioners a map with a road drawn across the Everglades to the Fort Lauderdale area. It would extend through just two counties—Collier and Broward. He asked Monahan if the SRD would back the road.

"Dade County would hang me," said Monahan. "This road would take all the district's primary road money. For just two counties."

An objection this mild would hardly slow down Guy Stovall. Monahan pondered, then added:

"It would have to be a toll road."

Broward and Collier Counties voted funds for traffic and revenue and engineering feasibility studies. The studies concluded that a two-lane road could be built for roughly $15 million and paid for with tolls.

By now Monahan was ready to run with the road. Big John was known as a man who got things done. Born in Polk County, he had to drop out of school in the sixth grade following the death of his Irish-born father. He moved then to South Florida where he launched a highly successful business career.

But seeing it through wouldn't be all that simple even for a bulldozer of a man like Monahan. Standing in the way would be a statewide firestorm of protest.

Every major daily newspaper in the state attacked it—with one exception. *The Naples Daily News* saw its home base benefitting from the road across the Glades.

By contrast, the *Fort Lauderdale News,* at the eastern end of the highway, opposed it even though Monahan contended it would be a big boost for Port Everglades and the Fort Lauderdale/Hollywood International Airport as well as the Farmers Market in Pompano Beach.

"Who in their right mind, we might ask," wrote Jack W. Gore in a *News* editorial, "would willingly pay $1.50 for the privilege of risking his neck on an arrow-straight, two-lane, high-speed highway bordered on both sides by deep canals?"

The heaviest attack came from the Peninsula Motor Club. Triple A opposes all toll roads but this clash went much deeper.

"The AAA believes," Dunn declared at a Rotary Club meeting, "that this project should be killed before it kills Florida motorists, if for no other reason. Besides the drag-racer threat, there are other hazards. It's supposed to be a 'limited access' facility—the superhighway type. But we find in the engineering report that in Collier County at-grade intersection will be permitted at every mile on the speedway."

Another possible problem alarmed AAA. Rep. William Cramer, a Congressman from the Tampa Bay area, warned that the project would "kill for an indefinite period" the extension of I-75 down the state's west coast and on into Miami. This brought out more dissenters—*The Miami Herald, The Miami News,* Channel 7 and the City of Miami, which was pushing for the extension of I-75 from the Florida west coast to Miami.

The safety of a high-speed, two-lane road in an era of multiple-lane parkways was the biggest concern. The risk of head-on collisions joined with deep roadside canals to create terrifying visions of a killer highway.

If the project had been proposed a few years later, environmentalists would also have joined in the attack. But in 1963 a ribbon of asphalt through one of Florida's richest wildlife areas attracted little reaction from conservation interests.

Through the roar of dissent Governor Bryant was hearing a few pro-toll road voices. Monahan pushed it as did many politicos in Broward and Collier Counties. No longer the small town of pre-war days, Fort Lauderdale now boasted some 85,000 residents. Adjacent Hollywood was pushing toward 40,000. Naples was closing in on the 5,000 mark.

In addition, the Seminoles and the Miccosukees, who wanted better access to their domain, had agreed to donate the right-of-way through their ancestral lands.

AAA charged that Gulf American Land Company, of Miami, reportedly the world's largest land development company, was behind the road. The highway would clearly open up Gulf American's Collier County developments, Golden Gate Estates and Remuda Ranch Grants. Monahan denied it.

On September 20, 1963, the six-man State Road Board meeting in Tallahassee unanimously approved the road with little public discussion. Approval came so quickly—in just two minutes, some accounts said—that *The Miami News* dubbed the road the "Chickee Quickee." A *News* cartoon by Don Wright depicted the State Road Department as a roadrunner which had laid an egg from which emerged a skunk.

Triple A had one more card to play. The City of Miami had joined the auto club in a Circuit Court lawsuit to block the validation of the $17 million bond issue needed to fund the road.

A key weapon to winning the case could well be a secret trust which owned Naples acreage near the road's western terminus. A report had reached AAA that Monahan was a member of the trust, a clear case of conflict of interest—if true.

Banker Edwin McDonald, trust officer of the First National Bank and Trust of Fort Lauderdale, was subpoenaed to the court hearing in Tallahassee to reveal the names of the land-owners.

Alligator Alley received a big boost from a supportive state highway sign. (Associated Press)

AAA attorney B. J. Masterson decided against asking McDonald to read the names aloud. A look at the trust officer's deposition revealed not the name of John H. Monahan of Fort Lauderdale but of another Irishman, Dr. John R. Mahoney of Fort Lauderdale.

"After the hearing I got in the elevator with the Triple A people," recalled Monahan. "I told them what I thought of their conflict of interest. I used some real bad words."

The validation was authorized first by the Circuit Court and then after appeal by the Florida Supreme Court in May, 1964.

Work on the toll road began in October, 1964. What a task lay ahead! The highway would have to be built through what was basically a freshwater marsh and a cypress swamp. The scarcest commodity along its path was dry land. Draglines would have to dredge deep canals for fill. Truckloads of dynamite would be needed to blast out stubborn rock.

To make matters worse, much of the land that lay beneath the shallow waters of the Glades was soft black muck, impossible to build on. By May of

1965 the state learned that the job of digging out the muck would cost an extra $1 million above the original cost estimates.

The first contract sent a work crew west from Andytown to the Collier County line. Workers, traveling in airboats, had to carry snakebite kits. Luckily only one man was bitten, a dragline operator who was rushed to a hospital via a swamp buggy.

Neither snakes nor gators proved to be the workers' toughest problem. Water, water everywhere was the real nightmare. An anonymous construction worker left behind a prayer in an Alley outhouse:

"Please, Lord, I've been a good man. So if I get cottonmouth bit, or attacked by some of Oscar the Alligator's brothers, and if I get to that Big Job in the Sky, oh, please, Lord, let it be on dry land. Amen!"

Work crews from Collier County used swamp buggies to slog through the Big Cypress Swamp. Poachers found it a dandy alley to the home of the gator.

Meanwhile, the Seminole Tribe of Florida honored Stovall for his 45 years of friendship to the Indians. The tribe gave him the title Chief Halpattah—Chief Alligator.

Stovall, in turn, gave the Seminoles a 10-foot mounted alligator which he had named Big John, in honor of Monahan. A thorough man, Stovall even designed a souvenir license plate for the Alley, featuring a gator named Big John.

Along the way the State Road Board decided it liked hearing its highway insulted. The phrase Alligator Alley had put the road on the map. In August, 1966, the board, at a breakfast meeting with the Collier County Commission in Naples, voted to change its name from Everglades Parkway, Monahan's original choice, to Alligator Alley. An insult had turned into a compliment.

Someone even suggested that giant alligators be manufactured to form arches at each entrance to Alligator Alley.

Finally on January 15, 1969, a little over four years after start-up, Alligator Alley was completed. John Easterlin, Broward County commissioner, became the first motorist to drive through the toll booth at Andytown at the eastern entrance to the Alley. He paid 75 cents, then had to pay another 75 cents to get off the toll road.

A full trip across the Alley, from Andytown to Naples, cost a motorist $1.50 then, just as it does today. Many drivers welcomed the faster trip across the Glades. Others were delighted at the view it gave them of the Everglades, the gators in the canals beside the road and the large wading birds seen in the winter in vast numbers.

Others were less pleased. Many complained that the monotonously straight drive bored them, lulling them into a dangerous stupor. Ahead lay the fear of a head-on collision.

Guy Stovall pats Big John, the symbol of Alligator Alley. (Fort Lauderdale Historical Society)

How dangerous did it prove to be? A 1974 study by the International Bridge, Tunnel and Turnpike Association declared it one of the safest toll roads in the country, based on figures for 1973, when 36 accidents resulted in two fatalities.

Four years later, however, the Florida Department of Transportation, which superseded the State Road Board, ranked it the most dangerous road in Broward County. Impatient drivers pulling out recklessly to pass slow-moving cars too often collided with oncoming autos at high turnpike speeds.

The worst such accident occurred on a Sunday in June, 1989. A pickup truck and a car filled with a mother and her children brought death to eight people in one crash.

"It's proven to be one of the most dangerous roads in south Florida," said state trooper Chris Hickel in the summer of 1992. He had worked on the Alley for a decade.

Looking ahead to the future, the original Alley-builders had acquired extra right-of-way for eventual four-laning. In 1986 building the new lanes began after the decision to fold the Alley into I-75. In contrast to the $17 million cost of the original Alley the price tag for the new lanes, which took three years longer to build, ran to $189 million when completed in 1993.

The bond issue for Alligator Alley was paid off in fiscal 1983–84, years ahead of its original payback date of 1991. The tolls, however, remained in place to repay DOT for maintenance expenses in previous years and also to fund panther-crossing tunnels underneath the highway. At $21 million, the wildlife mitigation program, as it is called, cost more than building the original road.

None of these problems any longer concern Stovall. He died in 1971 at 84. Two years later the Guy Stovall Wayside Park was dedicated on the north side of the Alley in Collier County.

Now the Guy Stovall Wayside Park is gone, swept away in the Alley's conversion to I-75.

Big John Monahan fared better. A bridge over the Okeechobee Waterway at Indiantown still bears his name. Retired, he lives now at Lakeport on the northwest side of Lake Okeechobee, where his toughest opponent is the largemouth bass.

VISIONARIES

Florida has long been a haven for dreamers of great dreams. A gentle, Utopian Koresh came to Florida a century before a bloodthirsty one came to Waco, Texas. The Sunshine State attracted a scientist whose discovery changed the world. And in the cypress swamps of Collier County a flock of visionaries banded together, one with a martini in her hand, to create a sanctuary for woodstorks.

CHAPTER 30

Koresh

Cyrus Teed tried to built
a Utopia near Fort Myers

Like a religious leader who followed a century later, Dr. Cyrus Reed Teed called himself Koresh. Unlike the destructive prophet of Waco, Texas, Florida's Koresh envisioned a mellower version of the Promised Land.

Teed was a man with big ideas. He dreamed of building a city of 10 million people near Fort Myers. And he planned to do it with his new "scientific" view of a cellular universe which taught that people lived not on the surface of, but inside, a giant hollow cell called Earth. He also created a new church, incorporating many of the teachings of Christianity and Judaism, and anointed himself the "Seventh Messenger"—the prophet who would usher in the millenium.

Though his dreams died with him, substantial traces of Teed's vision of a new world remain at Koreshan State Park in Estero, a small town just south of Fort Myers. Many of the buildings that Teed and his followers built nearly a century ago have been preserved as part of the park.

In 1882 an old German named Gustave Damkohler homesteaded on the Estero River. He lived in a shack with his wife and four children, surrounded by mango, lime and orange trees. To make a living, he sold honey, oysters and fish from the teeming waters of Estero Bay to people in Fort Myers, a growing town to the north.

In time, Damkohler's wife and three of his children died, leaving behind a lonely man. But during the winter of 1894 Damkohler welcomed to his modest homestead a distinguished visitor from Chicago, an intense, square-jawed man with hypnotic eyes that "burned like live coals."

His visitor was Dr. Cyrus Reed Teed, who mesmerized Damkohler with wondrous tales of Koreshan, a religious community he had founded in Chicago. But Teed explained that Chicago was not the right location for this special community, while Estero seemed ideal.

The old immigrant, far from his native land, listened to glowing claims that the land along the Estero River would become the "greatest commercial thoroughfare of the world" and a distribution center for international commerce. Overwhelmed, Damkohler gave his beguiling visitor 300 acres on the river. Teed's commune, known as Koreshan Unity, then bought an adjoining 1,000 acres, and Teed announced to his followers that his city, to be called New Jerusalem, would rise on the banks of the Estero River.

"It will contain 10 million people, white and black, and will become the greatest city in the world," Teed wrote. Streets would be 300 yards wide. He would allow "no bawdy houses, no tobacco shops, no distilleries, no breweries, no gambling houses, nor other forms or dens of vice."

Electrical wires would be installed underground so as not to mar the beauty of the city. A conveyor belt would transport waste products to a location 40 miles from New Jerusalem, where they would be reduced to fertilizer and returned to the soil.

"There will be no dumping of the public waste into the rivers, bays and gulfs," Teed proclaimed.

Within weeks of his announcement, devoted followers began to arrive in Estero, and construction began on a dining hall, dormitories and print shop. Gardens and fruit groves were planted.

His was not a revolutionary idea. During the 19th century many "utopian" communal colonies sprang up in the United States, including the Shaker communities, the Oneida community in New York State, and Robert Owen's experiment in New Harmony, Indiana.

Cyrus Reed Teed was born on October 18, 1839, to a Baptist family in Teedville, New York. He grew up to be a doctor, specializing in root and herb medical cures. His probing, doubting mind challenged the Bible, the Copernican concept of the universe and the competitive principles of capitalism.

One night in 1870 he experienced an "illumination." While meditating in his laboratory in Utica, New York, he was visited by an angel dressed in a gown of purple and gold who had "long, golden tresses of profusely luxuriant growth over her shoulders."

The angel revealed to Teed the secrets of the cellular universe and explained what his role in its realm should be. He renamed himself Koresh, the Biblical word for Cyrus.

Koresh's efforts to attract followers were unproductive until 1886, when he addressed the National Association for Mental Sciences in Chicago. His words electrified his audience, and the association unanimously elected Koresh president, giving him a free hand in shaping the future of the organization. That organization came to be known as Koreshan Unity.

Museum model depicts Koresh's belief that we live inside the Earth. (Florida State Archives)

Newspapers in Chicago took a skeptical view of Koresh, suggesting that this "smooth-shaven man whose brown, restless eyes glow and burn like live coals" had an unduly strong attraction to women. Of the 110 followers living at the community's home in Chicago, three-fourths were women.

There's no question that part of Koresh's appeal was personal magnetism. Part may also have been due to his characterization of God as a woman whom he often referred to as "the Goddess." Actually he believed God was male and female combined in one entity.

Koresh taught that the Goddess, the source of all spiritual life, had already sent six messengers to Earth: Adam, Enoch, Noah, Moses, Elijah and Jesus. The arrival of the seventh would usher in the millennium. The seventh messenger, of course, would be Koresh himself.

The constant criticism by Chicago newspapers led Koresh to seek a new home for his community. The location for Koreshan Unity, he said, would be a point determined by "the bitellus of the alchemico-organic cosmos."

A glowing account from a Fort Myers real-estate man at the 1893 Chicago World's Fair led Koresh to Florida's southwest coast and to Gustave Damkohler's home in Estero. The old German was not the only one to make a major contribution to Koreshan. Members of the group who moved to

Florida turned over all their possessions and agreed to work on whatever projects were required by the community. Although Koresh's followers numbered some 4,000, only about 200 followed him to Estero. Many of those were educated, talented people who brought a variety of skills to the colony. Members built machine shops, a concrete works, a general store, a boat landing, and a bakery that produced 600 loaves a day.

The Koreshans also brought culture to a frontier world. They started the area's first school. At their Art Hall, which is still standing today, they produced plays and concerts and attended art exhibits and lectures. The Guiding Star Publishing Company printed the colony's publications, *The American Eagle* and *The Flaming Sword*. Members also had their own band and a baseball team.

The colony's governing council, called the Planetary Court, consisted of seven men and seven women. Koresh was the sun, and Annie Ordway, a Catholic from Boston renamed Victoria Gracia, was the moon.

Celibacy was required of members of the Planetary Court. Perhaps because of separate dormitories for men and women, a misconception persists to this day that the celibacy requirement extended to all residents of Koreshan. This was not so, according to Jo Bigelow, president of Koreshan Unity, for the simple reason that it would have threatened the colony's survival, as it did the Shaker communities.

Koresh himself had been married, until his wife died of tuberculosis. Paintings of early Florida by their son, Douglas Arthur Teed, a well-known artist, still decorate the walls of the Art Hall.

Koreshan parents had to renounce all rights to their children. Boys belonged to the Unity until they were 21, girls until they were 18. At that age they were allowed to decide for themselves whether they would stay in New Jerusalem or leave to lead a different life elsewhere.

In his book *Cellular Cosmogony*, Koresh presented his case for life on the inside. He believed that the Earth is a hollow sphere, encompassing the entire universe. A huge electro-magnet called the sun occupies the center of the universe, sending out positive energy to the walls of the Earth. The Copernican theory held that the universe was infinite; Koresh saw a universe that was finite and, thus, within the grasp of the human mind.

The Earth's surface, he contended, was concave, with a curvature of about eight inches to the mile. In 1897 Koresh and his staff developed an instrument called a rectilineator to prove his theory.

At 8:50 a.m. on March 18, near Gordon Pass in Naples, a dozen Koreshans began eight weeks of measurements. The results, Teed believed, proved his case. Nonbelievers were unimpressed.

Koresh and Victoria Gracia at Koreshan. (Florida State Archives)

In general, the Koreshans were well-mannered people who worked hard at getting along with their southwest Florida neighbors. But in time they learned that New Jerusalem was not the utopia that Koresh had promised.

Trouble began to brew in 1897. Where was New Jerusalem? Gustave Damkohler wanted to know. The old German had donated his land and had been promised a great city of 10 million people; instead, the settlement had drawn barely 250. Damkohler filed a lawsuit to reclaim his property. Koresh settled the dispute by returning some of Damkohler's land.

More serious trouble began when Koresh collided with Lee County's political structure. In 1904 he sought to incorporate a city of 75 square miles. Since Koreshans would be required to vote as a unit, any non-Koreshans living in New Jerusalem would in effect have no voice. They managed to block the incorporation by fanning resentment against the Koreshan Unity throughout the rest of the county.

An all-out political war began in 1906 when Koresh challenged the county's Democratic leadership by creating the Progressive Liberty Party. Fearing an attack on his life, he began to travel with burly bodyguards, but they were helpless in one incident.

In the November election, one of Koresh's candidates became involved in a shouting match. After Koresh arrived it quickly erupted into a street brawl.

A Fort Myers police officer beat Koresh severely and dragged the "prophet" off to jail.

Despite this setback, the Progressive Liberty Party did very well in the election. But there was no joy in New Jerusalem because the health of the Koreshans' 65-year-old leader had begun to fail, possibly due in part to the beating he had received. On December 22, 1908, Koresh, the self-proclaimed Seventh Messenger, died.

Convinced that their leader was immortal, Koresh's followers kept a prayerful watch over his body, planning to wait for him to rise from the dead on Christmas Day and usher in the millennium.

The day after his death, however, county health officials informed the Koreshans that the rapidly decaying body would have to be buried. Koresh was placed by his followers in a bathtub and sealed in a brick-and-concrete tomb at the end of Estero Island.

Thirteen years later a storm washed the tomb out to sea. Some Koreshans felt this was a sign that their leader had at last risen from the dead.

After Koresh's death, Annie Ordway tried to keep his dream alive, but the Koreshan community's decline was rapid. Its last member, Hedwig Michel, died in 1982. Born in Frankfurt, Germany, she had arrived in the United States on the last ship Hitler allowed to leave in 1939. Michel was a Jewish educator who decided to seek out Koreshan, which she had heard about in Germany, and in 1960 she became its president.

Before her death at age 90, she provided for the preservation of the Koreshan Unity settlement. It is now designated a national historical site. Its conversion to a state park in 1962 preserved much of the physical remnants of the commune, evidence that a "prophet" had realized at least part of his dream on the banks of the Estero River.

CHAPTER 31

Plastic Snowbird

Baekeland's creation revolutionized the modern world

With his amazing brain protected from the merciless Florida sun by a white pith helmet, Leo Baekeland loved to sail on Biscayne Bay in his 48-foot ketch named *Ion* after the electrically charged atomic particle.

Dr. Baekeland was a scientific man who achieved what few scientists ever accomplish: he revolutionized the world. More precisely, what the old Biscayne Bay sailor did during the course of a long and productive life was to invent plastics.

In Coconut Grove, where Baekeland spent his winters, he would occasionally startle visitors by marching fully clothed into his swimming pool. Then he would let nature's evaporative powers cool him down.

Baekeland fancied white sneakers. He liked them so much, in fact, that he wore them everywhere, even in New York when he visited the Chemists' Club or the University Club. He didn't stand on formalities. Even when a sumptuous dinner was being served in his home, he would content himself with coffee, a bowl of soup and sardines eaten from the can.

Today, the product of Baekland's genius is found everywhere you need it most—from toilet seats and radios to clocks and airplane parts. And all too often it's found where you don't want it, in discarded cups, bottles, broken toys and all sorts of plastic items that the forces of nature are unable to break down.

Leo Hendrik Baekeland was born in Belgium in 1863. Later he studied organic chemistry at the University of Ghent and then became a chemical inventor. His first major invention was photographic paper on which prints could be made by exposure to artificial light, instead of strong sunlight. In 1899 he sold the process, called Velox, to Eastman Kodak for $750,000.

With a portion of the money, Baekeland bought "Snug Rock," a fine home in Yonkers, New York, and set up a well-equipped laboratory where he pursued whatever chemical puzzle intrigued him. The young scientist also treated himself to one of the town's first automobiles, which he reportedly drove in a fashion that terrorized his neighbors.

Baekeland concluded, as did many other organic chemists of the time, that a workable synthetic shellac might be made by combining phenol and formaldehyde. When he mixed them with other chemicals and materials under heat and pressure, it produced a substance that Baekeland believed would "make a substitute for celluloid and hard rubber."

What he came up with, in 1909, bore the chemical name of oxybenzlmethyleneglycolanhydride. He applied for a patent and gave his discovery a more practical name: Bakelite.

Baekeland's product could be molded, would not melt, resisted most acids and served as a superb electrical insulator. Its natural color was an attractive amber, but it could easily be dyed bright colors.

Its uses were so widespread that even the publicity-shy Baekeland could not avoid international fame. He wound up on the cover of *Time* magazine, won the Franklin Institute's Gold Medal as the "Father of Plastics," and joined Benjamin Franklin and Thomas Edison in the Business Hall of Fame. His Bakelite Corporation was the first Western industry to be established in Japan.

May Sarton, a famous poet, knew the scientist when she was a little girl growing up in Yonkers. Years later she wrote: "I never did feel Dr. Baekeland as a person I knew; rather he seemed to be some frightening masculine force—a god who must be placated, a piece of weather . . . with his fierce, shy eyes and black mustache, he looked something like Rudyard Kipling."

In the late 1920s, Baekeland bought the Anchorage, a plantation-style house on Biscayne Bay. It had been the home of the late William Jennings Bryan, "the Great Commoner." Bryan had moved to Coconut Grove in the early 1920s after three unsuccessful campaigns for the presidency. Among Baekeland's friends were the wealthy chemist William J. Matheson, who owned Key Biscayne, and David Fairchild, the horticulturist who founded Miami's Fairchild Tropical Garden.

In 1932 Baekeland joined the Biscayne Bay Yacht Club. Five years later club members picked him to serve as their commodore for the club's 50th anniversary. To the members' amazement, he turned them down. A clue to his decision can probably be traced to a 1908 entry in his diary, in which he wrote that his wife, Celine, "found out that they wanted to make our son George president of his class, but he refused, and afterwards when asked why by his mother, said he was satisfied with the thought that they had asked him."

Baekeland died in 1944 at age 81. His creation of plastic had opened a new world, affecting industrial design, the flashy styles of the Art Deco era, and in later years a huge range of products from nylons to Tupperware.

Leo Baekeland, founder of plastics industry, relaxes at Miami aboard his sailboat *Ion* in mid-1930s. (Historical Association of Southern Florida)

His grandson, Brooks Baekeland, believes that the old scientist would not have been happy with some of the ways that plastic is being used today. Said Brooks, "He certainly could not have foreseen the plastic-polluted world that has become such a monstrous joke. He would have recoiled."

If he had lived longer, Baekeland would have recoiled at more than plastic litter. He would have been particularly horrified at the use his great-grandson made of plastic. Future generations of Baekelands enjoyed the enormous wealth Leo had created for them, but none came close to the remarkable achievements of the old patriarch. Then on November 17, 1972, Tony Baekeland, a gifted but deranged psychotic, stabbed his mother to death. Nine years later, in prison, he took his own life by placing a plastic bag over his head, pulling the drawstring tight and suffocating himself.

When Tony's father heard about his son's death, he had just one, incredible comment: "It was a beautiful ending—and in plastic too!"

CHAPTER 32

Sanctuary in the Cypress

Dry martinis helped save wet swamplands in Collier County

Henry Ford wanted to give Florida the Big Cypress Swamp as a state park in the 1920s. Tallahassee turned the auto maker down. The state claimed it couldn't afford the roads and maintenance costs for a big park.

Today much of the swamp is preserved by the Federal government, which owns the Big Cypress National Preserve, by the state, which now owns the Fakahatchee Strand State Preserve; and by the National Audubon Society, which owns the Corkscrew Swamp Sanctuary.

Saving it hasn't been easy. Let's take a look at what was involved in preserving just the Corkscrew part of the vast swamp. It took some mighty efforts by the president of the National Audubon Society (who conveniently happened to have a winter home in Miami), a few soggy swamp slogs by the head of the National Geographic Society, two dry martinis by a Miami grande dame and, eventually, a hefty contribution by the Ford Foundation, long after Henry's death.

In Collier County the forests of virgin bald cypress stretched for 50 miles. Giant trees, some over seven centuries old, towered 130 feet above the swampy landscape. In 1913 the Lee Tidewater Cypress Company paid $1,400,000 for over 100,000 acres, which contained some two-thirds of all the marketable cypress in the county.

Nine years later the company gave an option to an agent of Henry Ford. The automobile manufacturer, who wintered in southwest Florida, wanted to buy a large piece of the swamp and give it to the state of Florida as a park. That's when farsighted state officials said no.

So the lumber companies stepped up their operations, particularly when World War II brought a heavy demand for cypress, a durable, rat-resistant wood. By the early 1950s the only virgin stand of cypress left in southwest Florida stood in the Corkscrew Swamp, near Immokalee. To save what remained, the Corkscrew Cypress Rookery Association was formed in 1954. It included some heavy hitters: John H. Baker, president of the National Audubon Society; O. Earle Frye, Jr., assistant director (later director) of the Florida Game and Fresh Water Fish Commission; Mrs. Eugene A. Smith of Fort Lauderdale, president of the Florida Federation of Garden Clubs; and Bill Piper, who owned Everglades Wonder Gardens, an attraction in Bonita Springs.

The association's goal was "the acquisition and preservation of the greatest remaining bald cypress swamp and its associated plant and animal life." The "associated animal life" included the largest rookery of wood storks and egrets in the country, numbering between 8,000 and 10,000 birds.

Baker moved into action none too soon. The Lee Tidewater Cypress Company, which owned much of the land, was preparing to bring its lumber crews into the Corkscrew. Surprisingly, J. Arthur Currey, Lee president, proved to be sympathetic to Baker's approach. He agreed to give the group a sizable piece of the company's land, grant options on additional acreage, and sell the rest at a fair market price.

By December, 1954, $170,000 had been raised to save the Corkscrew Swamp. It came from a variety of sources, among them such industrial magnates as Arthur Vining Davis (aluminum) and John D. Rockefeller, Jr., (oil). By now Henry Ford was dead but his Ford Foundation made a major contribution for a later acquisition.

For a dollar a year, 3,200 additional acres were leased from Collier County's largest landowner, the Collier Enterprises of Naples. Much of this land was later given to the association.

Henry P. "Hank" Bennett, already an Audubon warden and wildlife tour leader, was named manager of the Corkscrew Swamp Sanctuary. A one-room cabin with screen porch was built for him by Sam Whidden, a Corkscrew native who knew the swamp. He had hunted it for years.

Sam also proved to be the logical choice to build a boardwalk into the swamp. It would be a difficult task. The swamp was well patrolled by gators, cottonmouth moccasins, leeches, mosquitoes, bears and panthers.

Despite the welcoming committee, the new foreman was able to recruit a stouthearted boardwalk crew. Bennett himself was promptly put to work on the project, as was Alexander "Sandy" Sprunt IV. Sprunt just happened to be on the scene, making an inventory of plants and animals for the National Audubon Society's Research Department, which he now heads as a vice president of the national society. Sam lined up his brothers, Bob and Fletcher, to help, too.

The task was a large one. A 5,600-foot walk had to be constructed across a wet, sawgrass prairie, into cypress swamps and even across lakes. Digging postholes underwater was the toughest part of the job.

Foreman Sam Whidden supervises his uncomfortable brothers, waist deep in water, as they build boardwalk across Corkscrew Sanctuary lettuce pond. (Photo by Sandy Sprunt, courtesy of Corkscrew Sanctuary)

Said Sprunt: "Poor Hank was rather a short person. I think he stood about five foot six or seven. He was up to his chin a lot of the time."

Before the boardwalk was built, Baker had to lead special guests and potential donors out to the swamp on foot. Once he escorted an influential Miami group that included Dr. Melville Grosvenor, president of the National Geographic Society, Mrs. Grosvenor and Mrs. Marcia Tucker, an enthusiastic birder and contributor to Audubon causes who at the time was in her seventies.

The group walked through sawgrass, swamp and lakes, sometimes in waist-deep water. They came out of the Corkscrew dripping wet but glowing with dedication to the cause. After changing into dry clothes, they returned by jeep through cattle ranches until they reached the road where their cars were parked.

The lead car, belonging to Mrs. Tucker, was a shiny grey Daimler limousine. She traveled in style. Liveried chauffeur and footman. As the caravan returned to Miami, the Daimler stopped suddenly in front of a raunchy-looking roadside bar on the Tamiami Trail. The liveried footman disappeared into the saloon.

"Why have we stopped?" one of the directors asked the chauffeur. He was told that Mrs. Tucker had to have a dry martini, her favorite drink, every afternoon.

Soon the liveried footman reappeared, carrying a tray with a martini on it. Mrs. Tucker liked it. She ordered a second one.

By this time villagers and itinerant farm workers had clustered around the Daimler, the first they had ever seen. The martinis also were the first they had ever seen. It was a big day on the Trail.

With two cocktails under her belt, Mrs. Tucker gave the order to resume. The caravan continued on to Miami.

At today's Corkscrew Sanctuary, now owned and maintained by the National Audubon Society, no martinis are served; in fact, its guidebook states, "Please, no alcoholic beverages."

Besides, visitors these days are more interested in rambling along the boardwalk, which keeps them out of the waist-deep water, and observing the towering cypress, draped with Spanish moss, and a rich variety of wildlife which includes the country's largest nesting colony of wood storks.

The one question most asked, however, concerns not the birds but the name of the swamp. Actually it backed into its name. A river which rises in the swamp is so crooked in places it was once called the Corkscrew River. The river is now called the Imperial, but Corkscrew remains as the name for the swamp and for the sanctuary.

PLAYERS

Florida's first sportsmen were wealthy visitors who stalked the state's tarpon, deer, bear and panther. Later, sportsmen played baseball for hire at luxury hotels while wealthy guests placed bets on the games. And then came sportsmen who didn't have to be wealthy to place two-dollar bets on thoroughbred racehorses.

CHAPTER 33

Tarpon Country

Shultz's primitive hotel became "in" place for wealthy sportsmen

In the late 1800s, guests had to know this was a different kind of hotel when they saw a sign reading, "This is the end of the world, jump right off." Furthermore, the hotel's genial and obliging host, George Shultz, provided them with a convenient jumping-off place: a porch that sat high above the waters of San Carlos Bay, looking out toward Sanibel island and beyond to the Gulf of Mexico.

Of course, the smart guests didn't jump. They fished. At high tide they could sit on the porch and dangle their lines into waters that teemed with whiting, sea trout and redfish.

Perched atop 14-foot pilings, the Shultz Hotel, as it was called in the beginning, was a ramshackle, unpainted, salt-encrusted wooden building. Some said it looked like an abandoned barn. It was indeed a primitive hostelry, with rough walls, crude accomodations, barren floors, tin wash bowls and china slop jars. Obviously, a place for the down-and-outers of the world.

But Shultz, for some reason, was not attracting losers to his hotel. His guest list read like an international *Who's Who:* President Grover Cleveland; inventor Thomas A. Edison; Hugh O'Neill, a merchant prince whose New York department store by 1890 had become the largest store in the world; Walter N. Haldeman, owner and publisher, and Colonel Henry Watterson, editor of the *Louisville Courier-Journal;* Edward M. VomHoffe, one of America's most famous manufacturers of fishing tackle; not to mention a raft of financiers and captains of industry. From the British Isles came John Jameson of Dublin, revered for the Irish whiskey his company distilled, and the Duke of Sutherland from Scotland.

The Shultz Hotel may not have looked like much, but the rickety old barracks had some sort of strange chemistry that pulled in the rich and famous from all over the world. Part of that chemistry was the personality of the host, part the incredible building itself and part an epidemic, though nonfatal, disease called tarpon fever. By the late 1880s the southwest coast of Florida was "the place" to catch tarpon, and the "in place" to stay while seeking the silver king was Shultz's hotel.

George Shultz had simply drifted into the hotel business. Some might even say he lucked into it. In 1866 the International Ocean Telegraph Company was granted the franchise to lay a telegraph line from Jacksonville to Punta Rassa, and from there to Key West and on to Havana. George Renton Shultz, of Newark, 21 at the time, headed the crew that traveled via covered wagon down the peninsula, erecting telegraph poles. After three years they arrived at Fort Myers, which boasted a total of two small houses, and then moved on to the mouth of the Caloosahatchee River to a point of land called Punta Rassa.

When he took over the old Civil War barracks there, he found its thick plank floor charred from soldiers' indoor campfires. To keep mosquitoes out, he and his helpers had to plug up bullet holes in the building. One corner of the huge barracks was curtained off with a sheet to form the "telegraph office."

Since the region was virtually uninhabited, Schultz had few visitors. Most of them were cows, along with the cowboys who had driven them down from central Florida to Punta Rassa's cattle-loading pens. From there they could be shipped to Cuba.

At first the cowboys slept under the barracks, which were elevated on pilings to protect the structure from hurricane tides. For the cowboys, this method of sleeping had two serious drawbacks—high tide and more mosquitoes than a body could stand.

One day, the story goes, one of the cowboys sidled up to George and said, "Why don't you let us sleep inside? Fewer mosquitoes for us and a little extra money for you."

A shrewd soul, Shultz picked up on the advantages of the arrangement. He invited the cowboys in—as paying guests. Next he had his wife Josephine prepare meals for them. In short order, rave notices for her home cooking began to drift around southwest Florida.

Over a period of time Schultz set about improving the product. First off, he eliminated the snakes and wharf rats. Then he began to fix up other parts of the rambling old building which could serve as private hotel rooms for noncowboys.

In March of 1881 an event occurred which spread Shultz's fame outside of Florida. A famous cartoonist and writer, one Walt McDougald, was cruising with a party of friends along the coast on a fishing trip. A severe storm blew up, and the party headed into San Carlos Bay seeking shelter. They tied up at the wharf at Shultz's place. The Shultzes invited them in to find shelter from

Old Army barracks at Punta Rassa, future home of famous sportsman's hotel, the Tarpon Lodge. (Florida State Archives)

the storm. They stayed for the night and were treated to one of Mrs. Shultz's meals.

McDougald, in particular, liked the Shultz Hotel. When he returned north, he set about spreading the word. People began to learn that southwest Florida had a sporting inn of rare charm. Wealthy sportsmen poured into Shultz's, determined to enjoy Florida's fabulous fishing and the mellow hospitality of genial George. Somehow George Shultz just seemed to have the touch. A warm, enthusiastic man who sported a walrus moustache, he proved to be an excellent host, friendly without being fawning. His best rooms were called Murderer's Row. Wealthy guests were delighted by his irreverent joshing.

Instead of being derided for not painting the place, George was praised for not tampering with the rough Army barracks' primitive charms, whatever they were. Instead of calling his place rundown, they called it unique. Somehow Shultz had them roughing it—and liking it.

Fishing was unbeatable in the waters near Punta Rassa, but the one fish they all wanted to catch, the tarpon, seemed to be too much of a battler to be taken on rod and reel. Fishermen in the early 1880s caught their tarpon with a shark hook and a chain, or with a harpoon. Not very sporting, but it was the only thing that would work.

Some of the country's best fishermen, however, believed the silver king could be caught with rod and reel, but they agreed it would take a special design.

VomHoffe's tackle company was hard at work on a tarpon rig, as was

W. H. Wood, a New York sportsman reported to have caught more large bass than any other angler in America. In *Forest and Stream,* the leading outdoor publication of its time, Wood read of the great silver-sided streak of lightning called by Floridians the "tarpum."

Wood designed a special rod and reel for the silver king. The gearless reel, made of hard rubber and white metal, 5 1/8 inches in diameter and 2 3/16 inches wide, could hold 1,200 feet of 21-thread line. A thick, five-foot bamboo rod and a gaff hook mounted on an ash hoe handle rounded out the tarpon equipment.

When the gear was ready, Wood headed for the Shultz Hotel. He found waiting for him plenty of skeptical Florida anglers who were convinced he faced certain defeat with so fine a line and a rod less than seven feet in length.

Wood paid no attention but baited his hook with cut mullet, bound flesh side out with fine copper wire, a technique then in use among bass fishermen. He lost 10 good fish when the line was cut, so he added several feet of "safety chain," a strong brass chain with flat links, and made the last link into a swivel which revolved around the knobbed hook.

On March 19, 1885, Wood tried again. He ventured forth with Capt. John Smith whose sailboat towed a small dinghy. When they reached Tarpon Bay, near Sanibel Island, Wood transferred into the dinghy.

Wood uncoiled about 20 feet of line. He held the line in his hand after laying the rod down. His experience with fish had taught him he had to allow the hook to be swallowed. The bait was taken gently. Wood threw the coil of line into the water when he felt the bait move. He calculated that the bait would be swallowed by the time the line was run out.

At that time, he picked up the rod and set the hook. The battle began. The tarpon leaped into the air, a flash of burnished silver, and then dove with a sudden rush. Even the sea gulls, frightened by the frantic leaps of the fish, noisily left the scene.

Wood remained cool. Repeated practice in lifting weights with the rod and reel had taught him how to gauge the amount of pressure his thumb should apply to the reel. Holding the rod nearly upright, he placed the strain at 20 pounds and made the fish drag the boat.

At no time was more than 300 feet of line off the reel. Wood kept the pressure constant and the fish began to weaken. The leaps grew less high, the plunges less fierce.

After six leaps, Wood reeled the exhausted tarpon in. The gaff was applied to its gills and it was lifted into the boat. The fish was five feet, nine inches long and weighed 98 pounds. It had taken 26 1/2 minutes to land the first silver king ever caught on rod and reel. Wood returned to the Shultz Hotel with his trophy.

Accounts of his feat were sent to *Forest and Stream* and quickly picked up by other publications in the United States and Great Britain. Wood became a hero, and tarpon fever began to rage within the sporting community.

Two months after Wood's catch, a claim surfaced that a Mr. S. H. Jones of Philadelphia had caught a 174-pound tarpon with rod and reel in 1878 in the Indian River of Florida's East Coast. Delay in making the claim plus confusion about the size of the fish left Jones' reported feat somewhat discredited, so Wood's carefully authenticated catch has survived as the official first of its kind.

The rush of new business led Shultz to change the name of his hotel to the Tarpon House. Two years after Wood's historic catch George added still another new touch, hiring a French chef to cater to the cosmopolitan tastes of his illustrious guests.

The sportsmen at the Tarpon House were finding it harder to convince themselves that they were really roughing it, particularly after Shultz provided his wealthy visitors with a highly sophisticated service, thanks to the wonders of the telegraph. Guests could keep up with the latest stock market quotations and fire off buy and sell orders to their brokers.

For another two decades George Shultz enjoyed the prosperity of operating a famous and successful hotel. Then at 3 a.m. on December 30, 1906, Commodore Garret Van Horn, of New York, awoke to find his hotel room filled with choking smoke. He leaped out of bed and sounded the alarm.

Van Horn, the other guests and Shultz were forced to flee, leaving their belongings behind. Everything was destroyed—the main building, a warehouse and the wharf. All that remained was a 30,000-gallon rain barrel, and it was so badly warped it was useless. Boats stored under the building were destroyed.

Shultz had just completed improvements on the hotel which had cost him $2,000. He estimated his loss at $20,000. Shultz had paid for the improvements over the years, but the ground and the buildings were still owned by a telegraph company now known as Western Union.

The wealthy sportsmen who had wintered with Shultz for so many years quickly came through with new financing. On January 15, 1908, a new $40,000 hotel opened—40 rooms, all facing the water. It weathered a severe hurricane in 1910, then late in 1913 the second Tarpon House burned down. It was never rebuilt.

George Shultz died on January 25, 1921. An era died with him.

CHAPTER 34

Hunting in High Style

Cory and friends lived it up in the wilds of Florida

Seminole guide Charlie Willie was so good at his job that he could have bagged a panther for his millionaire client on the first day out. But that wasn't the idea, and they both knew it as well as they knew each other.

The well-heeled sportsman was a great burly bear of a man named Charles Cory. He was an accomplished hunter and fisherman and he was an author, a natural scientist, an ornithnologist—and a playboy carouser who wanted his outdoor pleasures to last as long as possible.

For Cory, who sported a flourishing handlebar moustache, the outing was the thing, a great lark in the woods to be stretched out and savored until the hunting party grew tired of the chase, usually after about 10 days. If it ended too quickly, Cory's guests would be disappointed. If it dragged on too long or became too much of a production, they would be bored.

And Cory certainly didn't want to disappoint or bore the kind of guests that he attracted—people such as President Grover Cleveland, Admiral George Dewey and, his favorite of all hunting companions, Joseph Jefferson, premier actor of the American stage.

It was up to Charlie Willie to pick up the signals, bring the hunt to an end with a successful kill and then send the hunting party back to Cory's luxury houseboat, anchored on the New River in a little frontier settlement called Fort Lauderdale.

A Cory hunt was unlike anything the South Florida of the 1890s had ever seen. Years later a friend wrote of the famed sportsman: ". . . when twenty years of age, Cory began a life of freedom and pleasure in the pursuit of natural history and sport which has scarcely been equalled and which might be the envy of many a man." When Charles Barney Cory went on a panther hunt, he did it in style. As heir to a wine and silk fortune, he could well afford to.

A Cory safari would set out from New River on horseback, accompanied by Charlie Willie and other Seminole guides. Supplies were carried in a wagon as the men proceeded along the County Road that linked Lantana and Biscayne Bay country. Where the road crossed the Hillsboro River, they found the camp of William Thornton, one of only a handful of people living in a tiny settlement called Deerfield. The community took its name from its impressive population of deer. Even more important for Cory's immediate venture, this was panther country.

The group set up camp near the Hillsboro River, which has since become the Hillsboro Canal. Only the latest and best in tents and cots were carried on a Cory expedition. Never let it be said that the guests of Charles Cory had to sleep on the ground.

From his 90-foot houseboat, *The Wanderer,* Cory took along his chef, skilled in the preparation of the plentiful game they planned to take and the fish they intended to catch from the river and the nearby Everglades. The chef was equipped with the most modern portable culinary equipment. "The most completely furnished camp that money could provide," an early account called it.

Cory's own accounts of his hunting forays skipped over the luxury-on-the-trail part. In *Hunting and Fishing in Florida,* one of 15 books he wrote, Cory described a south Florida panther hunt:

"It was our usual custom to start out at daylight and allow the hounds to run about as they pleased as we rode slowly through the woods. Every few minutes a hound would start off on a fresh trail of some animal and we would have to call in the other dogs and 'slow trail' it until we came to a place where the ground was clear and soft enough for us to see the tracks and learn what it was they were after. . . .

"In crossing a piece of open land, a panther walks directly across, while a deer would make a more or less irregular trail. . . . About eleven o'clock we usually returned to camp. Later than that, unless the day was cloudy, no dog could follow a trail on sandy soil in the hot, dry weather of Southern Florida."

Sometimes Cory, who took many of the pictures used to illustrate his books, moved in close to the cat to get the best possible shot.

"Cautiously moving to one side," he wrote, "I saw the panther crouching beside and partly under the fallen tree. She was not over twenty feet distant, and as she turned her snarling face towards me she presented one of the ugliest pictures I have ever seen. Her ears were drawn tightly back and she exposed a splendid set of teeth. A very pungent, musty odor was perceptible. As she turned towards me, all the dogs sprang at once. . . . She turned on them with a quickness that was astonishing, uttering a snarling roar while biting and clawing at them savagely; but just then I fired, once, twice, three times as fast as I could work the lever and the great cat lay kicking and aimlessly biting."

The panther measured just over seven feet from nose to tip of tail. When the hunt was over, the Cory party, which had been living it up on the trail, returned to the houseboat where living it up reached almost legendary levels.

With his 90-foot, $100,000, mahogany-paneled *Wanderer,* Cory brought Fort Lauderdale its first luxury housing: 12 bedrooms, magnificently appointed lounge and recreation rooms, a modern kitchen and dining room and the town's only grand piano—not to mention a gun room containing one of the most complete and elaborate collections of guns and fishing paraphernalia to be found anywhere in America. "Enough weapons," said one old-timer, "to have reopened the Seminole War at a moment's notice."

Warring with the Seminoles, however, would not have been Cory's style. He spent a great deal of time with them, studying their culture and their language. In *Hunting and Fishing in Florida,* he published one of the most complete Seminole vocabularies then in existence.

Fort Lauderdale took Cory in stride, apparently delighted that a rich celebrity had come upon the scene capable of attracting other rich celebrities. Jefferson, although up in years, still had the name and the charm to draw actors and actresses to the houseboat for what one observer called "some of the wildest parties ever witnessed on New River." The parties, which occurred about every two weeks, lasted for days and involved "wild young actresses."

Apparently, the scene was so dazzling that young Tom Bryan learned the facts of life by rowing out to the boat under cover of darkness and watching in amazement from the river. Young Tom must have learned well, since he later became one of the city's richest and most powerful citizens.

Jefferson enjoyed many glorious moments on *The Wanderer,* but one pleasure he missed out on completely. The old actor never reeled in a fish on New River.

* * *

Cory was born in Boston on January 31, 1857, the son of a wealthy and extremely successful importer of wines, silks and a variety of luxury items. An athlete from an early age, Cory received instruction in shooting, boxing, fencing and riding. Later in life he became one of America's better amateur golfers, capturing the prestigious North-South Amateur Championship at Pinehurst, North Carolina. He was also at one time the Florida champion.

His lifelong interest in natural history was triggered through a hunting and fishing trip to the Maine woods when he was 16. Four years later, while attending Harvard, he came to Florida, one of the first of many students who would make the state their destination during spring break.

Cory's first trip to Fort Lauderdale came in 1896 when he and his friend Jefferson accompanied Henry Flagler's party on the first Flagler train that

Charles Cory kneels beside fallen panther. (Fort Lauderdale Historical Society)

steamed into the New River community. They stayed only a few minutes but Cory liked what he saw. The New River became the home for his *Wanderer,* an old Mississippi River packet boat which he had completely refurbished at Titusville.

In those days Cory divided his time between Hyannis, Massachusetts, in the summer months and Palm Beach and Fort Lauderdale the rest of the year. In Palm Beach he established the Florida Museum of Natural History, near the Breakers Hotel. In 1903 it was destroyed by fire.

During his distinguished career Cory was Curator of Ornithology at the Field Columbian Museum in Chicago, president of the American Ornithologists' Union and an esteemed author of many books and scientific papers published in natural history journals. At least seven species of birds were named in his honor, as was the Florida panther. He was the first to identify *Felis concolor coryi.*

In 1906 Cory received an incredible jolt. Speculation in the securities of the "shipping trust" and the "sugar trust" suddenly wiped him out. At 49, a man who had never had to earn a dollar in his life found himself penniless.

At that point he turned to ornithology to earn his living. At Chicago's Field Museum his title as curator had been an honorary one, carrying no salary. The museum provided him with a salaried position as Curator of Zoology.

Cory took his incredible loss in stride, relying heavily on his noted sense of humor. The high life was over for him, so he settled down to a useful and productive career as a natural scientist. The only recreation he kept from the glory days was golf, played at a modest and inexpensive Chicago club. The days of the panther hunts and wild young actresses were gone forever. When Cory died on July 31, 1921, *The Auk,* journal of the American Ornithologists' Union, the group whose bird protection efforts had led to the establishment of the National Audubon Society, devoted 16 pages to his obituary.

CHAPTER 35

Black Baseball, Palm Beach Style

Henry Flagler brought in the best to play for his hotel teams

Diamonds and Palm Beach. They go together like champagne and caviar.

From the earliest days in the 1890s, diamonds graced the fingers and the milk-white necks of wealthy society women who gloried in the tropical luxuries of America's premier winter resort.

In the early 1900s Henry Flagler, the founding father of southeast Florida, added two more diamonds to Palm Beach's galaxy—one at the Royal Poinciana Hotel, the other at the Breakers Hotel.

They were baseball diamonds and they were home to some of America's finest players—not the white players winning fame and fat paychecks in the big leagues, but rather blacks who were still nearly a half century away from the opportunity to play in the majors.

Today their skills would draw salaries in the millions. Then, they waited on tables or worked as bellhops when they weren't playing baseball beside the rustling palms.

* * *

Arthur Spalding played the organ at the opulent mansion, Whitehall, to entertain Flagler and his wife, Mary Lily Kenan, and a steady stream of wealthy guests. A letter to his sister, dated January 25, 1907, describes a game:

". . . I went over to the baseball game and such sport I never had in my life. Both teams are colored and composed of employees of the Breakers and Poinciana Hotels, who however are hired because of their baseball ability and then incidentally given employment as waiters or porters. Many of them play on the Cuban Giants team during the summer so that the quality of baseball ranked with professional white teams.

"The greatest sport was in listening to the coaching and watching the antics of a full grandstand back of first base. Their sympathies were pretty evenly divided between the two teams, so accordingly whenever either team would make a hit, then was the time to watch the bleachers. The crowd would yell themselves hoarse, stand up in their seats, bang each other over the head, and even the girls would go into a perfect frenzy as if they were in a Methodist camp meeting. The third baseman on the Poinciana team was a wonderful ball-player and kept the whole crowd roaring with his horseplay and cake-walks up and down the sidelines."

* * *

In Cleveland Flagler had already made a vast fortune as a founder of Standard Oil of Ohio when he turned his attention, and his enormous resources, to Florida. In the mid-1880s the tycoon plunged into the business of building railroads and hotels and developing towns and farmlands in the Sunshine State.

At Palm Beach he attracted an international clientele of wealthy, socially prominent and often royal winterees to his ritzy hotels. These visitors, he knew only too well, demanded the best of everything: entertainment, food and drink—and sport.

In 1885 Frank P. Thompson, headwaiter at the Argyle Hotel on Long Island's south shore, formed a team of the hotel's black waiters to play for the amusement of the Argyle's guests. This was the start of the Cuban Giants, one of the best of the early Negro teams. Many black teams took the name "Giants," a confusing tribute to the popularity of the New York Giants.

Four years later the Cuban Giants spent the winter playing for a resort hotel in Jacksonville. *The Sporting News* had a light-hearted comment about them: "They can handle codfish balls with ease, serve fowls 'as you like 'em,' will take to their base on tips, and only draw the line on flies on the tables."

Another *Sporting News* writer, after covering an 1888 baseball tournament, wrote: "There are players among these colored men that are equal to any white players on the ballfield. If you don't think so, go and see the Cuban Giants play. This club, with its strongest players on the field, would play a favorable game against such clubs as the New Yorks or Chicagos."

Soon the waiter/baseballer phenomenon had worked its way down to St. Augustine, where Flagler owned hotels. From there it was a short leap to Palm Beach.

And Flagler had just the man to run his baseball program.

Ed Andrews, the son of a Great Lakes boat captain, starred in baseball at Western Reserve University in Cleveland, then moved up to play centerfield for Philadelphia. He was paid $3,800 in 1884. The best year for the five-foot-four speedster was 1887, when he hit .325.

Ed Andrews (National Baseball Library & Archive,Cooperstown, N.Y.)

Luckily for him, Flagler knew and liked him. In fact, when the Flagler interests created the first plat for Fort Lauderdale, they named the main north-south street of the new city after him—Andrews Avenue. Andrews, a close friend of Frank Stranahan, the founding father of Fort Lauderdale, visited the town often, though he never lived there.

When he retired from baseball in 1891, Andrews bought land on Indian River near Fort Pierce and went into the business of raising pineapples. After the freeze of 1895 wiped out his crop, he replenished his coffers by returning briefly to baseball as a National League umpire.

In 1899 he moved to West Palm Beach. Flagler had hired him to manage his yacht basin, a task for which he was highly qualified. His father had trained him well in boating skills and in his later years he became a respected and popular writer for yachting publications.

So, when Flagler decided to bring baseball to Palm Beach, he knew he had the right man aboard to run the program for him. Sometime in the early 1900s, Andrews began drawing on Giants talent to recruit players to fight off the terror of boredom among paying guests with names like Vanderbilt, Phipps, Carnegie, Whitney and Stotesbury.

They tapped the Cuban Giants, the Cuban X Giants, the Royal Giants and the Leland Giants—and perhaps a few other Giants—to create a team called the Breakers and a worthy opponent called the Poincianas.

Black waiters at resort hotels in those days were paid $23 to $33 a month, captains up to $40 and headwaiters, $75. Flagler also provided housing on the hotel grounds and meals.

In return, he received the services of players and managers whose names read like a Hall of Fame of black baseball. Elegantly clad socialites, sipping tea or Scotch in the Royal Poinciana and Breakers grandstands, cheered for—and bet heavily on—players who would have moved immediately into the big leagues if the barriers had been lowered.

They saw fastballs blown past batters by Smoky Joe Williams, regarded by many as better than Satchel Paige; homers belted by the likes of Louis Santop and Oscar Charleston; and grounders fielded by the greatest of the black shortstops, John Henry Lloyd, a Floridian who played for the Breakers.

Born in Palatka in 1884, the year Andrews signed with Philadelphia, Lloyd played semipro baseball with the Jacksonville Young Receivers before heading north in 1906 with $1.50 in his pocket to land an infield job with the Cuban X Giants.

For the Giants his highest average was .475 in 1911. As cleanup hitter with the best black team in baseball, he earned about $250 a month.

Lloyd was called "the Black Wagner," a comparison with Honus "Hans" Wagner, the great big league shortstop who was one of the first five players in-

John Henry Lloyd (National Baseball Library & Archive,Cooperstown, N.Y.)

ducted into the Baseball Hall of Fame at Cooperstown, New York. Said Wagner, whose 1911 baseball card drew the highest price of any card in history, over $100,000 in 1988:

"I am honored to have John Lloyd called the Black Wagner. It is a privilege to have been compared with him."

Perhaps one reason Wagner spoke so favorably of Lloyd was the respect he commanded throughout his long life. In a sport heavily laced with drunken rowdies, John was the exception. He never drank, smoked only an occasional cigar and astounded many because he never cussed.

Many who saw him play call him the greatest black player of all time. In his history of black baseball, *Only the Ball Was White,* Robert Peterson quoted the reply of an unnamed white St. Louis sportswriter when asked in 1938 to name the best player in baseball history:

"If you mean in organized baseball, my answer would be Babe Ruth; but if you mean in all baseball, organized or unorganized, the answer would have to be a colored man named John Henry Lloyd."

At Palm Beach Lloyd played in fast company. Catcher Louis Santop once hit a 485-foot home run off the not-too-lively ball used 1912. Always a showman, he sometimes called his home run shots in the classic Babe Ruth manner.

Oscar Charleston was not only a powerful hitter, .396 in the Negro American League in 1929—but also a superb centerfielder.

Smoky Joe Williams, six feet five, was a strikeout pitcher. He once fanned 25 Kansas City Monarchs in a 12-inning game. In 1915 he shut out Philadelphia's National League champions, 1-0. In 12 games against major league teams he won six, lost four and tied two.

The teams played two games each week, starting at 3 in the afternoon. Umpiring the games was the no-nonsense Connie Lewis. A former minor leaguer, Lewis was also famous in Palm Beach as the official Beach Censor. He patrolled the beach to make sure that black stockings worn by women bathers reached as high as their black bathing suits. His cry on seeing bare leg skin was, "Ladies, rules is rules."

If he could control the beachwear of fashion-conscious society women, he could call balls and strikes and make his decisions stick.

On occasion Lewis was known to call a game if the score became too one-sided, as in the case of a 1916 game when the Breakers opened up an 8-0 lead against the Poincianas. A local press account said, "Williams pitched gilt-edged ball for his nine and (John) Donaldson did not."

The paper reported "periods of anguish that filled the soul of Donaldson," referred to as "the dusky giant." Donaldson, however, was generally an effective curveball pitcher, as well as a hitter so powerful he played the outfield when he wasn't pitching.

Long after Flagler's death in 1913 black teams still played at the hotel diamonds. The fields were also used for other events such as the annual game between Philadelphia bluebloods and New York socialites.

Attendance at the games was not restricted to guests at the hotels or even to whites. John "Buck" O'Neil, who lived in Sarasota, recalls a 1923 trip he took as a boy of 12:

"My Daddy took me down to Palm Beach to see some black guys playing. These guys were representing the Royal Poinciana Hotel and the Breakers Hotel. They would work as waiters and bellhops for the rich folks. It was actually outstanding baseball, that's why they were down there."

Black baseball players take the field at Palm Beach's Royal Poinciana Hotel. (Historical Society of Palm Beach County)

O'Neil went on to star as a third baseman for the Kansas City Monarchs, then became a scout for the Chicago Cubs, signing Ernie Banks and Lou Brock. In 1962 the Cubs signed him as the first black coach in the big leagues.

The year 1928 was a fateful one for the Palm Beach hotel teams, starting the decline of black baseball at the resort. That year the St. Louis Browns of the American League began training over in West Palm Beach in the spring. Then in the fall the killer hurricane of 1928 struck the southeast coast, wrecking the Royal Poinciana, in its heyday the world's largest resort hotel. Blown away by the winds were its wooden bleachers.

Flagler would have wept at the damage to his grand hotel, but probably not at the loss of the bleachers. Why? Because in spite of his leadership in bringing high-quality baseball to Palm Beach he didn't particularly like spectator sports.

Asked why he seldom used his grandstand box, he invariably replied: "Why should I watch some colored boys hitting a ball with a stick?"

CHAPTER 36

Snakes, Mobsters and Ponies

Thoroughbred racing was slow out of the starting gate

The eyes of horse players around the world focus on Gulfstream Park whenever the track hosts thoroughbred racing's richest event, the Breeders' Cup, as it has twice. On hand are the best horses, jockeys and trainers from five continents, the richest owners, the fanciest dressed owners' wives and the sport's most knowledgeable wagerers. Network television and radio beam the races to a worldwide audience, and the leading racing writers descend on Hallandale to cover the most important sporting event ever held in Broward County.

The journey to this lofty thoroughbred pinnacle has hardly been a six-furlong romp for Florida racing. In America's subtropics the sport of kings did not exactly break fast out of the starting gate. In fact, when racing began here there were no starting gates in Florida.

But there were plenty of rattlesnakes.

Over the years a colorful cast of characters has paraded across the local racing scene: Jimmie Bright, cattleman; Joe Smoot, compulsive gambler; Joseph Widener, socialite; James Donn, nurseryman; Frank Nitti, Al Capone's executioner; and Rattlesnake Pete, snake catcher.

The founding father of Florida horse racing was James Harris Bright, a man no bigger than a jockey at five feet, two inches and 105 pounds. He started the state's first track at Hialeah, bred the first Florida thoroughbred at his farm in Davie, and talked a friend into starting a horse farm near Ocala, which has since developed into one of the nation's top breeding centers.

A fancier of the ponies since his boyhood days in Missouri, Bright came to Miami in 1909. On 3,000 acres to the west of the city, he started a cattle ranch. Riding his horse over the land, Bright observed that the black Allapattah marl could provide good footing for a track. In the early 1920s he promised Miami's power brokers that he would supply the track site and invest heavily in the venture—provided another substantial investor could be found.

The investor arrived in town in January, 1924. Dapper Joe Smoot, a fashion-plate with two-toned shoes, straw hat and cane, was just what Miami was looking for, a cash-rich sport who liked horse racing, gambling, red convertibles and blondes. Sporty Smoot had just sold his Buffalo, New York, brokerage firm for $300,000, a huge sum in those days. He was, he said, looking for "investment opportunities."

In the new boomtime city of Hialeah, Bright provided the land—200 acres sold to the Miami Jockey Club for a nominal $10—and work began on the track and clubhouse. Landscaping was provided by Exotic Gardens, a company owned by a Scotsman named James Donn. Donn agreed to accept as payment $25,000 in stock. Although he couldn't know it at the time, that stock certificate would launch him into a lifelong career in racing at three Florida tracks.

One of the biggest problems at the new track was the rattlesnake population. Bright hired a specialist, one Rattlesnake Pete, an enterprising soul who charged the track a quarter for each snake he caught, then resold them for $1.50. In paying him off, no one at the track ever questioned how many snakes Pete dropped into his gunnysack.

"You can count 'em if you want to," he offered cheerfully.

The rattlesnake crisis persisted right up to the time the track opened at the height of South Florida's manic land boom. Horses shipped to Hialeah were brought into downtown Miami by train and then were walked some ten miles through snake country to reach the track. Trainers and grooms carried pitchforks to clear a pathway for their valuable charges—and to save their own skins.

On January 5, 1925, one year and a day after groundbreaking, the track opened to a crowd of 17,000, a good turnout for a clubhouse and grandstand built to accommodate 5,000. Among the celebrities on hand were dancer Gilda Gray, who invented the shimmy, and boxer Gene Tunney, who would soon take the world's heavyweight championship from Jack Dempsey.

Parimutuel betting was illegal, but Hialeah came up with resourceful ways to outflank the state's anti-gambling laws. In 1926 the track sold picture postcards of every horse entered. If you held the postcard of a winner, the track would buy it back from you at a premium price—which just happened to coincide with the winning odds.

Church groups forced the closing of the track in 1927 and 1928, but Hialeah bounced back in 1929 with another innovative approach to wagering. The track was set up as a brokerage house. Each horse that was running was a separate "company." If your horse finished in the money, you could sell your shares back to the track, again at a figure that corresponded to the odds. If your horse lost, his company went into bankruptcy faster than you can say Secretariat.

Hialeah Park on opening day, January 15, 1925. (Historical Association of Southern Florida)

Although unhappy with Hialeah, Florida Governor John Martin left the track alone to place its illegal bets. But he showed no such restraint when the small farm town of Pompano tried to get into the racing business. At a cost of $1.25 million, Pompano investors built a one-mile track and a grandstand for 6,800 fans west of town.

The Pompano Race Track opened on December 25, 1926. Maybe the governor didn't like the way the "beanpickers" observed Christmas. A furious Martin called the little farming town "a center of lawbreakers" and threatened to "send the militia down there with a tractor and plow up Pompano track and plant it in cowpeas."

The threat worked. The horses ran there on just one day, opening day. Thirty-six years later another, and far more successful, track would be built on the same site. It would be called Pompano Park, which has hosted the Breeders Crown, the richest harness race.

Meanwhile, back at Hialeah, Bright had persuaded a wealthy Philadelphia and Palm Beach socialite named Joseph Widener to take over the track. Hialeah was running into difficulties as the Great Depression cast its shadow over Florida.

A collector of Rembrandts, Widener brought culture to Hialeah. The backside of the grandstand, which had been modeled after the Vienna Opera House, was further beautified by plantings of bougainvillea. Royal palms and

Seminoles watch races at Hialeah Park from infield. (Historical Association of Southern Florida)

a colony of pink flamingos beside the infield lake helped make Hialeah one of the world's most elegant tracks.

The Widener touch made Hialeah a destination for the Palm Beach crowd. In fact, the Palm Beach connection proved important in the early days of the track. When President Franklin Roosevelt declared a brief "bank holiday" in March, 1933, the action caught even the wealthy Widener without the funds to pay off the winners in cash.

To keep the track running, Widener called on the one man he knew who always kept a huge supply of cash on hand. Col. E. R. Bradley, who operated an illegal gambling casino in Palm Beach, sent an armored car to Hialeah to keep the horses running and the payoffs flowing.

When Widener took over the track in 1930, he mounted a massive campaign to legalize parimutuel betting. The following year, the state legislature finally made an honest woman of Florida horse racing—but not too honest. There were those who said that bribery and bootleg booze were used to influence the vote. And part of the inducement to gain the votes of the state's Bible Belt politicians was a provision that gave every Florida county, no matter how small, an equal share of the parimutuel taxes.

In making parimutuel betting honest, Widener caught the attention of an organization not noted for honesty—the mob.

A new Miami track called Tropical Park found itself taken over by major crime figures, including Frank Erickson, Owney Madden and Frank "The Enforcer" Nitti, who was Al Capone's chief hit man. The two-buck bettor might not have known which horse was going to win, but Capone's boys did.

Once again the name of James Donn appeared on the racing scene. In the pre-mob era, Exotic Gardens had been hired to landscape Tropical Park. The owners, however, were unable to pay Donn. In lieu of payment of $32,343, he had no choice but to accept a part interest in the track and a seat on the board of directors.

A Miami politician, State Senator Ernest Graham, whose son Bob would later become governor and still later a U.S. senator, induced Florida Governor Spessard Holland and the Racing Commission to withhold Tropical's license unless the mobsters were kicked out.

Rather than suffer a total loss, the mob sold. The only director whose hands were clean was James Donn. He continued his association with the track.

Donn was not the only person who kept showing up at south Florida's race tracks. In 1938 Joe Smoot reappeared, this time without money, but fortunately in the company of young Jack Horning, who had plenty. They built a new track at Hallandale, just over the Dade County line in southern Broward, and called it Gulfstream Park. A fancy tent served as the clubhouse.

The first Gulfstream was doomed from the start. Racing interests who didn't think three tracks could operate profitably in south Florida gave the new kid on the block dates in conflict with "old, established" Hialeah.

On opening day, February 1, 1939, Gulfstream drew 18,000 fans, the biggest turnout ever to watch racing in Florida up to that time. In fact, there were so many people they battered down the fences. Like Pompano, however, the track knew just one day of glory.

The second day, the crowd and the betting handle plummeted. Horsemen who had won purses were not paid. On the fourth day the syndicate that supplied money for mutuel play withdrew its support.

Gulfstream died.

Then in 1944 a familiar face reappeared—not Smoot, not Bright, but the canny Scottish landscaper James Donn. He had been associated with Hialeah and Tropical and by now he knew his way around the race track scene. He formed a syndicate and bought Gulfstream by buying out Horning and making deals with creditors.

Said Donn, "We offered to buy them out for a percentage. Or they could just sit there and get washed out in bankruptcy court. They all accepted."

Joe and Rose Kennedy, parents of a president, place their bets at Hialeah Park, which they visited regularly in the 1930s. (Historical Association of Southern Florida)

Suddenly, the modest landscaper had become one of the big names in horse racing.

James Donn was born in Lanark, near Glasgow, Scotland, on February 7, 1887. His father was Big Donn the blacksmith. Six feet tall and weighing in at 240 pounds, he was also the village strongman.

Rather small himself and lacking the great strength of his father, James decided not to pursue blacksmithing. In 1909 he immigrated to New York, then moved to Florida. He found work as the manager of a large nursery near Jacksonville.

After marrying fellow Scot Nellie Whiteside, he moved to Miami. When the great land boom of the 1920s arrived, he was in place with his company, Exotic Gardens, ready to landscape Miami's real-estate explosion.

While Donn was expanding his landscaping and flower-shop business, he was also learning more and more about his accidental career—racing. When he took over Gulfstream he already understood the importance of working with the state government. Donn was determined to get racing dates that did not conflict with Hialeah's.

The state agreed but gave Donn what appeared to be bad dates, the first 20 and the last 20 days of the racing season. Once again Donn's luck held. To save gasoline during World War II the federal government shut down racing after the first 20 days, so Gulfstream was the only track to operate that season.

After the war South Florida started to grow. And Donn grew with it.

Naturally, he made sure the landscaping at Gulfstream was lush and tropical. The Kentucky Derby had its "Run for the Roses." At Gulfstream the Florida Derby had become the "Run for the Orchids."

Since those difficult days in 1944, Gulfstream has gone on to overtake Hialeah as Florida's most successful race track. Its premier annual event, the Florida Derby, is considered by many to be the most significant prep race for the three-year-olds that compete for the Triple Crown.

All his life James Donn fought for the winter racing dates. They had always gone to Hialeah until he finally attained them in 1972. He enjoyed them for only one racing meet. That summer he died at age 86.

After his death Gulfstream remained in the Donn family through three generations, operated first by his son, James, Jr., and then by his grandson, Douglas. Then, after the track was awarded one of racing's highest honors, the opportunity to run the Breeders' Cup, the Donn connection to South Florida racing was finally broken. Gulfstream Park was sold to Bertram Firestone, who also owned Calder Race Course, in nearby Dade County.

BIBLIOGRAPHY

Akin, Edward N. *Flagler: Rockefeller Partner & Florida Baron*. Kent, Ohio, and London: Kent State University Press, 1988.

Ballinger, Kenneth. *Miami Millions: The Dance of the Dollars in the Great Florida Land Boom of 1925*. Miami: Franklin Press, 1936.

Bartlett, Patricia, and Prudy Taylor Board, *Lee County: A Pictorial History*. Norfolk, Donning Company, 1985.

Blake, Nelson M. *Land Into Water—Water Into Land*. Tallahasee: University of Florida Presses, 1980.

Bramson, Seth H. *Speedway to Sunshine: The Story of the Florida East Coast Railway*. Erin, Ontario: Boston Mills Press, 1984.

Brooks, Abbie (Sylvia Sunshine, pseudonym). *Petals Plucked from Sunny Climes*. Nashville: Methodist Publishing House, 1880.

Buker, George E. *Swamp Sailors: Riverine Warfare in the Everglades, 1835–1842*. Gainesville: University Presses of Florida, 1975.

Burghard, August. *Alligator Alley*. Fort Lauderdale: Lanman Company, 1969.

—— and Philip Weidling. *Checkered Sunshine: The History of Fort Lauderdale, 1793–1955*. Gainesville: University of Florida Press, 1966.

Burke, John. *Rogue's Progress*. New York: G.P. Putnam's Sons, 1975.

Burnett. Gene. *Florida's Past*. Three volumes. Sarasota: Pineapple Press, 1986, 1988 and 1991.

Cabarga, Leslie. *The Fleischer Story*. New York: DaCapo Press, 1988.

Cash, W.T., and Dodd, Dorothy. *Florida Becomes a State*. Tallahassee: Florida Centennial Commission, 1945.

Chandler, David Leon. *Henry Flagler*. New York: Macmillan, 1986.

Cory, Charles B. *Hunting and Fishing in Florida*. Boston: Estes and Lauriat, 1896.

Curl, Donald W. *Mizner's Florida: American Resort Architecture*. New York and Cambridge: Architectural History Foundation and MIT Press, 1984.

——. *Palm Beach County: An Illustrated History*. Northridge, California: Windsor Publications, 1986.

Daley, Robert. *An American Saga: Juan Trippe and his Pan Am Empire*. New York: Random House, 1980.

Douglas, Marjory Stoneman. *The Everglades: River of Grass*. New York: Rinehart and Company, 1947.

Dunn, Hampton. *Yesterday's St. Petersburg*. Miami: Seemann Publishing, 1973.

——. *Yesterday's Tampa*. Miami: Seemann Publishing, 1972.

——. *Florida: A Pictorial History*. Norfolk, Virginia: Donning Company, 1988.

——. *Highway to Success: The Story of the Peninsular Motor Club*. Norfolk, Donning Company, 1989.

Fitzgerald-Bush, Frank S. *A Dream of Araby: Glenn H. Curtiss and the Founding of Opa-locka*. Miami: South Florida Archeological Museum, 1976.

Fritz, Florence. *Unknown Florida*. Coral Gables; University of Miami Press, 1963.

Graves, Richard Perceval. *Robert Graves: The Years with Laura, 1926–1940*. New York: Viking Penguin, 1990.

Hanna, Alfred Jackson and Kathryn Abbey Hanna. *Florida's Golden Sands*. Indianapolis: Bobbs-Merrill, 1950.

Hemenway, Robert E. *Zora Neale Hurston: A Literary Biography*. Urbana and Chicago: University of Illinois Press, 1980.

Henshall, James A. *Camping and Cruising in Florida*. Cincinnati: Robert Clarke, 1884.

Higham, Charles. *Ziegfield*. Chicago: Regnery, 1972.

Hortt, M.A. *Gold Coast Pioneer*. New York: Exposition Press, 1953.

Huston, John. *An Open Book*. New York: Knopf, 1980.

James, Marquis. *The Life of Andrew Jackson*. Indianapolis: Bobbs-Merrill, 1937.

Johnson, Lamar. *Beyond the Fourth Generation*. Gainesville: University Presses of Florida, 1974.

Johnston, Alva. *The Legendary Mizners*. New York: Farrar, Strauss and Young, 1953.

Kearney, Bob, Editor. *Mostly Sunny Days*. Miami: Miami Herald Publishing Company, 1986.

Kirk, Cooper. *William Lauderdale: General Andrew Jackson's Warrior*. Fort Lauderdale: Manatee Books, 1982.

Lazarus, William C. *Wings in the Sun: The Annals of Aviation in Florida*.Orlando: Cobb's Florida Press, 1950.

McCabe, John. *Babe: The Life of Oliver Hardy*. Secaucus, New Jersey: Citadel Press,1989.

McGoun, William. *A Biographic History of Broward County*. Miami: Miami Herald Publishing Company, 1972.

McIver, Stuart B. *Coral Springs: The First 25 Years*. Norfolk: Donning Company, 1988.

——. *Fort Lauderdale and Broward County: An Illustrated History*. Northridge, California: Windsor Publications, 1983.

——. *The Greatest Sale on Earth: The Story of the Miami Board of Realtors, 1920–1980*. Miami: E.A. Seemann Publishing, 1980.

——. *Hemingway's Key West*. Sarasota: Pineapple Press, 1993.

——. *One Hundred Years on Biscayne Bay, 1887–1987*. Coconut Grove: Biscayne Bay Yacht Club, 1987.

——. *Yesterday's Palm Beach*. Miami: E.A. Seemann Publishing, 1976.

McKay, D.B. *Pioneer Florida*. Tampa: Southern Publishing Co., 1959.

Mahon, John K. *History of the Second Seminole War, 1835–1842*. Gainesville: University of Florida Presses, 1967.

Mahoney, Lawrence. *Early Birds: A History of Pan Am's Clipper Ships*. Miami: Pickering Press, 1987.

Martin, Sidney Walker. *Florida's Flagler*. Athens: University of Georgia Press, 1949.

Matthews, T.S. *Under the Influence*. London: Cassell, 1977.

Monaghan, Jay. *The Great Rascal: The Life and Adventures of Ned Buntline*. Boston: Little, Brown and Company, 1952.

Munroe, Ralph Middleton and Vincent Gilpin. *The Commodore's Story*. Miami: Historical Association of Southern Florida, 1985.

Nelson, Richard Alan. *Florida and the American Motion Picture Industry*. New York: Garland Publishing, 1983.

Nolan, David. *Fifty Feet in Paradise: The Booming of Florida*. New York: Harcourt Brace Jovanovich, 1984.

Parks, Arva Moore. *Miami, the Magic City*. Tulsa, Oklahoma: Continental Heritage Press, 1981.

Peters, Thelma. *Biscayne Country: 1870–1926*. Miami: Banyan Books, 1981.

——. *Lemon City: Pioneering on Biscayne Bay: 1850–1925*. Miami: Banyan Books, 1976.

Pettingill, George R. *Story of Florida Railroads, 1835–1903*. Boston: Railway and Locomotive Society, 1952.

Pierce, Charles W. *Pioneer Life in Southeast Florida*. Donald W. Curl, editor. Coral Gables: University of Miami Press, 1970.

Pratt, Theodore. *The Story of Boca Raton*. St. Petersburg: Great Outdoors Publishing Co., 1963.

Remini, Robert V. *The Life of Andrew Jackson*. New York: Harper & Row, 1988.

Riley, James A. *All-Time All-Stars of Black Baseball*. Cocoa, Florida: TK Publishers, 1983.

Roseberry, Cecil R. *Glenn Curtiss: Pioneer of Flight*. New York: Doubleday, 1972.

Seymour, Harold. *The People's Game*. New York and Oxford: Oxford University Press, 1960.

Smiley, Nixon. *Yesterday's Florida*. Miami: Seemann Publishing, 1974.

Strickland, Alice. *The Valiant Pioneers*. Miami: University of Miami Press, 1963.

Tebeau, Charlton W. *A History of Florida*. Coral Gables: University of Miami Press, 1971.

——. *Florida's Last Frontier*. Coral Gables: University of Miami Press, 1971.

Weigall, T.H. *Boom in Paradise*. New York: Alfred King, 1932.

Woodward, C. Vann. *Tom Watson: Agrarian Rebel*. London, Oxford and New York: Oxford University Press, 1938.

Publications

The list of Florida publications that have proved invaluable include:

Florida Historical Quarterly,
Broward Legacy,
South Florida History Magazine,
New River News,
Sun-Sentinel,
Miami Herald
Miami News,
Fort Myers News-Press
Key West Citizen.

INDEX

Illustrations are indicated by italics.

CPSIA information can be obtained
at www.ICGtesting.com
Printed in the USA
BVOW08s0455060317
477680BV00001B/1/P